PREMIUM

QUALITY

M.G.P.A. JACOBS, W.H.G. MAAS

HISTORION

THE MAGIC OF HEINEKEN

HEINEKEN NV / AMSTERDAM 2001

MAN

1864
Gerard Adriaan Heineken
The first generation of the Heineken
family of brewers

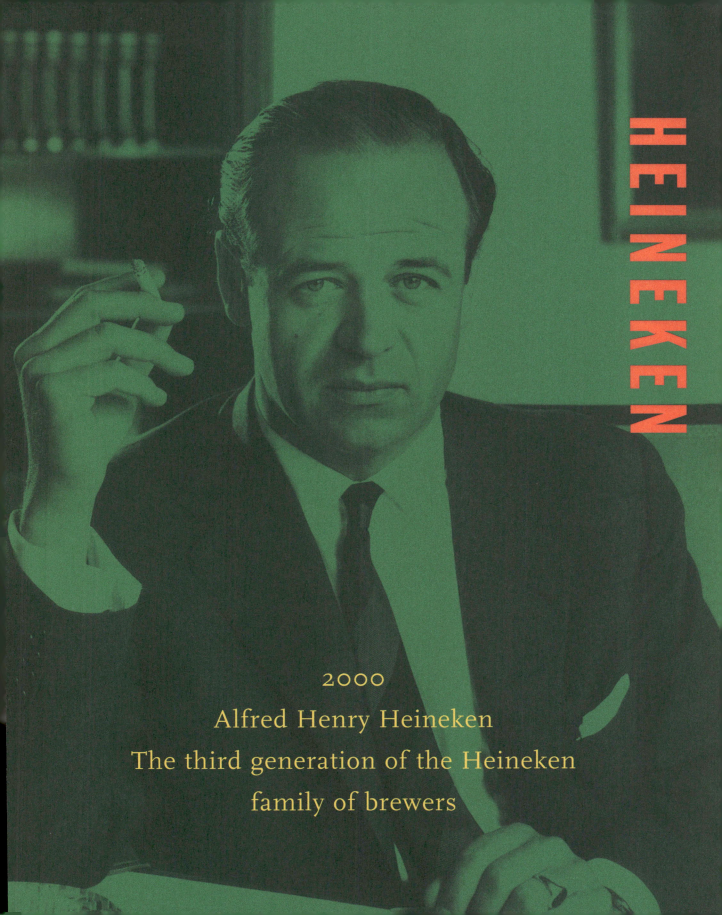

2000
Alfred Henry Heineken
The third generation of the Heineken
family of brewers

COMPANY

1873

The Heineken logo

2000

The Heineken logo

BRAND

1900
Heineken pilsner

HEINEKEN

2000

Heineken pilsner

C	
>	1864 …
1	AMSTERDAM 1864
2	ROTTERDAM 1873
3	PARIS 1889
4	BRUSSELS 1927
5	SINGAPORE 1931
6	NEW YORK 1933
7	UTRECHT 1948
8	LAGOS 1949
9	NOORDWIJK 1954
10	LOENEN 1968
11	STRASBOURG 1972
12	SHANGHAI 1988
13	CORK 1992
14	AMSTERDAM 2000
>	2001 …

TABLE OF CONTENTS   P

THE MAGIC OF HEINEKEN

THE FOUNDING OF A TRADITION / PASSION   1.1

FAITH IN YOURSELF / DARING   2.1

NAME AND FAME / ATTENTION   3.1

THE ROAD TO COOPERATION / SOCIAL   4.1

AN ACTIVE ROLE ON THE WORLD STAGE / WORLD CLASS   5.1

THE AMERICAN DREAM / STATUS   6.1

THE BATTLE FOR THE DUTCH BEER MARKET / AUTHORITY   7.1

PIONEER IN AFRICA / RESPECT   8.1

THE MAN AND THE BRAND / PERSONALITY   9.1

A BUSINESS OF NATIONAL IMPORTANCE / FRIENDSHIP   10.1

STAR STATUS IN EUROPE / CONSISTENCY   11.1

WORLD-CLASS PERFORMANCE / AMBITION   12.1

COLORFUL CHARACTERS WITH FROTHY HEADS / EXPERIENCE   13.1

CROWNING ACHIEVEMENT / HEINEKEN   14.1

THE MAGIC OF HEINEKEN

THE MAGIC OF HEINEKEN

The magic of Heineken was first felt in 1864. The story of the Heineken family, the brand and the company is no ordinary one. By the 21st century, this small 19th-century local Amsterdam brewer has grown into a worldwide business with a global brand.

Its noble pilsner, in its attractive green bottle, captivates the senses. This book invites you to take a journey through time and an appetizing trip around the world. Discover the world of Heineken and experience the magic for yourself.

THE
FOUNDING
OF A
TRADITION

The Heineken story starts on February 15, 1864. On this date, Gerard Adriaan Heineken founded the company Heineken & Co., taking over the De Hooiberg brewery in Amsterdam. Gerard Adriaan Heineken was a well-dressed young man with an impeccable moustache and whiskers, whose bearing exuded decisiveness. Nevertheless, the outside world must have viewed this bold move with some misgivings. Could someone of just 22 years of age have developed sufficient qualities to lead a new company? Also, not being a brewer himself, would his heart really be in the venture? The young director may have had little experience, but he possessed courage, self-confidence and entrepreneurial spirit in abundance. The brewing industry became his life. Gerard Adriaan Heineken knew exactly how to go about his business – able to see the big picture, he treated his personnel and clients correctly and ensured consistent high quality in the product. This is how the Heineken tradition started, in the port of Amsterdam.

A BREWER WITH AN IDEAL

The Heineken family has its roots in Germany. Early in the eighteenth century, Christiaan Heineken was a prominent citizen of the city of Bremen in northern Germany, where he owned extensive property, including a brewery. His two sons, Nicolaus and Diderik, saw little future in the family mercantile tradition and were more interested in spiritual pursuits. They set off for the Netherlands to study theology. Nicolaus went on to become a professor of philosophy, Diderik a minister in the town of Doornspijk. It was Diderik's son, Adriaan Gilles, who brought the Heineken family to Amsterdam. Towards the end of the eighteenth century, he settled on the Brouwersgracht as a merchant and started a business exporting butter and cheese. Business was good, he had an entrepreneurial spirit and, after his death, the company passed to his children. One of these was Cornelis, born in 1799. Sometime in 1838, he married Anna Geertruida van der Paauw. Their first child, Gerard Adriaan Heineken, was born into this marriage on September 28, 1841. It is he who went on to found the Heineken brewery.

Following his father's death in 1862, Gerard Adriaan started looking around for a suitable investment for the family's money. The idea of a brewery appealed to him – although he knew little about the brewing business. But then, how difficult could it be? He knew of someone who had bought and built up a brewery with no experience at all. 'Anything he can do…', the young Heineken must have thought. His move into the brewing trade was to a certain extent also prompted by idealism, however. During the nineteenth century, alcoholism was a big social problem in the Netherlands. Cheap Dutch gin ('jenever'), 40 percent proof, could be bought on virtually every street corner. More than 60 percent of alcohol consumption was accounted for by spirits. The popularity of beer – still a favorite drink during the Middle Ages – was in heavy decline. Many breweries led  a precarious existence. To combat the misuse of strong drink, the government was promoting beer instead of the hard stuff. Gerard Adriaan Heineken agreed with this strategy and saw beer as a responsible beverage: delicious, good to drink and with a low alcohol percentage. He was convinced there had to be a market for such a product. His mother shared his enthusiasm and agreed to provide financial support.

Portrait paintings of the parents of Gerard Adriaan Heineken, Cornelis Heineken (1799-1862) and Anna Geertruida van der Paauw-Heineken (1804-1881).

HEINEKEN & CO.

In 1863, 22-year-old Heineken commenced negotiations for the purchase of brewery De Hooiberg, located on the Nieuwezijds Voorburgwal in Amsterdam. The company had been founded in 1592 and had once been among the most prestigious breweries in Holland. De Hooiberg had been incurring heavy losses for years, but this did nothing to discourage Heineken's plans. To ensure a good working environment, he needed to have complete control of the company. He rejected out of hand advice to settle for only some of the shares. 'So that I can acquire a share, perhaps earn good interest and pay out dividends? That's not what I want. It has to be all or nothing! Anything else is nonsense. If I need a new machine, I would have to go to the shareholders for their blessing! No, that's not the way!'

So all or nothing was the stake… and all was the result! On December 16, 1863, Heineken reached an agreement with the Supervisory Board of De Hooiberg. The company Heineken & Co. was founded on February 15, 1864, with the official transfer of De Hooiberg taking place in May. Gerard Adriaan Heineken paid in excess of 80,000 guilders for ownership of the brewery buildings. The new owner made no bones about his plans for the future, 'I have set myself the task of continuing this business with the utmost effort and painstaking care and will leave no remedy untried to persist in supplying the best quality beer in the long term.' The adventure could begin.

OUR NAME IS OUR BOND

1.6

The good name of the company and the product were of great value to Gerard Adriaan Heineken. Following the take-over, he presented himself to his customers in a letter, 'By reason of the Company having been honored in the past by pleasant orders from Your Esteemed Self, and with a view to my most excellent November beer, I do not hesitate to entreat Your Good Self to once again take a sample; should this not be satisfactory to Your Respected Taste (of which I am in no measure afraid), the same may be returned at my expense.' In modern English, the brewer is saying: my beer is good – if you are not satisfied, you can have your money back!

Irreproachable customer service and a generous complaints procedure were integral components of the company's standards of decency. Minor conflagrations were doused before they could develop into forest fires. Following a poor delivery, Gerard Adriaan Heineken wrote to a customer in Leeuwarden: 'An accident occurred with the wort from which Your beer was brewed, and if I had been able to anticipate this having such an outcome, I would have preferred to have had You wait a few days more.' The brewer also made a proposal to the dissatisfied customer, 'Naturally, it would not suit me to have to accept the return of full barrels to the brewery, and I therefore kindly request that You throw the beer away, and this as much as possible in a discrete manner, so that no-one shall see it, and I will send You replacement in full measure.' It is better to incur a loss oneself, than to cause a loss for a customer because of a bad product – this was clearly the motto. Such an approach engenders confidence: whereas De Hooiberg sold a total of 2,100 barrels of beer in 1862, during the first year under Heineken, turnover rose to some 5,000 barrels. At that time, the company employed 20 people. Not bad for a beginner.

THE MOVE TO THE STADHOUDERSKADE

A year after the take-over, the Amsterdam municipal authorities charged the brewery with causing a nuisance. A resident of the neighborhood had complained about the hoppy odor and pollution of the water in the canal. During this period, the city was busy covering up a lot of canals with cobbled streets. It therefore seized with both hands this opportunity to fill in the

The new Heineken & Co. brewery on the Stadhouderskade in Amsterdam, 1868.

canal on the Nieuwezijds Achterburgwal. The brewery was forced to look for new premises. In fact, this was not such a bad thing: the large increase in turnover meant that expansion had become inevitable anyway.

Heineken was given permission to build a new brewery on the Stadhouderskade. The progressive brewer asked architect J. Gosschalk to design the buildings and, on May 17, 1867, the foundation stone was laid. Gerard Adriaan bestowed this honor on his mother. The splendid celebrations then continued in a wooden beer shed, the Vijfhoek, on the brewery site. The directors treated their guests to a meal and a party was held, together with all the personnel – with foaming beer and drinking songs sung at full volume.

Less than a year later, the project was complete: a new building had been erected at plot YY123 in the municipality of Amsterdam, Steam Beer Brewery De Hooiberg, belonging to Heineken & Co. The new brewery boasted four brewing coppers and several coolers. The first product was heartily tasted by invited guests on January 22, 1868... and met with their approval. Now the serious life of the brewery could begin.

THE BEER DRINKER WANTS GENTLEMEN'S BEER

In around 1850, a number of new imported beers reached the Netherlands. Beer-drinking palates were tickled by the new tastes from Bavaria; Münchener and Gerste (barley beer). From Pilsen in Bohemia, a clear beer arrived – pilsner – and by the end of the nineteenth century pilsner went on to completely dominate the market. Both the Bavarian beer and pilsner were

1.8

'Die Port van Cleve' is one of Heineken's oldest customers. The café/restaurant is located at the site of the former brewery De Hooiberg on the Nieuwezijds Voorburgwal.

produced by the bottom-fermentation brewing process, which results in a clearer beer with a longer life. The new brewing process differed considerably from the top-fermentation technique Dutch brewers had been using for centuries. For this reason, most of these decided to continue brewing their traditional beers. Hardly surprising, really, as the new bottom-fermentation process involved a great many 'tricks of the trade' and required considerable investment. Beer drinkers took to referring to top-fermented beers as workman's beer, and the preferred bottom-fermented beers as Gentlemen's beer. In 1850, the Netherlands still only imported 1,280 hectoliters of bottom-fermented beer from Germany, but by 1865 this figure had risen to 14,800 hectoliters.

Initially, Heineken stuck with the top-fermentation technique. In 1868, the range included 'White' and 'Brown' beer (Princess and Double Princess), 'Hollandsche' Ale, 'Hollandsche' Porter, Pharoe and Old Brown. In addition, during the haymaking season, there was a Hay Beer, a reasonably light beer. The brewery saw little reason to be pessimistic about its top-fermented beers. A letter dated January 27, 1868 assures the Chamber of Commerce that there

	¹/₁ T.	¹/₂ T.	¹/₄ T.	¹/₈ T.
ƒ 12.— Wit of Bruin BIER (dubbel Princesse)	ƒ 16.15.	ƒ 8.15.	ƒ 4.15.	ƒ 2.19.
„ 8.— „ „ „ „ (Princesse)	12.15.	6.15.	3.15.	1.70.
„ 6.— „ „ „ „	10.15.	5.15.	2.65.	
„ 5.— „ „ „ „	9.15.	4.65.	2.40.	
„ 4.— „ „ „ „	8.15.	4.15.	2.15.	
Hollandsche ALE	24.—.	12.—.	6.—.	3.—.
„ PORTER	24.—.	12.—.	6.—.	3.—.
No. 37	24.—.	12.—.	6.—.	3.—.
Faro en oud Bruin	16.15.	8.15.	4.15.	2.19.

A price list from 1868 with the range of top-fermenting beers by Heineken & Co.

is little evidence 'that the Dutch Bavarian beer is diminishing consumption of the old Dutch types.' In spite of this optimistic attitude, the company started to feel the increasing pinch of competition from Bavarian beer in its home market. Although Heineken managed to provide the citizen with a good workman's beer at a good price with his 'Hollandsche' Ale and Princess, demand for bottom-fermented Gentlemen's beers increased steadily.

Gerard Adriaan Heineken knew what he had to do. He shifted his attention to these new Gentlemen's beers. In the autumn of 1868, he sent his confidential clerk, Paul Adrian Huet, on a study trip through Germany, the leading country at the time in the bottom-fermentation brewing process. Huet arrived at the significant conclusion that the company Heineken & Co. would have to start tapping into the bottom-fermentation process. It is likely that, during his journey, Huet also contacted the German master brewer Wilhelm Feltmann jr. This powerful figure joined Heineken in 1869 and, with his ambition and iron will, went on to sweep the brewery up in the course of world history.

THE CUSTOMER IS ALWAYS RIGHT

Feltmann prepared thoroughly for his new position. In 1869, he visited a large number of German and Austrian breweries. During his absence, Gerard Adriaan Heineken kept him informed of events at Heineken & Co. by means of lengthy letters. It was in this way that Feltmann learned that the brewery was to participate in the international exhibition in the 'Paleis voor Volksvlijt' (Palace of Arts & Crafts) in Amsterdam. The brewery had a stand in the hall at this exhibition and a small beer tent on the square in front, amidst a host of other small beer tents, coffee houses, snack vendors and stalls. Gerard Adriaan Heineken noted with dismay that the bottom-fermented beer at the beer pavilion of Viennese brewer Dreher was selling much better, and noted that Heineken's competitor 'has tapped more beer in three days than in the past two months.' In a letter dated August 13, 1869, he wrote, 'Our beer is receiving little attention at the exhibition, which is not surprising, as Dutch beer is not greatly popular, particularly in its unbottled form.'

The exhibition was a large-scale event, held in his home town, involving a great many laughing, fun-loving and beer-drinking visitors, the majority of whom preferred the competitors' beers. This was a great blow to the ambitious Gerard Adriaan Heineken. It was time for action. If the market wanted a clear, bottom-fermented beer, then the brewery would supply such a beer. If beer drinkers liked the color of the German beer, then Heineken & Co. would brew a beer that color. On January 17, 1870, the range was expanded: 'In view of the increasing consumption of Bavarian beer, we consider it necessary to brew this product alongside our normal product, and have taken the necessary measures to this end. We have commenced production of Bavarian beer to coincide with the start of the new year.' This decision was to mark a significant turning point in the history of beer-making.

DUTCH OLD MASTER

As a result of the outbreak of war between France and Germany in 1870, imports of German beer to the Netherlands dried up. This caused a great increase in the turnover of Heineken & Co.'s bottom-fermented beer. Regretfully, the brewery was forced to inform potential customers that 'we will be unable in the near future to accept new customers for Bavarian beer, as this would give rise to problems in fulfilling the ever-increasing demand from our regular customers.' This blossoming situation was also reflected in the number of personnel. In February 1871, the brewery already had forty employees, including some ten Germans. These master brewers knew the bottom-fermented beer process inside out, and played a vital role within the company.

In 1870, Heineken entered into negotiations with the city of Amsterdam regarding the purchase of land for expansion of the city. Villa Soeracarta, the Heineken family's country residence, was one of the buildings that disappeared beneath the rubble. According to the urban planning design by city architect J.G. van Niftrik, large numbers of residential buildings were to be erected around the brewery on the Stadhouderskade. New streets were constructed, named after well-known Dutch painters such as Frans Hals, Jan Steen, Bartholomeus van der Helst, Gerard Dou and Jacob van Campen. The brewery in Amsterdam now nestled among the Dutch Old Masters. Brewing entrepreneur Gerard Adriaan Heineken could be justly proud of the result. However, his own masterpiece was yet to come.

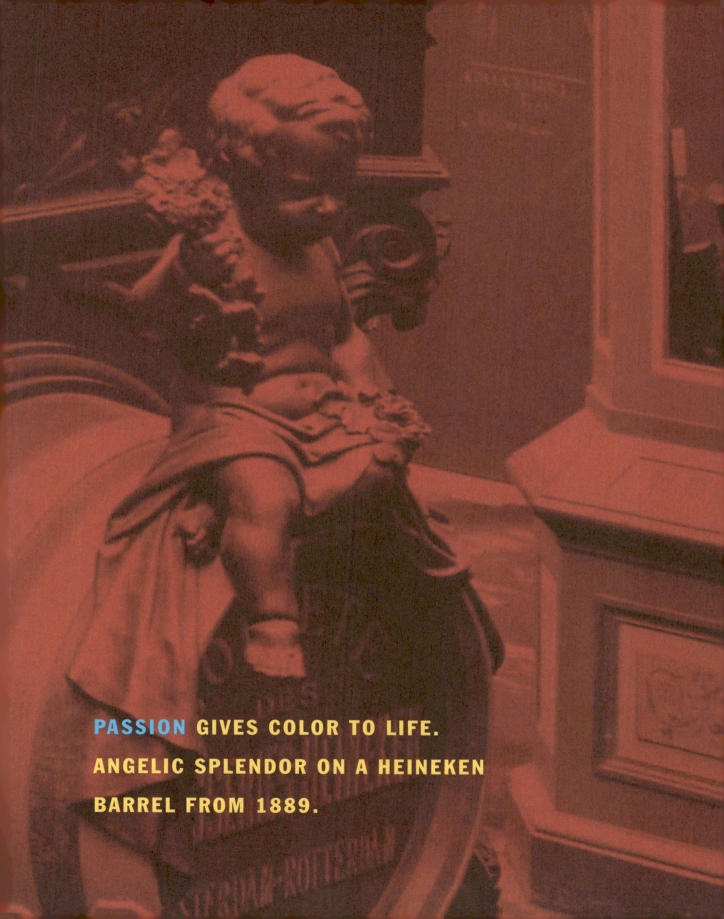

PASSION GIVES COLOR TO LIFE.
ANGELIC SPLENDOR ON A HEINEKEN
BARREL FROM 1889.

JOSEF ISRAËLS

RUYSDAEL

VINCENT VAN GOGH

THE HEINEKEN BREWERY IN AMSTERDAM IS LOCATED IN THE RESIDENTIAL AREA

VAN OSTADE

'DE PIJP', WHERE THE STREETS ARE NAMED AFTER FAMOUS DUTCH PAINTERS.

FRANS HALS

THE MASTER OF LIGHT AND DEEP, GLOWING GOLDEN TINTS IS WITHOUT DOUBT

PIETER AERTSZ

REMBRANDT VAN RIJN (1606-1669). HIS 'NACHTWACHT' (THE NIGHT WATCH),

MESDAG

PAINTED IN 1642, IS WORLD-FAMOUS AND JUST ONE OF THE MANY

1ᴱ JAN STEEN

MASTERPIECES HOUSED IN THE 'RIJKSMUSEUM' (NATIONAL MUSEUM),

GERARD DOU

JUST A STONE'S THROW FROM THE BREWERY. REMBRANDT VAN RIJN PAINTED

SAENREDAM

SOME HUNDRED SELF-PORTRAITS. ON THIS PAINTING FROM 1636, WE SEE THE

1ᴱ VAN DER HELST

PAINTER WITH HIS WIFE SASKIA, A GLASS OF BEER PROMINENT IN HIS RIGHT

FERDINAND BOL

HAND. THE PASSION OF A TRUE MASTER.

JACOB VAN CAMPEN

GOVERT FLINCK

MARIE HEINEKEN

KADE
KADE
STRAAT
STRAAT
STRAAT
STRAAT
STRAAT
STRAAT
PLEIN
STRAAT
STRAAT
STRAAT
STRAAT
STRAAT
PLEIN

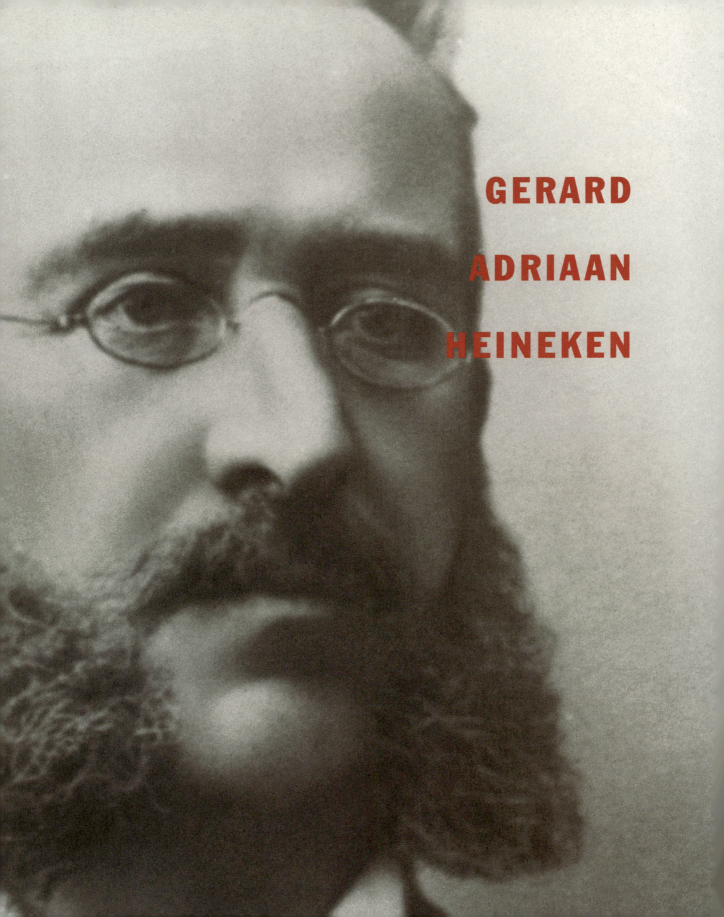

STARTED BREWING PILSNER IN 1870. THE BREWER WANTED TO CREATE A PILSNER UNSURPASSED IN TASTE, CLARITY AND COLOR.

THE TASTE, CLARITY AND COLOR OF ITS PILSNER ARE THE CORE OF THE HEINEKEN TRADITION. THANKS TO THE PASSION OF GERARD ADRIAAN HEINEKEN.

PASSION

SOCIÉTÉ DES BRASSERIES DE LA MEUSE

HBM

BIERE HOLLANDA

AMSTERDAM-ROTTERDAM

FAITH 2 IN YOURSELF

ROTTERDAM

What bold decisions Gerard Adriaan Heineken took. And at such an early stage in his life! These included an impressive villa he had built only a hundred yards from the Amsterdam brewery, allowing him to supervise and contemplate the business of the brewery in peace and quiet. On January 11, 1873, he signed the papers to officially incorporate 'Heineken's Bierbrouwerij Maatschappij NV'. The same year saw the foundation of Gerard Adriaan's masterpiece, the construction of an imposing new brewery, this time in Rotterdam. Having breweries in both Amsterdam and Rotterdam meant that Heineken could put the squeeze on its Dutch competitors. Thanks to its brewery in the port city of Rotterdam, the brewer finally had huge areas of the world at its feet. All of which thanks to the vision of Gerard Adriaan Heineken. To expand a company requires more even than this, however. Fortunately, 26-year-old Wilhelm Feltmann, a technical genius, combined strength of personality with an iron will. Heineken and his fellow director were like fire and water, but united by a single thought: to expand the brewery into the largest, and the best, in Europe.

'HEINEKEN'S BIERBROUWERIJ MAATSCHAPPIJ NV'

The emergence of bottom-fermented beer galvanized Gerard Adriaan Heineken into action. The capacity of the brewery in Amsterdam was inadequate to keep up with demand. For this reason, in 1872 he developed plans for the construction of a new brewery, specifically for bottom-fermented beer. Rotterdam caught his eye as a site with potential. This rapidly expanding port city could form an ideal base for future beer exports; the Heineken director always thought a few steps ahead. Furthermore, Rotterdam itself was a significant beer market, with its many workers in and around the docks. The cost of the new brewery was colossal, however. When Gerard Adriaan Heineken heard that some-

one else was contemplating similar plans, he decided to get in touch: two breweries for bottom-fermented beer in one city seemed a bad idea. The second party with ambitions in this area was the energetic Willem Baartz jr, director of the local Oranjeboom brewery. He had set his sights on a new brewery as his company was then geared up to brew top-fermented beers.

Baartz and Heineken decided to combine forces. On January 11, 1873, 'Heineken's Bierbrouwerij Maatschappij NV' (HBM) was founded in Rotterdam. The Board got down to brass tacks right away. A new brewery was to be set up, at which the two breweries would jointly produce bottom-fermented beer. The Oranjeboom brewery in Rotterdam would continue to produce exclusively top-fermented beers. HBM's total share capital amounted to 1,200,000 guilders, divided into 240 5,000-guilder shares – an incredible fortune in those days. The capital of a traditional top-fermenting brewery at the time would seldom have exceeded 100,000 guilders. Gerard Adriaan Heineken acquired 166 shares and was appointed President/Director of the new company. The technical management of the brewery in Rotterdam was entrusted to Wilhelm Feltmann, along with the technical supervision of Amsterdam. As compensation for giving up their own plans, Hubertus François Hoyer and Willem Baartz of Oranjeboom were allocated seats on the Board and Supervisory Board of the new company, along with a share package.

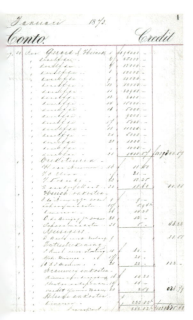

The first cashbook of 'Heineken's Bierbrouwerij Maatschappij NV', Amsterdam 1873.

Two photos of the Heineken brewery in Rotterdam, under construction (1873) and following its completion (1874).

Construction work on the Crooswijkse Singel in Rotterdam, under architect A.W. van Dam, got under way in the spring of 1873. The first stone was laid on June 23. 4,000 piles, 6,200,000 bricks, 1,500 cubic meters of wood and a similarly mind-boggling amount of metal later, an extensive complex of buildings had been built, with a floor area of no less than 3,000 square meters. The building was insured for 478,000 guilders. The yeast cellars had a total capacity of 3,000 hectoliters, the eight maturing cellars could each hold in excess of this amount. An awe-inspiring building. In March 1873, Gerard Adriaan Heineken informed his 400 customers in Amsterdam and further afield that he was ceasing production of 'Hollandsche' Ale and the other workman's beers. HBM was to become an exclusive brewer of the bottom-fermented Gentlemen's beer. With brewing premises in both Amsterdam and Rotterdam, the company set out on a new chapter in its history.

WILHELM FELTMANN – A FORCEFUL PERSONALITY

Technical director Feltmann was closely involved with the new Rotterdam brewery from the very start. Such was his impatience to start brewing, that he was giving out orders even before the construction work had been completed. On March 28, 1874, the brewery completed its first wort. The director was triumphant, stating, 'Soon, no more alien beer will be sold in this place!' His verdict upon delivery of the first beer in June 1874: 'It was great.' He was a man with a mission: his aim was to brew the best beer in the world. 'The days when all good beer came from Bavaria are at an end!', he confidently proclaimed.

Wilhelm Feltmann, master brewer and technical director of Heineken between 1869-1897.

The ambitious technical director saw the Rotterdam brewery as his creation, as well as a means of demonstrating his true worth. Anything that stood in his path had to go. He was merciless in his dedication. In 1869, he once picked up a worker and, in a fit of rage, threw him out of the window. He expected the personnel to be as perfect as the product. This applied equally, in Feltmann's uncompromising view, to the managers. In Feltmann's opinion, it was the management in Amsterdam that brought about a significant fall in profits for HBM in the 1874/1875 financial year. He could see only one solution: at Feltmann's insistence, in April 1876, J.G. van Gendt – who had in fact been appointed by Feltmann himself – resigned as technical director.

The Van Gendt incident prompted Gerard Adriaan Heineken to write at length to the supervisory directors. He expressed his dissatisfaction in a letter dated February 9, 1876. Heineken and Feltmann had been at odds since the foundation of HBM. The two men avoided one another as much as possible, and when their paths did cross, they aggravated one another. Heineken realized, however, that he needed the terrific capabilities of his former master brewer. But Gerard Adriaan Heineken felt himself to be entangled in a web spun by the technical director. He was sick and tired of the constant bickering. The fact that the existence of HBM appeared to depend on a 'wrestling match with tremendous effort', meant that Heineken no longer enjoyed running the company. He did not throw in the towel, but retreated somewhat into the background. He waxed nostalgic for the best years of his life, those of Heineken & Co.

Feltmann was crucial to the company. With his indisputable knowledge of brewing, he rivaled everyone. His dedication to the company and love of his craft were boundless. He was one of a kind. Following Van Gendt's resignation, he took over the technical management in Amsterdam, together with master brewer Stuer. Together with Gerard Adriaan Heineken, this triumvirate ran the Amsterdam branch. Stuer was the perfect counterpart to Feltmann. He combined fervor with technical skill and was famed for his stringent demands in terms of order and tidiness. Although the workers realized that a clean brewery is one of the preconditions for good beer, they were subjected to a terrifying daily ritual: master brewer Stuer would check the floors with his fingernail to make sure that they were spotless. Feltmann was in his element.

COMPETITION!

The arrival of several large bottom-fermenting breweries made competition on the beer market in the Netherlands all the fiercer. Turnover had to be boosted in order to recoup investments. And the struggle between the various brewers was not always played out according to the rules. HBM was regularly confronted by second-rate beer being sold under its name. This was a serious blow to a brewery that was trying to market its product on the basis of guaranteed quality. In other cases, other brewers maintained that HBM's beer had been produced in their brewing plants.

The greatest competition to HBM came from Amsterdam brewery De Amstel. The two brewers regularly came across one another not only in Amsterdam, but also in the northern provinces of the Netherlands. Outside of the larger cities, De Amstel managed to shake off many of its competitors by supplying free ice for refrigeration with its beer. Heineken and De Amstel regularly attempted to steal one another's customers. The management wrote to a potential customer in September 1874, for instance, 'Regarding a matter of which Your Esteemed Self may already be aware; we in any event consider it our duty to draw your attention to this, in order that you may profit by it. What De Amstel supplies, is green beer and not good; the time is therefore ripe to seize this opportunity.' The tone is polite, but the intention somewhat less noble. De Amstel, however, proved a worthy opponent, with a thorough understanding of brewing techniques.

Lower prices became an important weapon in the competitors' arsenal. The management was against this as a matter of principle, convinced that a good product would always win in the longer term. Even in the countryside setting of the province of Brabant, the brewery made no concessions on price, as it informed a customer from the town of Waalwijk in October 1877. 'That the price is high compared with the local "Brabantsche versche" beer, we do not deny,' HBM writes, 'but we aim to keep the quality as high as possible, and adhere to the motto: a good product for a good price.' And in a cutting tone, a customer from the city of 's-Hertogenbosch was informed that the brewery had even more expensive beer, but that 'the people of Brabant are accustomed to receiving a lot of beer for a little money.' The southern provinces of the Netherlands in fact conducted a silent boycott against Heineken, although the management was of the opinion that the innkeepers of Brabant had little to complain about. After all, they paid the brewery fifteen cents a liter, while from each liter they could pour five glasses, which they then sold for fifteen cents each.

Initially, HBM maintained this stance: the prices for the more expensive Bavarian beer and pilsner would remain unchanged. When sales began to stagnate, however, Feltmann advised creating a cheaper beer. He was of the opinion that HBM should not only purvey high-class beers. For this reason, in 1882 the brewery launched Gerste beer – a lighter, bottom-fermented beer with a lower alcohol percentage. It proved a success. HBM's sales increased considerably. Whereas sales in the Netherlands during the financial year 1880/1881 amounted to 46,015 hectoliters, in the financial year 1883/1884 this rose to 68,203 hectoliters. The beer enjoyed immense popularity and bulk customers in Rotterdam, such as the cafés Loos, Kroon and De Witte Sociëteit on the prestigious Hofplein square, ordered predominately Gerste beer. The technical director concluded with satisfaction: 'On Saturday alone, the city of Rotterdam took 300 Hectoliters in the familiar little barrels. Ach, if only it could last.' Unfortunately, this sunny disposition was not to endure.

A 'FIGHTING BEER'

The introduction of the cheaper Gerste beer was inadequate to stem the tide of ever sharper competition. HBM had to join in the battle for the beer market. In 1885, the price of the Gerste beer was reduced, and the prices of the pilsner and Bavarian beers were revised for particular areas. HBM was acutely aware of the heady fumes of competitors such as Van Vollenhoven, Oranjeboom, De Amstel and a number of German breweries breathing down its neck. A price war broke out. HBM felt the uneasy constraints of its position.

These price reductions on the part of HBM did not immediately have the desired effect. What could the brewery do? Drop prices even further? Feltmann refused, but came up with an alternative solution: to introduce a 'fighting beer' to the market. Alongside the existing Gerste beer, an extra light, even cheaper Gerste beer was produced. The names were not far to seek: Gerste No. 1 and Gerste No. 2. Feltmann was not actually very enthusiastic about having to brew such a flaccid beer, but the degree of competition left him no other choice: in this case, the interests of the brewery were paramount. Neither was master brewer Stuer prepared to allow this beer into the Rotterdam vats without a fight. He saw Gerste No. 2 as an insult to his qualities as a brewer. But the technical director reported on April 3, 1889 to Gerard Adriaan Heineken that, 'Decisions taken by the Board must be put into practice', whereby the technical director could not afford to 'tolerate the resistance of a master brewer. The test worts have already been made.'

The strategy was to win over the 'price drinkers' with the cheap beer, while the old clientele would continue as far as possible to purchase the higher-class beer. HBM did not wish to make too much noise about Gerste No. 2. The Board preferred not to sell it in Amsterdam at all, and in the provinces 'it should not be marketed with too much industry.' The new beer was necessary, but kept at the back of the shop. Nevertheless, it was a great success. This beer had potential, particularly in Rotterdam, where HBM achieved turnover in excess of 8,000 hectoliters during the first seven months, and demand showed no signs of drying up. The cheaper beer was a big hit with workers – 'a section of the consuming public that was more or less a stranger to us to date,' according to the HBM management in 1890. Feltmann had a good nose for what the market wanted. His only problem was the low profit margin on the lighter beer; the brewer was selling Gerste No. 2 almost at cost price.

RESULTS COUNT

In Rotterdam in particular, the introduction of the cheaper Gerste beer led to a heightening of competition with Oranjeboom. Both breweries put all hands to the pumps. Each tried to lure customers away from the other, often by delving deep into their coffers. A huge sigh of relief reverberated around the boardrooms each time a customer was won over. The café owners did well out of the situation: they were increasingly able to ask for cash and favors for stocking a particular beer. As the banks were not interested in providing credit to the catering sector, an unknown market for them, the brewers took over the role of banker. In exchange for credit and other facilities, the café owners were willing to sign an exclusive supply contract.

Allying the café owners in this way assured the brewers of fixed custom and guaranteed beer sales. The breweries' expensive production apparatus gave the best return when running in a stable fashion, at optimum capacity. HBM too was forced to give substantial incentives. The members of the Board were not entirely happy with this state of affairs. 'Substantial sales cannot be maintained without making advance payments and giving credit, it is an inevitable down-side of the business,' the Board concluded in 1894. If HBM refused to give credit, another brewer would be standing by waving a sack of money and a keg of beer. The market operated according to its own rules: expanding sales had to go hand-in-hand with the provision of credit.

At the same time, the management relaxed its policy in relation to the acquisition of its own outlets. In 1892, HBM acquired ownership, for 500,000 guilders, of a 'Company for the operation of coffee houses, hotels, restaurants and buffets.' With this purchase, HBM became the proud owner of a number of beer houses in Amsterdam and Utrecht, including the celebrated Café Monopole on the Heiligenweg and Mille Colonnes on the Rembrandtplein.

Purchasing outlets had become an important weapon in the competition war. This also kept cafés and restaurants with a certain allure or large turnover within the company. HBM bought beer houses in the towns of Zutphen, Groningen, Rotterdam and Nijmegen. The brewery even bought a few properties on the boulevards of Paris, where the brand sparkled like a star.

2.11

Interior of the Amsterdam alehouse 'Die Port van Cleve' in 1889.

HBM was able to keep its head well above water among the competitive maelstrom on the beer market. Domestic turnover rose from some 175,000 hectoliters in 1893 to more than 350,000 hectoliters in 1914. The results engendered a feeling of satisfaction, annual dividend payments could be increased and the company's financial standing was reinforced. The general picture of HBM at this time was therefore a positive one. The 'fighting beer', Gerste No. 2, protected the quality beers against a fall in prices. The brewery persisted in its belief that a superior quality beer would eventually see off its competitors. This was the best strategy for maintaining the company's reputation and building on its good name.

FOREIGN AFFAIRS

Soon after its establishment in 1873, HBM started exporting kegged beer to England, Belgium and northern France. Demand for a good beer also existed outside of the Netherlands, it seemed. Initially, the perishable nature of the unpasteurized kegged beer restricted its radius of travel. Attempts by brewers to export beer overseas resulted in a great many problems with quality.

2.12

From 1875, the Rotterdam brewery concentrated on creating a non-perishable bottled beer by means of pasteurization. Stuer, the traditional master brewer in Amsterdam, swore by the traditional kegged beer, and wanted no part in pasteurized bottled beer. Feltmann on the other hand was much more open to innovations in brewing technology, and embraced the technique of 'pasteurizing' developed by French chemist and bacteriologist Louis Pasteur. This involved the bottled beer being heated to between 50 and 60 degrees Celsius, thus killing the bacteria and greatly improving the beer's shelf life. Ideal for transporting beer to far-off countries. On January 11, 1882, the management reported to Leversen & Co., a company in Rotterdam, that 'Our bottled beer remains in a very good condition for six months or more, while the slightest leakage in a shipment of kegged beer renders the entire barrel useless.' That this was no idle boast is demonstrated by a letter sent to the brewery in June 1880 by a domestic agent: 'Here, we can show you beer that has been in the attic since 1877, i.e. that has experienced the heat of three summers, and still has good effervescence and a good taste.'

By the end of the nineteenth century, HBM beer was being shipped all over the world. The beer bottles had a label on the neck showing the name of the importer. The two suppliers, the brewer and the importer, guaranteed the quality of the Heineken beer.

The pasteurizing process made shipment of bottled beer possible to regions such as the South of France, Spain, Southern and Central America, the Dutch East Indies and India. Before the brewery in Amsterdam had realized it, the Rotterdam brewery had taken over control of exports. To begin with, the new activity exceeded all expectations. In 1883, more than 25 percent of turnover was generated outside of the Netherlands. Profits at this stage were small, however, as competition on foreign markets was intense. In addition, the export process itself was not entirely without problems. Both the brewer and the customers constantly had complaints about transport, price calculation and the treatment of the beer. The brewer had less control over its foreign customers, and depended heavily on their good will. In some cases, the brewery didn't even know to which countries the beer was going: large quantities of beer were sold to sea carriers trading for themselves.

THE CANCAN, MEDALS AND SONGS OF PRAISE

France was HBM's principal export market during the nineteenth century. Gerard Adriaan Heineken had fallen under the spell of this country, and in particular the capital city, Paris. He saw the 'city of light' as the center of the world, and as a brewer with a certain reputation, he wanted a presence there. In a private capacity, and more or less outside of HBM, he started to 'tinker about' in this market. It was in Paris, in 1875, that Heineken came into contact with Mr. Tarut, who was appointed as importer for the city.

Heineken wanted to get into the French market at all costs. The beer was supplied to the importers at a very favorable purchase price. Some of the beer was supplied under a plethora of different names, as the label 'HBM Rotterdam' had a negative effect in competition with the highly popular German beers. Dispirited, Gerard Adriaan Heineken concluded that, in France, every brand of beer sold well, as long as its name ended with the German 'bräu'. In fact, there was even a plan at one time to introduce a 'Heineken-bräu' to the market. The plan never came to fruition, however. There was as yet no uniformity of operation on the export markets. The brewers were finding their way, and had to adapt to local circumstances. On the English market, the beer was known as Light Export, on the Belgian market as Bock Ale.

During the 1870s, HBM sold several thousand hectoliters in France. Heineken's successful participation at an exhibition in Paris in 1878 had a positive effect; one of the results was the signing of a contract with the Folies Bergères for an annual supply of 2,000 hectoliters. Heineken and the cancan. Exports to France also led to great costs and a mountain of administration. During transportation by train, both full and empty barrels were getting damaged; some were even disappearing altogether. How was this possible? The brewer blamed the French way of working. In 1877, four freight wagons were therefore acquired to transport beer abroad. Deliveries to Paris took place once a week. By 1882, 8,000 hectoliters were already flowing into France – some 10 percent of total turnover. Paris, Lille, Le Havre and Bordeaux accounted for the lion's share of sales. Exports were made from the brewery in Rotterdam, except for the beer for Paris, which came from Amsterdam. Gerard Adriaan Heineken viewed the French capital as his own territory, in addition to which an 'Amsterdam' label had greater appeal to the beer drinkers of Paris.

Although the Heineken beer was more expensive than the French product, sales were quite reasonable. The beer had a good reputation and was specifically aimed at 'une bonne clientèle bourgeoise.' The management wrote to the importer on May 23, 1882, 'Rest assured that we will spare no effort to supply to You a beer, that in each and every respect can compete with the best in Paris. We are proud that now, following years of struggle, our quality has also triumphed in Paris; we will therefore not be quick to endanger our newly acquired position. You may be sure that our quality will not diminish, but rather we continue to strive to improve wherever possible.' Quality was a permanent topic of conversation. On October 20, 1886, a letter to a French beer agent stated, 'J'aime beaucoup à vendre de la bière, mais encore de plus j'aime mon nom et ma bonne réputation comme brasseur.'

2.15

Uniformity of labeling, as applied by Heineken today, was not practiced in the nineteenth century. In blue: the official export label of HBM, showing the name of the French importer. In red: a French variant on the HBM label.

By 1885, HBM was the biggest exporter of beer to France, but sales were made or broken by Tarut, who gradually began to neglect his position as an importer. Financial mismanagement on the part of the importer led to a rapid deterioration in the situation: sales in the financial year 1889/1890 fell to 5,372 hectoliters. Following Tarut's death in February 1892, the position was passed on to another importer, but he proved even worse than Tarut. Several years later, a Heineken director declared, 'We have such a job finding good people in this country, how should we find such a person among the canailles de Paris?'

From the 1890s, HBM's exports to France and other export countries tailed off heavily. Protectionist measures and stiff competition from German beers played a role in this, but more significantly, the brewery did not follow the trend to cut prices. According to the management, the competition only had to win market share, while HBM's reputation was at stake. There was another reason why exports gradually declined: the company undertook no advertising at all. Heineken may have been a pioneer when it came to brewing, but advertising was a dirty word. 'A good product is recommended by its use alone. Only when an article is taken up without the accompaniment of a chorus of praise can we be assured that it deserves its reputation; and will find its way, inconspicuously.' In this, we hear an authentic voice from the nineteenth century.

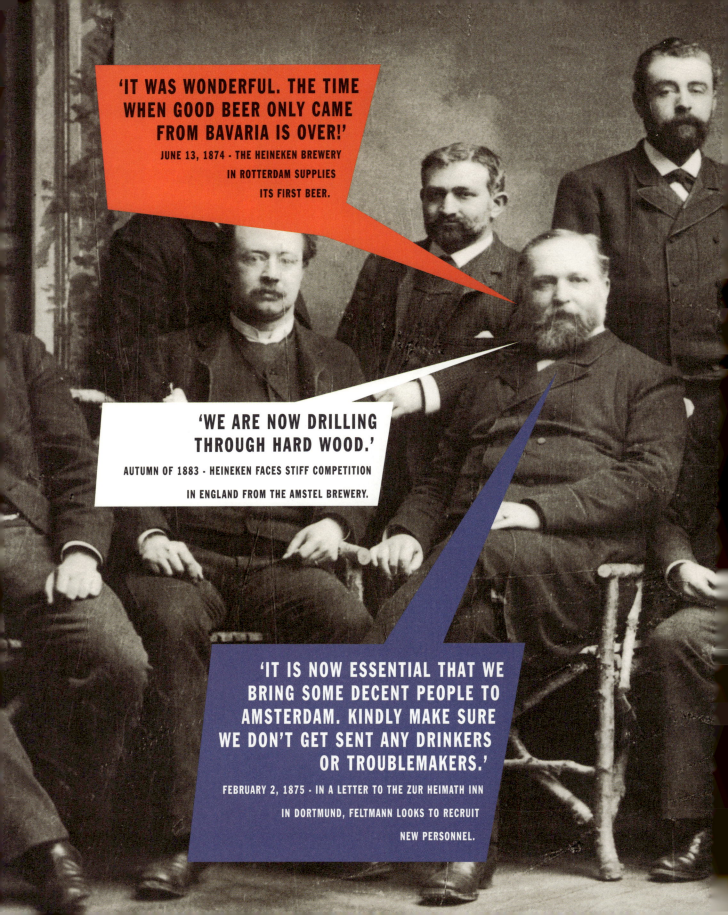

WILHELM FELTMANN

MASTER BREWER AND TECHNICAL DIRECTOR OF HEINEKEN

BETWEEN 1869-1897

THE HEINEKEN SKITTLES CLUB, 1887

THE HEINEKEN RANGE APPEALED TO EVERYONE IN THE
NINETEENTH CENTURY:
EXCLUSIVE 'GENTLEMEN'S BEERS' FOR THE MIDDLE CLASSES AND
CHEAPER 'TABLE BEERS' FOR THE WORKERS

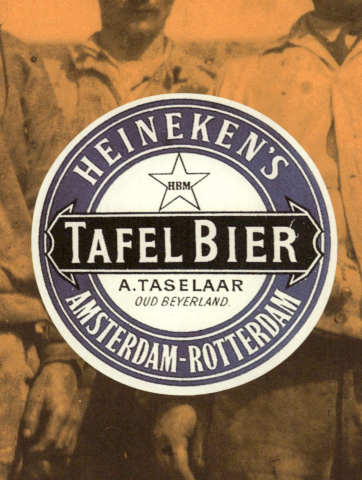

THE HEINEKEN RANGE APPEALED TO EVERYONE IN THE NINETEENTH CENTURY: CHEAPER 'TABLE BEERS' FOR THE WORKERS AND EXCLUSIVE 'GENTLEMEN'S BEERS' FOR THE MIDDLE CLASSES

1884

1884

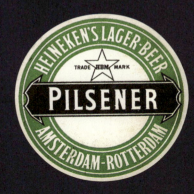

1884

1884

1884

1884

1884

IN 1884, THE HEINEKEN BREWERY REGISTERED ITS EXPORT LABEL. QUALITY IN THE BEER WORLD NOW HAD A NAME, A COLOR AND A STAR.

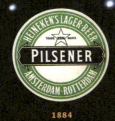

THE HEINEKEN NAME,

THE GREEN COLOR AND

THE RED STAR MAKE UP

THE LOGO OF THE MOST

SUCCESSFUL EXPORT

BEER IN THE WORLD.

2000

DARING

NAME
3
AND
FAME

'It gives us pleasure to inform you that we were awarded the Very Highest Distinction for Dutch Beers at the World Fair in Paris, the Diploma of Honor' – these were the words the brewery proudly used in a letter to its Dutch customers in August 1889. But why were they so proud? Because the brewer regarded the prize as a reward for years of passionate research into ways of improving the brewing process and of getting to the bottom of the 'secret' of beer. Heineken was implementing important technical innovations such as refrigerating equipment, a company laboratory and an experimental brewery. The most important factor, however, was that the company fell in love with the magic of brewing. Of course, the brewer did not discover everything – but enough to surprise the world of beer in 1886 with its Heineken 'A' yeast. It was as a result of this that pilsner beer acquired its special, pure character. Two prizes were subsequently won in Paris: the Grand Prix de Paris in 1889 and, one year later, the supply of Heineken beer to the Eiffel tower restaurant, justifying talk of the 'highest' distinction.

3.4

WERELDTENTOONSTELLING PARIJS 1889.
GRAND-PRIX,
Eenige hoogste onderscheiding voor Nederlandsche Bieren.

The rise of pilsner was accompanied by intense competition in the area of quality. Heineken won many prizes, including the important Grand Prix at the Paris World Exhibition in 1889. The brewer still proudly exhibits this on its label.

A DELICIOUS COOL BEER

Cooling is essential for the bottom-fermentation brewing process. The main fermentation process takes place at temperatures of 5 to 10 degrees Celsius and without cooling equipment the brewing of bottom-fermentation beer was impossible in countries such as the Netherlands, with their relatively mild climates. Originally, brewers used natural ice. During severe winters, HBM had ice hacked from the frozen canals in Amsterdam and the outer reaches of the IJ river. This work, known as 'ijzen' (icing), had to be carried out quickly. The task was subcontracted to firms that then had to ensure 'that, whenever a new freeze commenced, they send at least twelve men to the brewery at 9 o'clock in the morning, which team will have to be expanded at one o'clock in the afternoon to comprise at least one hundred men, in order to pack full the cellar and ice houses...'. If the winter was not severe enough, the brewers had to order additional natural ice from Norway. The price of the 'Norwegian ice' was, on average, four to five times higher than 'domestic ice.' 'The winter has yielded no ice and this caper has cost us approximately 25,000 guilders more than in other years,' HBM lamented after the sluggish winter of 1872.

The development of refrigerating equipment was a godsend for the world of brewing. Such equipment made it possible to brew bottom-fermented beer all year round, even after a mild winter. During the autumn of 1873, technical director Feltmann ordered an absorption refrigerator from the German company Vaass & Littmann for the mechanical production of ice. This ice was used in the brewing process. In order to cool stored beer, HBM was still reliant on natural ice. The machine functioned quite well and in 1874 a second was ordered at a cost of 16,000 guilders for the brewery in Rotterdam. The purchase of the machines partially compensated for the cost of ice provision, but expenditure on this item remained considerable. Moreover, the original enthusiasm dampened within a number of years: the machines malfunctioned regularly, did not work satisfactorily in warm weather and eventually produced too little yield.

The management wanted a better machine. A properly functioning refrigeration system was, in its view, vital for the further development of HBM. The brewery sought contact with Dr. Carl von Linde, lecturer in theoretical mechanical engineering at the Polytechnic School in Munich. Since the beginning of the 1870s, he had been collaborating with Gabriël Sedlmayer of the Munich Spaten brewery and Deglmayer of the Viennese Dreher brewery on the perfection of a French refrigerator. Von Linde succeeded in constructing a prototype of a new refrigerator. HBM kept a close eye on his research. In 1879, Feltmann visited the Carlsberg brewery in Copenhagen where two Linde machines were operational at that time. He was ecstatic: 'Those two Linde machines are functioning brilliantly in Copenhagen', he wrote to the Munich brewer Sedlmayer. In close cooperation with Von Linde and the Carlsberg brewery in Denmark, HBM helped to perfect the machine. For Feltmann, a dream had come true – in a letter dated November 17, 1880 to Dr. Von Linde, he wrote, 'One of my greatest desires, namely the replacement of natural ice with artificial cooling, is close to being fulfilled.'

3.6 The introduction of the Linde refrigeration machine at the end of the nineteenth century radically changed the brewing process.

'HEINEKEN ICE'

In December 1880, the members of the Supervisory Board of HBM approved the proposal by the management to purchase a Linde ice machine for the Amsterdam brewery. The total investment amounted to 86,000 guilders. 'Hopefully,' wrote Feltmann after the machine had been made operational in June 1881, 'the absence of winter has caused me ice worries for the last time, at least with regard to the brewery.' A number of months later he remarked excitedly, 'Our Amsterdam ice machine is working brilliantly!' The new ice machine created quite a stir. Requests for information and details rained in from locations in the Netherlands and abroad. Originally, HBM was pleased to cooperate – the world of beer would, in his view, be assisted by as much openness as possible with regard to technical improvements – but a lack of time meant it was forced to refer guests to the Von Linde company in Wiesbaden. The members of the Supervisory Board of HBM were extremely pleased with the results achieved and heaped the highest praise upon their technical director. In 1883, he was allowed to purchase a second machine, this time for the brewery in Rotterdam.

Mechanized ice production meant that HBM was no longer dependent on expensive natural ice and no longer needed to equip large cellars for the purpose of ice storage. Beer production could be increased since work could be carried out throughout both summer and winter. In addition, HBM turned into an ice seller and competitor of the traders in Norwegian ice, thereby recouping part of the investment. On July 1, 1881, potential clients received a circular informing them: 'Within a couple of days, the Amsterdam newspapers will have brought the fact to your attention that our ice factory (1,000 kg per hour) in Amsterdam has been rendered operational. From now on, we will be supplying ice from Amsterdam, as crystal clear (as the purest Norwegian ice) in rectangular blocks of approximately 1 meter in length, approximately 17 centimeters thick and wide, with each block weighing approximately 25 to 26 kilos. The ice is to be supplied in single crates 0.75 meters wide and high and 1.05 meters long which can therefore hold well over 400 kilos. Since the blocks are positioned tight up against each other and because the ice is crystal clear, the losses due to melting (in relation to Norwegian ice) will be minimal.'

A worker using machine-made ice in the Amsterdam Heineken brewery.

The brewery became a formidable player in the ice trade and entered into contracts with, among others, butter and margarine factories and fish traders. In order to reinforce its 'ice position', the company purchased a third machine in 1891, although ice – of course – continued to be a by-product. The main objective was the company's own ice supply and the brewing of beer. 'Ice trading is very, very attractive,' explained Gerard Adriaan Heineken, 'but, in our view, must only be regarded as occupying second place; the principle business is the acquisition of a reserve machine in order to guard as much as possible against calamities.' The technical director developed a modern refrigeration system based on the Linde machine, with which the yeast stores and conditioning cellars could be cooled. Blocks of ice were no longer necessary, meaning that the brewery's ice trade came to an end. HBM had won the icy fight hands down.

HBM was the first brewery in the Netherlands to switch to the Linde system. Its example was soon copied by other large-scale bottom-fermentation breweries. For most smaller breweries, the installation of a cooling system was far too expensive, whereby production of the popular bottom-fermentation beer remained beyond their means. They were forced to continue producing top-fermented beers or brew seasonal beers.

HEINEKEN 'A' YEAST

From the brewing technology point of view, HBM played a very stimulating role in a number of areas. The brewer wanted to get to grips with the brewing process. And in the brewing process, yeast played a decisive role. The brewing of beer had, for centuries, been an incomprehensible process. On one particular day the beer was of a good, on another of a lesser quality – without it always being clear why. Was the weather the reason, the raw materials or had the wort been boiled for too long? The master brewers – the great 'magicians' – worked with a fickle product, meaning that they were never sure how the wort would turn out.

Wilhelm Feltmann did not want to give in to the incomprehensibility of beer. He thought it bizarre that the brewery knew hardly anything of the effects of yeast, for example. Why did the yeast used by HBM lose its strength as time passed? The consequence was that the beer went off all too often. Quite regularly, batches of yeast purchased in Germany were spoiled by the time they arrived in Amsterdam and were therefore worthless. In 1884, the brewery received complaints from clients about the beer's mediocre quality and bitter aftertaste. The technical director invested a great deal of time in studying this problem, but to his exasperation he failed to penetrate the mysteries of yeast culture.

On January 1, 1886, Dr. H. Elion was put in charge of the new Heineken laboratory. He introduced the Heineken 'A' yeast to the world. It is still used to give Heineken beer its characteristic taste.

Left: Dr. H. Elion's testing flask. It was in this vessel that the famous Heineken 'A' yeast first saw the light of day in 1886. The culture methods have changed, but the 'A' yeast is still the same.

Jacob Christian Jacobsen, owner of the Carlsberg brewery in Denmark, chose to use a scientific approach to tackle the problem of yeast. In 1877, he set up a laboratory and appointed Dr. Emil Christian Hansen to the post of head of the research department. His assignment was to focus the research exclusively on yeast. Hansen expanded on the scientific results produced by Louis Pasteur. In his 1876 publication entitled 'Etudes sur la bière' (Studies on Beer), Pasteur already referred to the existence of numerous yeast strains that can add a variety of characteristics to beer. Only a few types are suitable for the preparation of beer. In his laboratory, Hansen concentrated on the cultivation of a pure type of yeast from a single cell. He succeeded in cultivating several types of yeast in flasks he had designed specially for the purpose. In 1884, he had the opportunity of testing the types of yeast he had cultivated when the yeast used in the brewery was found to be contaminated. The result was excellent and brewer Jacobsen was won over to this 'pure culture'. Because Hansen did not entirely know how to solve the difficulties related to the cultivation of yeast, Jacobsen appealed to the international brewing world to join forces to tackle the problem. Feltmann was amenable to this proposition.

During these same years, he paid regular visits to the Carlsberg brewery in connection with the development of the Linde ice machine. He was greatly impressed by his Danish colleagues' laboratory. He could see that, compared with Carlsberg, HBM was just muddling along at this stage. Things had to change. Responding to a proposal put forward by the technical director, HBM engaged a physicist in July 1885 for the purpose of yeast research. His name was Dr. H. Elion. This turned out to be an important decision. Following study trips to the Carlsberg brewery and after the setting up of a HBM laboratory, Dr. Elion started his major project on January 1, 1886. He was soon able to present some significant results. He improved the cultivation equipment constructed by Hansen, and cultivated two pure strains of yeast – 'A' yeast and 'D' yeast. HBM was the second brewery to start applying pure culture on a large scale. This enabled the company to manage the brewing process more satisfactorily. The 'A' yeast – the brewery's pride and joy – was initially only used for Heineken pilsner. The 'D' yeast, which was used for lighter beers, disappeared from circulation after a time. Dr. Elion's successors managed to continue cultivating 'A' yeast of the same quality. As a result, Elion's pioneering work still forms the basis for most bottom-fermentation beers and the characteristic pure taste of Heineken beer.

In October 1886, the first barrels of beer prepared using the new 'A' yeast left the brewery for Paris. In a letter dated March 21, 1887, the management wrote to the Parisian representative: 'The use of pure yeasts has rendered our beers so exceptionally pure and sweet that they are "extremely light" on the palate. At the moment, our beers are definitely no less full-flavor than good Munich beers and the frothiness is second to none.' The 'A' yeast was of a supreme quality. HBM exported many thousands of kilos of 'A' yeast to foreign breweries for many years.

The larger German brewers were also among the brewery's clientele, as they were not yet capable of cultivating yeast of a comparable quality. Due to increasing international competition, the brewery stopped its yeast deliveries in 1930. HBM yeast was the reason why some brands of beer became the successes they are today. From that time onwards, Heineken kept the 'A' yeast exclusively for its own use.

CARE FOR THE PRODUCT

To HBM, quality also meant using the best raw materials and setting up an internal quality control system. The brewery preferred to purchase its barley, malt and hops from the same, reliable suppliers. It had no desire to do business with unofficial sources. The brewery did not want a product with 'trade-appeal', but rather one with 'customer-appeal'. Supplies were not allowed to be of any less quality than the samples. The art was to find the proper balance between a high-quality product and a reasonable cost price. The best quality barley at the best price could be supplied primarily by the company Pfister-Mayer & Co. in Munich. However, during the 1930s, HBM started using a lot of barley cultivated in the Netherlands due to the certainty of supply, among other reasons.

Originally, the brewery imported malt from England. However, this raw material was consistently of an unsatisfactory quality and, at the start of 1900, the required malt was primarily imported from Germany and Austria. Due to the quality aspect, the brewery attached more and more importance to its own malting house. In 1883, the Rotterdam malting house expanded to enable a production capacity of 100,000 hectoliters of beer. For a number of reasons, HBM never bought hops via middlemen. In the first place, in order to keep the lines of communication with the producer as short as possible, since rapid delivery times were, after all, of considerable importance in preventing loss of quality. In the second place, the trade in hops

3.12

The pitching workshop and cooperage of the brewery in Rotterdam, 1927. Here, the wooden beer barrels were made – a labor-intensive process that required a great deal of skill.

demanded highly specialized knowledge and it was very difficult to find the right people. Purchasers therefore did business principally on the basis of trust in a supplier. Once the brewery had established a reliable relationship, it preferred not to disrupt it by starting to work in a different manner. HBM's preferred suppliers were the companies Schröder-Santfort and Heijden-Heimer & Co.

When the bacteriologist Jan Emmens joined the company on October 1, 1920, he was assigned the task of implementing a meticulous quality control system. The initial focus was on detecting beer infections, which resulted in a considerable reduction in the product's quality. The problem turned out to be related to the barrels. When clients returned the empty barrels, residues of beer remained inside and these started to rot. The brewery needed the barrels badly and therefore cleaned them too quickly before re-using them. The barrels were cleaned on

1933 saw the commencement of radical renovation to the Amsterdam brewery, for which part of the Jacob van Campenstraat was demolished in 1930. In the center is the overhead bridge joining the two sections of the Amsterdam brewery with one another. Following the renovation, these were joined together.

the outside, rinsed with hot water and then again using cold water. Thereafter, the barrels were refilled with fresh beer. Critical examinations revealed that droplets of the residual rinsing water were clouded with wild yeasts and bacteria, which had not been killed off during the short cleaning process. Emmens did not have to look any further to detect infections: this was the one and only source that had to be eliminated. The solution lay in the fastidious sterilization of the wooden barrels using steam and the application of a coating on the inside. Although this was an expensive measure, the brewery decided nevertheless to carry it out.

The building of an experimental brewery in Rotterdam, in 1932, was an important step as far as the quality of the beer was concerned. It was a world first. The brewery could take all manner of samples here without this being to the detriment of the normal production process.

3.14

Construction workers working on the roof of the new building for the Amsterdam brewery at the beginning of the 1930s. In the background on the right the contours of the 'Rijksmuseum'.

BUILDING WITH BREWING IN MIND

Technical developments led to enormous changes in the brewery. Rebuilding and extensions were the order of the day in Rotterdam and Amsterdam. For example, the introduction of the Linde refrigerator in Rotterdam resulted in the construction of four new storage cellars and a reorganization of the brewery building. In 1884, the brewery acquired a new boiler house with a tall chimney, and the Amsterdam factory acquired its own malting house shortly afterwards. 'Extensions or alterations take place every year,' the technical director lamented in 1886. The company had to modernize in order to keep up with increasing sales. At the same time, expensive machines necessitated continuous increases in turnover. Woe betide the brewer who failed to maintain his position in this costly race!

However, the alterations made during these first years were peanuts in comparison to the large-scale projects carried out after 1888. In that year, the Board of Directors and the supervisory directors decided to reserve a large portion of the profit for future alteration work. If HBM wanted to continue as a first class brewery, it had to keep ahead of the competition. First of all, the factory in the Dutch capital replaced its existing conditioning cellars with new, larger ones. Then new storage cellars were constructed and a new double refrigerator was installed at the Rotterdam brewery. Both brewery buildings expanded to include a second brewhouse. In 1890, electric lighting was installed at the Amsterdam brewery, with the same development taking place in Rotterdam in 1894. During the 1920s, the brewery became the largest in the Netherlands, both with respect to turnover and size. Between 1922 and 1933, the Rotterdam brewery carried out further alterations costing a further 4.5 million guilders. Among other features, a new brewhouse was built which, due to its immense structure, soon acquired a new nickname: the beer cathedral! A new fireproof office building was also constructed. The company not only aspired to the construction of a building that was justified from a business point of view, but also sought to implement artistic solutions. The result elicited the following comment from a local newspaper: 'It is not only an office building, but above all, as far as the main section is concerned, almost a monument.'

The new Heineken brewery on the Stadhouderskade in Amsterdam, at the end of the 1930s.

There were plenty of changes in Amsterdam as well. In 1924, HBM purchased the private residence of the Heineken family on the Weteringplantsoen in order to accommodate office staff. From 1927 onwards, HBM entered into negotiations with the municipality of Amsterdam regarding the exchange of part of the Jacob van Campenstraat for three premises on the corner of the Dam square. Up to that time, the Jacob van Campenstraat had split the brewery into two parts, linked by an elevated bridge. When the local council approved the plans on May 8, 1930, the brewery was able to commence radical alterations. The old building and the chimney were demolished and, on the corner of the Ferdinand Bolstraat and the Stadhouderskade, a building was erected in a business-like, late Amsterdam School style, in accordance with a design by B.J. and W.B. Ouèndag. The building had no windows because the temperature had to remain constant in the yeast cellars, which were located on the second and third floors. Windows were only to be found on the uppermost floor where the wort was cooled in the cooling trough. These were open all the time so as to accelerate the cooling process. Today, this building is the characteristic face of Heineken in the center of Amsterdam.

CONCENTRATION SHARPENS THE SPIRIT.
PAINTING HEINEKEN ADVERTISEMENTS
IN 1917.

THIS MICROSCOPIC VIEW SHOWS THE BREWER'S BEST-KEPT SECRET: THE HEINEKEN 'A' YEAST FROM 1886.

THE HEINEKEN 'A' YEAST HAS BEEN ENSURING THE PURE TASTE OF HEINEKEN BEER SINCE 1886. THE BREWER CHERISHES THE SECRET OF THIS TRADITION.

MEDAILLE D'OR,
PARIS 1875

DIPLOME D'HONNEUR,
AMSTERDAM 1883

GRAND PRIX,
PARIS 1889

HORS CONCOURS MEMBRE DU JURY,
PARIS 1900

THE FACT THAT HEINEKEN WAS ASKED IN 1900 TO JOIN THE JURY INCREASED THE BREWER'S PRESTIGE AND THAT OF HEINEKEN BEER. THE OTHER SIDE OF THE COIN WAS THAT FROM THEN ON THE BREWER COULD NOT COMPETE IN THE COMPETITION FOR THE VERY BEST BEERS.

PURVEYOR TO THE ROYAL HOUSEHOLD SINCE 1927

ON OCTOBER 7, 1927, QUEEN WILHELMINA OF THE NETHERLANDS GRANTED HEINEKEN THE DESIGNATION PURVEYOR TO THE ROYAL HOUSEHOLD. THE EMBLEM STILL PROUDLY HANGS ABOVE THE ENTRANCE TO THE HEADQUARTERS IN AMSTERDAM TO THIS DAY.

ATTENTION

KEN'S

REN

THE ROAD TO 4 COOPERATION

World citizen, doctor of chemistry, artist, a passionate pianist... and, above all, a team player. More of an intellectual than the classic brewer. In 1914, a highly multi-facetted personality was added to the brewery Board in the form of Dr. Henry Pierre Heineken, representing the second Heineken generation. From 1917 to 1940, Dr. Heineken was Chairman of a cast iron Board of Directors that was to steer the brewery safely through the crisis of the 1930s. Henry Pierre Heineken was very internationally oriented – he spoke and wrote fluent French, German and English – and was perfectly at home abroad. The purchase of a brewery in Brussels in 1927 was the first step HBM took on the world stage. But other frontiers were being pushed back too. The company was pursuing a progressive social policy. Thanks to his social involvement, Henry Pierre Heineken acquired an even more colorful reputation; he was known as 'the red brewer'.

A NEW GENERATION

Gerard Adriaan Heineken died, very unexpectedly, on March 18, 1893. A shareholders' meeting had been planned for that day, before which a Board meeting was to have taken place. Before this meeting had started, Heineken and Wilhelm Feltmann exchanged a few words 'and he had not even finished his sentence,' wrote the technical director three days later, 'when he suddenly collapsed and a few minutes later lay motionless in my arms.' Death had taken the man who was so rarely ill by surprise and he died in harness. He had made the brewery great. Not, in the first place, by wanting to make the brewery profitable, but by wanting to improve it, as was stated in his funeral oration. 'The desire for improvement remained with him constantly and was the reason he continually set up new companies, throughout his entire life. He did not consider financial benefits to be a prerequisite. His wish was to establish satisfactory grounds on which building could continue.' Heineken's vision helped the brewery to progress.

Lady Mary Tindal, wife of Gerard Adriaan Heineken.

Feltmann did not consider it immediately necessary to find a new director to succeed Gerard Adriaan Heineken. He regarded an appointment for the sake of form or a name to be 'a useless and unnecessary adornment'. The technical director had other plans. He thought his own son would be the ideal successor to Gerard Adriaan Heineken. It was possibly with this wish in mind that he regularly visited Heineken's widow, 43-year-old Lady Mary Tindal. He showed exceptional interest in the block of shares she had inherited. Given that she was a majority shareholder, she in effect held the reins of power within HBM. Everyone was kept in the dark about the intentions of 'Her Majesty', as she was known, for a considerable time. In January 1894, she announced that a friend of the family, J.D.A. Petersen, was to become the third director. The shares were to remain, much to Feltmann's disappointment, within the family.

On February 14, 1894, Petersen was appointed as a director. Feltmann's influence waned. Health problems forced him to make a number of visits to a German health resort and he finally died on April 10, 1897. Without him, the brewery would have been very different today. Petersen married Heineken's widow on January 12, 1895 and became stepfather to 8-year-old Henry Pierre Heineken. The future of the Heineken dynasty now rested on the shoulders of this young man. At that moment in time, the Board of Directors consisted of Chairman Petersen, A.G.W. Berkemeier and G. Dalmeyer. These three were to guide the company into the twentieth century.

The bottling line of the brewery in Amsterdam, circa 1900. The swing-top bottles used were closed by the employees by hand.

WORKERS' UNREST

Around the turn of the century, the voice of the labor movement was becoming louder and clearer. This was equally true within HBM. One of the problems the brewery personnel faced was that there were no explicit contracts of employment. Each case was assessed separately by the Board, taking the employee's marital status, number of years of service and behavior into account. Due to the fact that HBM was still a small company, a certain balance was maintained between business and human aspects. The staff were, for a long time, perfectly content with this system but were, in a sense, jolted into activity by the rise of Socialism.

Filling wooden barrels, 1912. At the beginning of the 1960s, the wooden barrels were replaced by metal ones.

In 1899, the – formerly German – barrel-makers submitted a request for a wage increase, which the Board bought off with a small concession. But on May 1, 1900, amidst Labor Day celebrations, the situation became a lot more serious. The brewers' trade associations of the Amsterdam brewery communicated their displeasure to the Board and demanded, in addition to a wage increase, a satisfactory regulation with regard to 'working on Sunday' and the setting up of an illness and invalidity fund. The top directors refused to meet these demands, whereupon the workers suspended operations for a couple of hours. Director Dalmeyer was enraged and wrote to his colleague Petersen on June 19, 1900, 'The people, incited by those from other breweries, are demanding a day of rest on Sunday or payment for those hours. It is, of course, nonsense, since work on Sunday is already included in their weekly wage. In any case, the matter has been put to rest and we can discuss it when you return.' The Board did not give way.

The first major strike occurred in August 1901, following the dismissal of a stable hand. A pamphlet even urged the public to boycott the brewery and no longer drink Heineken beer! Dalmeyer was hardly able to suppress his rage and wrote to Petersen that HBM had to 'clear out' some staff because 'a house that is divided from within cannot continue to stand.' Dalmeyer and Berkemeier were employers of the old school. They found it difficult to adapt to a situation that entailed workers making demands. Petersen, however, was more diplomatic and progressive and viewed the social developments in a different light. He strove for dialogue, which resulted, in September 1901, in an agreement to increase the minimum weekly wage to 12 guilders and to pay for overtime worked. When the Oranjeboom brewery gave its workers the right to holidays in 1902, Berkemeier regarded this as proof 'for the company to seek favor with members of the working class who were the ones who primarily drank their beer.' Dalmeyer sneeringly added, 'The only thing that isn't included is free traveling money.'

In April 1903, strikes broke out again at a large number of breweries. With 'only' 25 striking employees in the Amsterdam brewery and 62 in the Rotterdam branch, HBM had few problems. Because the Board was also able to find replacements, the strike at HBM failed. A day later, the strikers reported to the gate. They were allowed to resume their work because the Board regarded them as 'victims that had been misled'. The upshot was that relationships thereafter were less turbulent. The employees organized themselves better and acted more and more often as a permanent partner in consultations with the Board. Moreover, working conditions rapidly improved. In 1904, for example, a day of rest on Sunday was introduced. In 1909, the first collective bargaining agreements were established. Oranjeboom and HBM entered into an agreement for Rotterdam: a working week of 54 hours and four days off per year. They did want something in return, however: every worker's right to four liters of free beer per week was abolished. More's the pity!

Dr. Henry Pierre Heineken, 1886-1971.
This photo is from circa 1920.

THE RED BREWER

On October 1, 1914, Dr. Henry Pierre Heineken, then aged 28, was appointed as a director. Three years later he was appointed Chairman of HBM. Until the middle of the 1930s, the Board of Directors consisted of Chairman and chemist H.P. Heineken, engineer J.Th. Berkemeier, technical brewer A.W. Hoette and lawyer C.P.H. Ras. Apart from Ras, they had all succeeded their fathers onto the Board. The combination of practical experience and academic education, family tradition and personal ties made the four men a very close-knit team. Heineken also acted as a source of inspiration and – where necessary – conflict manager. He was simply made for the role of impartial chairman.

4.8

Under the leadership of Henry Pierre Heineken, the brewery reinforced the social path it had embarked upon. At his explicit request, a pension fund was set up to mark the company's 50-year anniversary in 1923. In addition to an old-age pension, HBM also started paying out widows' and orphans' pensions. During the crisis years in the 1930s, the brewery introduced a reduced working hours system and workers aged 58 and older were allowed to take early retirement. The remaining personnel earned less, but were able to continue working. The magazine 'De Fabrieksarbeider' (The Factory Worker) reported favorably on this system in October 1932. 'We admit, the way in which the Oranjeboom brewery and HBM have resolved the issue of excess workers should serve as an example to other employers. Workers at these companies are given a pension worthy of the name when they reach the age of 65 and for which the workers themselves do not have to pay a single cent.' There was a patriarchal bond between the employees and the company management. Within this system of one big happy family, Henry Pierre Heineken acted as a caring family head.

Advertising billboards for the three largest Dutch breweries during the 1920s and 1930s.

STRENGTH THROUGH UNITY

In response to the increasing degree of cooperation among the workers, the breweries also started organizing themselves. Within the framework of the 'Bond van Nederlandsche Brouwerijen' (Association of Dutch Breweries), joint agreements were made concerning such matters as Sundays off, wages, working hours and other shared interests. At the end of the First World War, the breweries were even more motivated to work together. A lot of breweries emerged from the war years weakened and were reluctant to resume the expensive struggle with competitors in the hotel and catering market. The fact that the situation was difficult is revealed by the reduction in the number of breweries: from 440 in 1910 to 257 in 1920.

On March 18, 1920, Heineken, Amstel and Oranjeboom – the three largest breweries – formed their own association known as the 'Driehoek' (Triangle). The result of this cooperation was that the big three shifted the competition to other breweries. Director Peters of the 'Zuid Hollandse Bierbrouwerij' somewhat accusingly wrote on March 12, 1921 to the HBM Board, 'You, as brewery directors, know just as well as we do that when your representatives are forbidden from acquiring customers from the two other affiliated breweries, these representatives will focus on those customers which can be acquired, namely those of breweries outside the Association, including our customers.'

The Triangle became the most powerful faction within the Association of Dutch Breweries. This annoyed the other brewers in the Association, but they were forced to accept the situation. What could they have done otherwise? Start a beer war? A lot of small breweries would then have been obliterated. The alternative was to seek protection within the Association and hope for the best. In a sense, HBM was able to relax within the Association: its product quality and good name ensured that the best customers usually approached HBM first.

Despite the Association contract, each brewery still attempted to create its own niche as far as possible and to circumvent the agreements wherever it could. The flourishing beer market of the 1920s led to the breweries once again embarking on a hunt for hectoliters: the café proprietors were enticed with all manner of loans and facilities. In 1927, brewers invested an estimated 47 million guilders in cafés; in 1930 this figure had risen to 50 million. The unbridled investment policy was getting out of hand. It was for this reason that, from 1927 onwards, those within the Association started devising a new and more rigorous contract for the affiliated members. This was intended to put an end to the existing abuses, illicit trading and fraud. Each brewer was faced with the same dilemma: do I opt for competition or the Association's beer cartel? Eventually, most brewers made the best of a bad lot. The expectation was that any disintegration of the Association would result in chaos: a situation that was to be avoided at all costs.

On May 30, 1930, almost all the affiliated breweries – including HBM, Amstel and Oranjeboom – signed the Reorganization Contract. This agreement was based on a proportional distribution of turnover. If the average turnover of the breweries was to increase in any particular year by, for example, five percent, those members that had experienced an increase of more than five percent would make payments to those members whose growth in turnover was less than five percent. In this way, therefore, a financial restriction was imposed on increases in turnover at the expense of others. The aim of the system was to maintain beer prices and slow down the hunt for hectoliters. With this contingency system in place, breweries would hesitate before increasing turnover by lowering prices, for example. The extra turnover they could achieve in this manner would, after all, be deducted in the form of a penalty payable to the disadvantaged breweries.

In 1930, the affiliated breweries represented around 80 percent of the total beer market in the Netherlands. Given that the Reorganization Contract was valid for 10 years, the affiliated breweries expected it to guarantee peace on the beer front for a considerable period of time. However, reality was to prove otherwise.

Cardboard advertising boards for Heineken beers from the 1930s.

A CHANGING PERSPECTIVE

Individual beer consumption in the Netherlands grew from 10.4 liters per capita in 1918 to 28 liters per capita in 1929, and many breweries experienced considerable growth. HBM's beer turnover increased during this period from 182,650 hectoliters to 611,064 hectoliters. An additional advantage for the brewery was that the majority of beer drinkers were starting to drink more expensive, heavier beers, such as pilsner and Münchener. On January 23, 1925, the HBM Board commented with some satisfaction 'that the consumption of heavy beer is increasing while that of light beers is decreasing. This phenomenon started last year and is proving how inaccurate the belief is, expressed at a meeting of pub owners in Rotterdam, that the public do not care that much about quality.' The increased purchasing power of workers played an important role in their preference for pilsner.

The 1930s were an inverse reflection of the 1920s. The economic crisis also affected the brewing industry. The malaise became even more serious when, in 1934, a temporary increase in excise duty took effect and, in 1935, import duties on malt were also increased. Average beer consumption dropped disastrously: from 28 liters in 1929 to 14 liters per capita in 1936. While the beer industry's home market turnover in 1929 was still 2,150,000 hectoliters, by 1936 it had fallen to just 1,165,000 hectoliters. HBM's turnover also dropped during this period by almost 50 percent. A calculation made by director Berkemeier showed that, if the decline were to continue apace, the brewery would have to close down by 1940.

It was primarily the more expensive beers that were under pressure. More and more beer drinkers were switching to cheaper and lighter Lager beer. The share of sales of Lager rose from 45.8 percent in 1929 to 56 percent in 1939. As far as HBM was concerned, this was an unfavorable development, since the majority of its sales involved heavy beer. Some brewers considered lowering the first wort content of pilsner – secretly resulting in a reduction in price – in order to halt the popularity of Lager beer. HBM was, understandably enough, very much against such a move – the company had become great on the basis of the reputation and quality of its pilsner. There was unrest in the world of brewing; that much was sure. An idea put forward on September 23, 1932 by the Amstel brewery almost pushed HBM's Board over the edge. 'Amstel has already discussed the possibility of not producing any more heavy beer, but only Lager. This would result in HBM's lead being decimated in one fell swoop, as well as destroying all the work that has been carried out over many decades to increase the quality of Dutch beer to make it equivalent to German beer. It would be suicide!'

THE BEER PRICE WAR

The Reorganization Contract was signed in 1930 by those at the top of the beer market and was designed to ensure equal distribution of the growing beer turnover. But the crisis led to beer turnover diminishing and the system started to operate in an entirely different way than had been intended: breweries with the least rapidly diminishing turnovers had to pay a penalty to breweries who had experienced the most marked decreases. The policy had turned the world upside down! Because HBM was doing better in relative terms, the brewery had had to pay penalties from the very beginning. In 1933, the HBM Board reached the absurd conclusion that, despite seriously declining sales, they would have to restrict sales because they would otherwise have to pay a considerable amount to the Association. The situation was made additionally complicated due to the fact that the members not affiliated to the Association had a more or less free hand. They could partially cope with reduced turnover by means of price reductions. This would reduce sales of the affiliated breweries more rapidly than those of unaffiliated companies.

Together with other affiliated breweries, HBM nevertheless remained an advocate of the existing affiliation contract. The motto was: it is better to sell fewer hectoliters at a good price than sell more hectoliters at reduced prices. The members of the Association kept rigidly to the Association prices: and suffered as a result. Beer prices were too high for the workers' seriously depleted incomes. The Association's pricing policy further reduced sales. The breweries did not have a ready-made solution: lowering the beer price would only result in a fierce price war with all the unpleasant side-effects this would bring, while maintaining prices would give the initiative to those breweries not affiliated to the Association. 'The puzzle remains as unsolved, as it always has been', the HBM Board concluded somewhat dismally on October 9, 1936. There was nothing to do but wait and simply hope that the crisis would blow over quickly. One silver lining was that HBM was doing better than many other breweries. In the financial year 1930/1931, HBM accounted for 35.5 percent of domestic market turnover, and three years later this had risen to 37.2 percent. HBM counted its blessings.

This enamel board bears the new Heineken logo introduced in the 1930s: a hand holding a glass.

A UNITED FRONT

The crisis passed its nadir in 1936 and the breweries began to crawl out of the abyss. HBM's sales grew from 316,934 hectoliters in 1936 to 388,059 hectoliters in 1939. Now that the crisis seemed to be over, however, an entirely different danger reared its terrible head. The threat of imminent war caused all the breweries to close ranks once again. HBM was asked by the Association to set up a new brewery organization to unite all the breweries.

On September 18, 1939, the 'Centraal Bouwerij Kantoor' (Central Brewery Agency, CBK) was set up in Amsterdam. All the breweries joined. The motto was: start the war together and end it together. The quantity of raw materials the government made available during the war was distributed among the breweries by the CBK. The breweries' organization also determined the quantities of beer the breweries were permitted to brew, including the proportion of light and heavy beers.

An equally important function of the CBK was that of protector against the occupying German forces. All breweries were allowed to continue working, provided that beer was also supplied to the German troops. The breweries agreed to this rule in order to prevent the disbanding of the breweries and the requisition of workers. The CBK spread these forced deliveries equally among the breweries. A positive side effect of these beer supplies was that German troop concentrations could be ascertained fairly accurately and the CBK could then pass this information on to the allies.

4.14 Although the breweries were able to obtain barley from within the Netherlands, the CBK nevertheless decided to use raw materials sparingly. As early as January 1941, the breweries therefore halted production of Lager beer. In the case of heavy beer, the CBK lowered the first wort content in three stages. From 1942 onwards, the content was reduced from 12 percent to 8 percent and eventually to 4 percent. In comparison with pre-war quality, the beer produced was very weak. However, in the absence of drinks such as coffee, tea, wine, spirits and lemonade this 'war-time beer' was very popular. From 1944 onwards, brewing production declined dramatically. The brewing industry was having to deal with serious shortages of raw materials, packaging and spare parts. Liberation on May 5, 1945 was therefore a godsend, for the nation and also for the brewery. The Netherlands was able to start the process of rebuilding.

FEELING TO WARM THE HEART.
HBM MANAGEMENT AND PERSONNEL
IN THE 1930S.

DIRECTORS, WE THANK YOU

FOR THIS HAPPY NEWS

A PENSION FUND, MOST LOFTY IDEAL,

HAS BEEN SET UP BY YOU!

NO LONGER OF OLD AGE IN DREAD,

WE MARCH COURAGEOUSLY AHEAD

THE FUTURE HOLDS NO FEAR OR WORRY,

WE ARE ALL CARED FOR BY THE BREWERY.

THE COMPANY MAY IT

MANY CENTURIES SURVIVE

WHATEVER AFFAIRS AROUND MAY FAIL

LET IT FORGE ON AND THRIVE.

TO LET THE FLOW INCREASE FOR EVERMORE

IS ALL THAT WE DESIRE.

WHATSOEVER MAY DECAY OR FALL,

NEVER LET IT BE THE BREWERY!

ON FEBRUARY 13, 1923, THE HBM BREWERY CHOIR SUNG THE ABOVE SONG TO THE DIRECTORS AS THANKS FOR THE SETTING UP OF A PENSION FUND. THE BRAND BREWERY IN WIJLRE, THE NETHERLANDS, A SUBSIDIARY OF HEINEKEN, STILL MAINTAINS THE TRADITION OF ITS OWN CHOIR.

HENRY PIERRE
HEINEKEN

HAS HIS HEART IN THE RIGHT PLACE. AS EARLY AS 1923, THE BREWERY SET UP A PENSION FUND FOR ITS EMPLOYEES.

HEINEKEN LIKES TO BE A GOOD EMPLOYER. WORLDWIDE, ALMOST 38,000 EMPLOYEES ARE INVOLVED IN THE COMPANY'S SOCIAL TRADITION.

For many years, the brewery was a male environment. A.G.W. Berkemeier, director from 1897 to 1914, adhered to the principle: no women in the office. However, to appoint a male telephonist was considered rather odd. A telegraph was sent to Berkemeier, who at that moment was in Switzerland, asking whether the office in Amsterdam could take on its first female employee, as a telephonist. The director's answer was: alright, as long as she's ugly.

SOCIAL

— time for a
Tiger

5

AN
ACTIVE ROLE
ON THE
WORLD STAGE

SINGAPORE

Luck, daring and wisdom – a splendid combination. It was luck that Heineken director Pieter Rutger Feith met up with John Fraser and David Chalmers Neave in Singapore in 1931. That same year, Heineken and Fraser & Neave set up Malayan Breweries Limited. It took some daring to establish a brewery on the other side of the world. And it was wisdom that led Dr. H.P. Heineken to appoint Dirk Uipko Stikker as a new director on July 1, 1935. In his 13 years with the brewery, this former banker grew in stature to become the absolute number one. So much so that he acquired the nickname 'Field Marshal Forward March'. Stikker moved around the company and the world like a tornado. He ensured that HBM became a permanent feature on the world map. The brewery became a permanent feature of financial centers such as Zurich, Brussels and London. Ingenious networks enabled the company to acquire ownership of Cobra, an international breweries investment company. After the war, the main priority was to expand exports. Luck, daring and wisdom certainly proved to be a splendid combination as far as the brewery was concerned.

QUALITY HAS ITS PRICE

When Gerard Adriaan Heineken took over De Hooiberg in 1864, part of this Amsterdam brewery's turnover came from exports to the Dutch East Indies. The new owner continued this policy. In 1876, the HBM Rotterdam brewery installed a bottling plant for, among other things, exports to Java. However, this business did not go well. HBM felt at the mercy of the whims of the various trading houses that had a strong position in the Dutch East Indies. Middlemen raised beer prices as they saw fit. The brewery Board believed that they used the imported beer 'to blackmail thirsty customers.' In addition, Heineken beer was regularly placed on the market under all manner of strange labels. Some trading houses were good enough to ask whether they could sell Heineken beer under a different name, but the brewery resolutely refused such requests: Heineken beer was not to be supplied under a different label.

Right from the start in 1864, the brewery concentrated on exports to the Dutch East Indies. The beer was packaged with straw in wooden export crates. Import and sales in the Dutch East Indies were provided by various merchants.

The mediocre degree of success overseas was not only due to the way in which business was conducted but also, surprisingly enough, to the high quality of the Heineken beer. In tropical countries cheap, long-life beer was most in demand. It was no easy task to brew a beer that could be kept for a long time in extremely hot conditions. Some brewers chose the easy way out by using less expensive raw materials of a lesser quality and adding preservatives. HBM was neither willing nor able to compete with such beers. Director Berkemeier explained the heart of the matter on August 4, 1899 to his two fellow directors. 'We have always believed that our forte was the brewing of the purest beer made from malt and hops alone, and we will

Beer activities at the end of the nineteenth century by merchant house Geo Wehry, one of the Heineken importers in the Dutch East Indies.

therefore desist from the use of any surrogate so as to follow the example of the Bavarian brewers, in whose country the use of surrogates in the brewing of beer is forbidden.' The trading houses regularly asked HBM to supply less expensive surrogate beers, but the brewery stuck to its principles. It supplied a natural product, and the shorter shelf life had to be accepted as part of the deal. The relatively high price of this beer and the limited storage life were, however, preventing successful sales – competition from the lower priced surrogate beers was simply too great and made beer exports to tropical countries unprofitable for HBM.

Packaging beer for Surabaya in the Rotterdam brewery, circa 1910.

TIME FOR A FRESH START

5.6

At the start of the twentieth century, the brewery pursued a rather cautious export policy. Home market sales were going well and the Board did not wish to undertake expensive and uncertain export adventures. The brewer regarded foreign trade as a luxury, an added bonus. Mr. Keidel, the German head of the export department, did not have a great deal to do. He primarily sent wooden barrels to his old contacts in London, Brussels, Paris and Liege. Now and again Keidel was required to go to London: this was such an undertaking that the department was in commotion for weeks beforehand. One of his colleagues described him as 'one of the most impractical people I have ever seen. Every morning he could be seen walking to work down the Crooswijksesingel with his jacket wide open. Once he had puffed and panted his way through the mail, he took time out to read The Times at his desk with the door to his office wide open. If a letter went missing, which was repeatedly the case, he would become so annoyed he would grab a fist-full of papers and fling them onto the table, moaning indignantly as he did so, while the papers swirled around.'

Keidel's death in 1928 was an opportunity to approach things in a different way. The Board wanted a 'strong man' for exports, and this man was Pieter Rutger Feith. His appointment meant extra attention to exports. One of his first deeds of note was a Heineken advertisement 'written in the sky' by an aircraft during the 1928 Olympic Games in Amsterdam. Feith looked after export activities from his base in Rotterdam, in close cooperation with J.A. Emmens who, at that moment in time, was the head of the company laboratory. The latter succeeded in radically improving the storage life of export beer. The brewery decided to take exports more seriously.

BREWING IN THE TROPICS

The Dutch East Indies was HBM's most important export market in the Far East. The brewery found it difficult to get to grips with this market, however. Local beer traders were not that enthusiastic about the sale of Heineken beer. If the brewery was to become properly established, a different approach would have to be tried. Perhaps the establishment of a brewery in the Dutch East Indies would provide a solution?

In 1929, the banker baron C.J. Collot d'Escury, a friend of HBM director Ras, established contacts between the Board and René Gaston Dreyfus. This French banker/brewer had set up the 'Société Financière de Brasseries' (Brewers' Financial Association, Sofibra), which had interests in breweries in tropical and subtropical countries such as Egypt, Morocco and Indo-China. Dreyfus was keen on a brewery in Java and hoped that he could interest a Dutch brewery in such a project. After he had his fingers burned at the Amstel brewery, the Frenchman found HBM to be more open to the idea. The brewery responded enthusiastically to the idea of a branch in Java. This represented an ideal opportunity to gain experience of brewing beer in tropical conditions. Professor Pierre, a Sofibra expert, technical engineer G.J.J. van Goor and Feith traveled to Java to assess the possibility at first hand. Medan was rejected as a possible location because the authorities would not grant permission. Surabaya seemed a good alternative but, when it transpired that the investment company Cobra already had an option on the same site, the investigating team abandoned its plans. Once the former Batavia had also been rejected as a location, the three men returned home disappointed. Cobra started building a brewery in Surabaya on September 14, 1929. Production started two years later.

On the way back to the Netherlands after his adventure in the Dutch East Indies, Feith stopped off in Singapore. Here, he came into contact with Fraser & Neave, a local soft drinks factory. This company was convinced that a locally brewed beer would sell well in Singapore and Malacca. But before Fraser & Neave were willing to engage in any business, they sent a telegram to London and Amsterdam requesting detailed information about the Dutch brewery. The name HBM was practically unknown in Singapore, and Fraser & Neave wondered whether they could safely enter into a joint venture with this brewery. The information provided reassured them and negotiations commenced. The companies complemented one another perfectly: Fraser & Neave had the necessary capital, a good distribution network and knowledge of the local market, while HBM possessed the technical brewing knowledge. It was

5.8

Pre-war advertising for Tiger beer, brewed in Singapore since 1932.

an ideal basis for cooperation. The two parties set up Malayan Breweries Limited on April 15, 1931. Fraser & Neave were responsible for the commercial and administrative management while HBM was assigned the technical responsibilities. It was a magnificent alternative for the failed brewery project in the Dutch East Indies.

Singapore was HBM's first tropical brewery project. In order to avoid any risks, the beer was not sold under the Heineken brand, but under the name 'Tiger' instead. The Chinese associated the tiger with power and the power of Tiger beer soon became apparent. Once sales started on October 1, 1932, the beer's quality and smooth sales organization made sure that Tiger became a big hit. Within no time at all, Singaporean beer was also available in Hong Kong and Thailand. HBM in the Netherlands received good dividends and payment for its technical support and the conclusion was obvious: Singapore had been a brilliant move.

Advertising for Heineken beer, initially imported then from 1937 to 1960 brewed locally in the Dutch East Indies, present-day Indonesia.

INTERNATIONAL SPRINGBOARD

During the 1930s, three investment companies were active in the international brewing world. Sofibra, set up by the French banking house Gaston Dreyfus & Cie was based in Zurich. There was also the Swiss-German-Belgian 'Brasserie Coloniale' (Cobra) and the 'Société International de Brasserie' (Interbra), based in Brussels, with interests in breweries in Belgium, France, the Belgian Congo and Angola. In addition, these three investment funds were interlinked through cross-shareholdings. In a sense, it was a financial maze.

In 1931, HBM partially financed the establishment of the Malayan Brewery by taking a shareholding in Sofibra. Two years later, HBM also took a small stake in Interbra. HBM was, however, a distant shareholder, rarely becoming involved in events in Brussels and Zurich. The arrival, on July 1, 1935, of the dynamic Dirk Uipko Stikker changed all that. This banker originally had no interest in a directorship at HBM. It was only once he had gained insight into the brewery's balance sheet that he became curious. This balance sheet surpassed anything he had seen before. A great deal of money had been written off to debtors that were in credit, while so much had been paid in advance to creditors that they had become debtors. It was as if HBM was a bank! The brewery's conservative financial policy was a great asset, since Stikker realized the company's enormous potential – the beer's golden color was the final piece of encouragement he needed. The ex-banker was assigned responsibility for HBM's foreign activities, including contacts with the investment companies.

Mr. D.U. Stikker, director of Heineken from 1935-1948.

Stikker wasted no time getting to work. The Banque de Bruxelles wanted to relinquish its majority share in Interbra. These shares were of interest to HBM because they would enable it to gain control of a brewery in Surabaya that it coveted very much. In December 1935, the Interbra share package was acquired by Sofibra and HBM. For a relatively minor amount – less than a million guilders – the brewery became a joint owner of breweries in the furthest corners of the world. In subsequent years, Stikker reinforced HBM's overall position. After all, the brewery was making an important contribution by providing technical assistance to a variety of breweries. Stikker believed that HBM was justified in exerting greater influence in exchange for this support. In 1937, this resulted in a reorganization. Unprofitable companies were sold and the remaining interests were consolidated in Cobra, which was based in Amsterdam. Within a period of less than two years, the brewery's position abroad had completely changed, with interests now existing in breweries in Belgium, France, the Dutch East Indies, Singapore, French Indochina, Egypt, the Belgian Congo, Morocco and Palestine. HBM had been given a facelift and could now boast a worldwide image.

A DILEMMA

During the pre-war years, imported German beer was very popular in a lot of tropical countries. Beer from Beck's Brauerei had a particularly good reputation. In 1932, this brewery took over the 'Archipel Brouwerij Compagnie' (ABC) in Batavia and also established a new brewery under the same name in Singapore. From 1933 onwards, it started selling locally brewed beer: Anchor and Diamond in Singapore, Anker and Diamant in the Dutch East Indies.

The ABC brewery in Batavia was competing with the Cobra brewery in Surabaya. The Cobra brewery brewed its beer using an abridged brewing process involving a short storage time, highly suitable for the tropics. The brewing process was, however, still at an experimental stage, which meant that the quality of the beer tended to be unreliable. Beck's therefore won the battle with its competitors in the Dutch East Indies. In Singapore, the reverse was the case. There, Beck's faced a challenge from Malayan Breweries, which had a fail-safe trump card in the guise of its Tiger beer. The Anchor and Diamond beers from the Singaporean ABC brewery did not catch on among Singaporean beer drinkers. The brewery tried to use price reductions to gain a larger market share. Beck's financed this price war in Singapore with the profits from its brewery in Batavia. HBM was unsure how to tackle this troublesome competitor. The conclusion was drawn that Beck's should be tackled in the Dutch East Indies, the market where it gained its profits. What was the best form of attack? Eventually the brewer decided that a locally brewed Heineken beer was the solution. The weapon the brewery in Singapore had not yet dared to use – namely supplying the Heineken brand – was the one applied in Batavia. Local production of Heineken was intended to destroy Fortress Beck's. This was the idea behind the attack. The Cobra brewery in Surabaya, which was in difficulties, now became an important pawn in the battle against the German competitor. After complicated transactions had taken place, HBM acquired control of this brewery in 1937. 'Heineken's Nederlandsch-Indische Bierbrouwerij Maatschappij' (Heineken's Dutch East Indies Brewing Company, HNIBM) heralded the start of the battle for East Indian beer drinkers.

5.11

The three HBM brands from 1937 in the Dutch East Indies: Heineken's, Rex and Java.

LOCALLY BREWED HEINEKEN

HNIBM decided to combat Beck's hegemony with three different beers. For those with little purchasing power there was Java beer, brewed according to a special accelerated process. In addition, the brewery introduced the traditionally brewed beers Rex and Heineken. Imported Heineken beer was discontinued. With Heineken and Rex, HNIBM had two very high quality beers. On December 24, 1937, HBM director Berkemeier complimented the master brewer of the Indian brewery, Dr. F. Mendlik with the words, 'Yesterday, two crates of Heineken and Rex beer arrived in Amsterdam. We had just had a HNIBM meeting and all the gentlemen present, including Dr. Heineken, tasted a bottle of each. First and foremost it has proved possible to brew two beers with entirely different characters, as we planned, and moreover these beers are actually a success. Both beers are pure of taste. The Rex beer is full of flavor, properly bitter, although the bitter taste does not remain on the tongue for too long, and the Heineken beer smells of our yeast and has a soft rounded flavor. Now Rex and Heineken have to start their race across the Indies, and we all hope that they will be very successful, that there will be plenty of supporters from all sides and that the race will be a noble one, with both parties achieving good results.'

Heineken and Rex were launched on the market in December 1937. Less than one month later, master brewer Mendlik reported enthusiastically, 'Both beers are a great success here, a greater success than anyone actually dared expect. We were sold out within no time and had to organize rationing: fortunately, we will be drawing off beer again tomorrow. We certainly need to!' A minus point was that the sales of Rex, after having made a flying start, slowly declined. The unknown name and the taste, which was similar to Beck's – the 'ABC aroma' – played a role in this. However, it turned out that the advertising campaign had been set up wrongly. Rex beer was launched on the market as 'the beer for better circles.' The suggestion to Indian beer drinkers that better circles existed had an adverse effect. The ABC brewery successfully counteracted this with the slogan: 'Diamant, for people of all classes'.

Diamant's mocking was not enough to save the ABC brewery, however. The German brewery lost ground to HNIBM, which saw its sales rise from 37,000 hectoliters in 1937 to 60,000 hectoliters three years later. HBM's goal had therefore been completely achieved: combating Beck's' pricing policy in Singapore by increasing competition in the Dutch East Indies. Beck's suspended its beer war in Singapore in 1938. The two breweries, controlling the largest share of the beer trade in the Far East, made their peace. The war on this beer front was over.

SOLDIERS' BEER

After England and France had declared war on Germany on September 3, 1939, the British government in Singapore seized the ABC brewery from the German company Beck's on the grounds that it was enemy property. HBM and Fraser & Neave eventually purchased this brewery in 1941. Matters progressed slightly differently in the Dutch East Indies. Here, the local authorities confiscated the ABC brewery in May 1940. In March 1941, HNIBM offered 3.5 mil-

5.14

Crates of Tiger beer being loaded into the train for transport to customers, Singapore 1961.

lion guilders to acquire its former competitor. There was, however, an additional competitor. A trading company, Borsumij, offered 1 million guilders more, thereby gaining control of the brewery, which it renamed the Oranje brewery. Stikker regarded this as a wasted opportunity. 'The two breweries under the control of a single company are a great deal more valuable than the situation that now exists in the Indies. A million more could certainly have been paid than the price paid by Borsumij.' Reluctantly, he had to accept the reality of the situation in the Dutch East Indies: there was no monopoly position, but rather competition.

The brewery in Singapore played an important role at the end of the war in supplying beer to Allied troops in the Far East. In Europe, the war ended on May 8, 1945, but in the Far East intense fighting continued, and the British were on the point of recapturing Singapore. Concerned British Members of Parliament wondered whether the soldiers would have sufficient beer to drink after the town had been recaptured. Churchill calmed their fears, however, saying, 'I promise there shall be beer.' A few days after the liberation, Stikker traveled – at the explicit request of the British government – to the War Office in London. His assignment was clear: the brewery in Singapore had to become operational as soon as possible so that beer could be supplied to the soldiers. The British authorities promised full assistance and supplied

Packaging bottles of Anchor beer into export crates, 1961. Anchor was the brewery's second brand in Singapore.

the necessary raw materials and resources. In June 1945, a special army unit searched defeated Germany for usable materials at the breweries that had been destroyed and those that had been spared. In September 1945, a Heineken team started work in Singapore and Surabaya. Despite the serious damage the breweries had suffered, the first crates left the factory site within a couple of weeks. The beer was soon disappearing down thirsty soldiers' throats.

In postwar Singapore, business was booming for Malayan Breweries. 'The situation in Singapore is in many respects ideal. On the surface, the consequences of the war were invisible, except that in general the houses needed a coat of paint. The shops were full of goods and the prices did not, in themselves, seem high. However, people were living the good life and spending was up,' director Feith stated following his visit to the city in 1949. The takeover in 1941 of the former ABC brewery meant that the Singaporean brewery had acquired a monopoly position in this British colony. Improvements in the economy caused the two breweries to flourish and sales rocketed. Tiger was primarily drunk by the British army, while Anchor was mostly consumed by the local population. The brewery also sold stout under the brand names Tiger, Lion and Elephant. In addition, a great deal of beer was exported to countries such as Japan, Hong Kong, Thailand, Pakistan and the Seychelles.

In the Dutch East Indies, on the other hand, the situation was far from peaceful. On August 17, 1945, Sukarno and Hatta proclaimed the 'Republic of Indonesia'. The Dutch government resisted independence and refused to acknowledge this republic. When negotiations failed, the authorities sent Dutch army units to the archipelago. Stikker traveled to Java in the wake of these troops. During his stay in May, June and July 1946, he succeeded in ensuring that HBM regained control of the brewery in Surabaya. On April 17, 1947, the first Heineken beer reappeared on the market. The political situation was confusing, but this did not adversely affect beer sales. In this region as well, there were plenty of soldiers waiting for their thirsts to be quenched. However, on December 27, 1949, centuries of colonialism came to an end when the Netherlands transferred sovereignty to the new Indonesian government. The name of the brewery in Surabaya was changed to 'Heineken's Indonesische Bierbrouwerij Maatschappij NV' (Heineken's Indonesian Brewery Company). It was the start of a new period in the company's history.

GLOBAL THINKING PUSHES BACK BOUNDARIES. EXPANSION OF THE BREWERY IN SURABAYA IN 1938.

IS IN THE DUTCH BLOOD

HEINEKEN WAS EXPORTING BEER TO THE DUTCH EAST INDIES AS EARLY AS 1864 AND SET UP ITS OWN BREWERY THERE IN 1937

1937 WAS THE FIRST TIME HEINEKEN BEER WAS BREWED OUTSIDE OF THE NETHERLANDS. BREWERS FROM HEINEKEN MONITORED THE BREWING PROCESS.

TODAY, HEINEKEN BREWERS MONITOR THE BREWING PROCESS IN EUROPE, SOUTH AMERICA, ASIA AND AFRICA. HEINEKEN CAN JUSTLY CALL ITSELF A 'WORLD BREWER'.

INDONESIAN INDEPENDENCE ON DECEMBER 27, 1949 LED TO THE 'INDONESIANISATION' OF THE LOCAL HEINEKEN BREWERY. THE BREWERY'S NAME IS NOW MULTI BINTANG INDONESIA, AND INSTEAD OF HEINEKEN IT BREWS BINTANG, INDONESIAN FOR STAR.

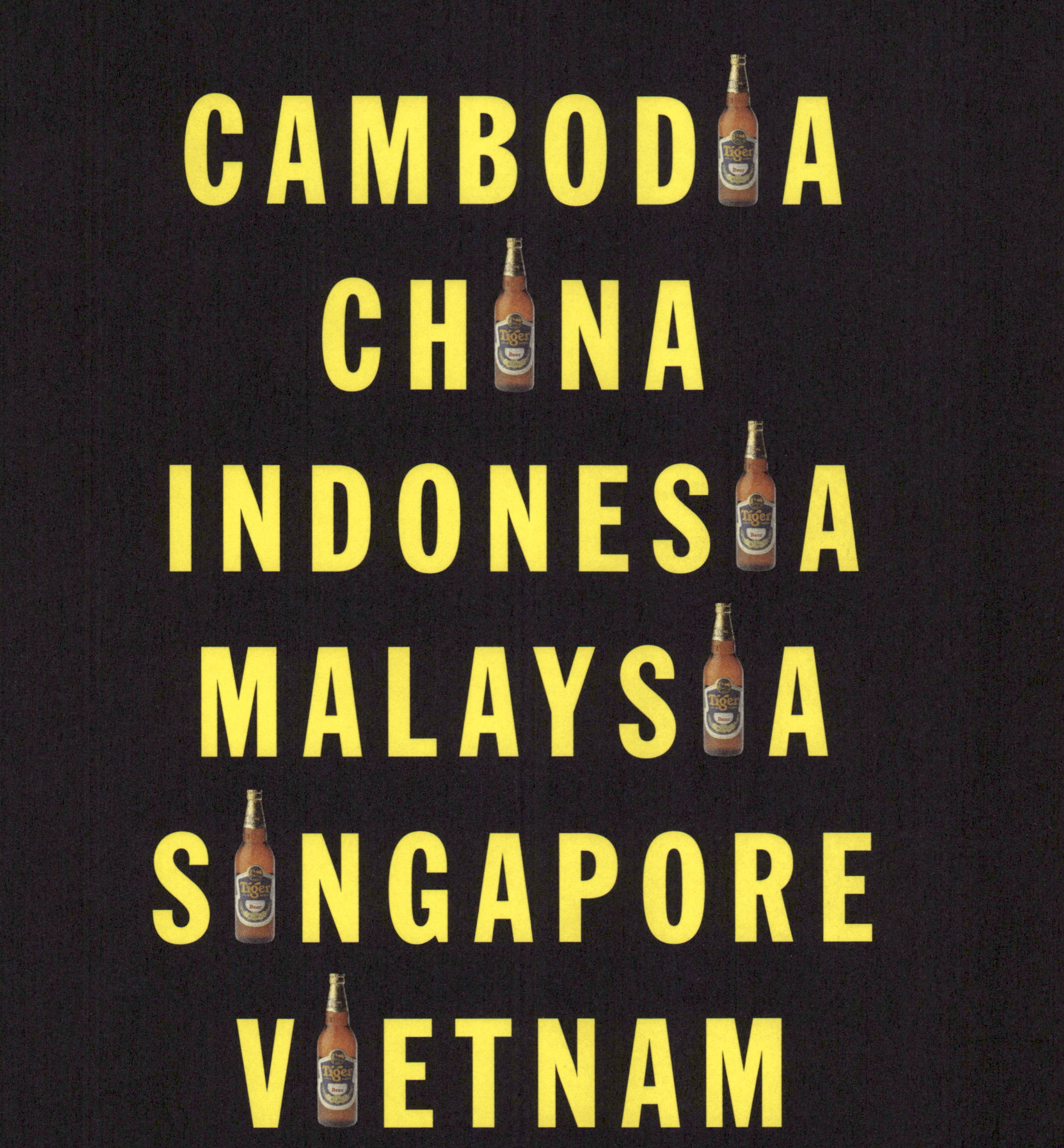
CAMBODIA
CHINA
INDONESIA
MALAYSIA
SINGAPORE
VIETNAM
Tiger
Beer

WORLD CLASS

6

THE AMERICAN DREAM

NEW YORK

Heineken was the first imported beer to reappear on the American beer market following the end of Prohibition. On April 11, 1933, 25 barrels and 50 crates of bottled beer were unloaded at the docks in Hoboken. The following day, the New York Times marked the event with a tiny article. Initially, the brewery faced many setbacks. A number of consignments of beer were even dumped in the New York water system. The brewery, however, had two trump cards up its sleeve: Heineken beer and 'the Dutch Baron', colorful Heineken importer Leo van Munching. This Dutch-born beer-lover achieved the classic dream of paperboy to millionaire. Partly thanks to his unstinting effort, Heineken became the best-selling imported beer on the American beer market. The ingredients of this success story are: a green bottle, a characteristic taste and an exclusive image. 'Imported from Holland' – a success story in the United States.

PERFECT TIMING

6.4

The first barrels of Heineken reached the USA during the 1880s. This was more a question of chance than conscious planning. The directors considered the Heineken beer too 'European' and characteristic in taste for American beer-drinkers. The American beers, following the example of Budweiser, introduced in 1876, had a neutral, light taste, that corresponded to the preference of the masses. So it was hardly surprising that the Dutch brew was not a spectacular success. In addition, two events hampered further development, namely the outbreak of the First World War in 1914 and the instigation of Prohibition in the United States in 1920. Any beverage containing more than 1.5 percent alcohol was forbidden as a danger to society. It soon became clear that the measure did not work – what did work was bootlegging and organized crime. Al Capone & Co. made a fortune from the illegal trade in alcoholic beverages.

In 1931, the Democrats adopted the abolition of Prohibition in their electoral manifesto. 'Perhaps we can gain some advantage by being quick with our imports,' was the response of the brewery directors on September 11, 1931. A few months later in Paris, export director Pieter Feith met Colonel Johnston, Vice President of Maynard & Child of Boston. The American gave him some useful advice. Following victory by Democratic presidential candidate F.D. Roosevelt, it was announced that Prohibition would officially come to an end on April 11, 1933, initially for lower-alcohol products only. This was music to American brewers' ears, but Heineken was also listening closely. The brewery was not exactly brimming over with optimism, however, since only beer with an alcohol content of 3.2 percent or less could be imported, and outstanding results were not expected from such a weak brew.

Poster accompanying the launch of the passenger ship S.S. Statendam in 1929, designed by the French artist Cassandre.

Unperturbed, Heineken nevertheless prepared for serious competition. Which foreign brewery would be the first to gain a foothold on American soil? Cargo ships from several European countries prepared for the crossing. With 25 barrels and 50 crates of Heineken beer, Feith boarded the S.S. Statendam of the Holland America Line. And on April 11, 1933 – his timing could not have been better – Heineken became the first non-American beer to land at the quay in Hoboken, New Jersey. An English competitor, sailing on the Majestic, and the brewery's great Dutch rival Amstel were just behind in a very tight race. But what did it matter – now the real work could begin.

LEO VAN MUNCHING

During the crossing, Feith ran into Leo van Munching, born in 1903 in the Dutch town of Harderwijk and employed at that time as a steward in first class on board the Statendam. Feith had met Van Munching a few times at the export division of the Rotterdam brewery, on which occasions Van Munching had expressed his interest in an American adventure. Thanks to his line of work, the Harderwijk man had good contacts at a number of important American East Coast hotels. Feith, who appreciated his compatriot's enthusiasm, had plenty of time during his Atlantic crossing to get to know Van Munching better. One thing soon became clear to him: the steward could tap beer with the best, had the gift of the gab and knew how to get along with anyone of any social rank. Van Munching was the perfect salesman.

6.6

Shortly after arriving in America, Feith appointed the Boston firm Maynard & Child as the official Heineken importer. Initially, things did not go smoothly. On April 18, 1933, the United States abandoned the Gold Standard and devalued the dollar. In addition, the American government introduced an import tariff of 1 dollar per gallon and restricted the strength of beer to 3.2 percent. The first order, for 3,000 crates of 72 30 cl. bottles of Heineken light Lager, was delivered in May 1933 but the extremely high import duty meant that sales never really took off – the beer was too expensive. Unsold batches were tipped into New York harbor. The first offensive had failed. Heineken beer needed a little extra support. On September 11, 1933, the brewery appointed Leo van Munching as its sales promoter for the United States. Together with an American, James Clark, Van Munching was awarded the agency for HBM cask beer for the states of New York, New Jersey and Pennsylvania in October 1933. Maynard & Child dealt purely with bottled beer.

In December 1933, Van Munching left for the United States on the S.S. Statendam, accompanied by his wife, their son Leo jr and daughter Anne. The cost of the tickets – 450 dollars – was paid by Heineken, subject to the understanding that Van Munching and his family traveled tourist class. To Van Munching's surprise, once on board he became acquainted with a Captain Krol, a former captain of the Holland America Line, who – traveling first class – had been charged with establishing Amstel in the United States. Both men were facing an intrepid adventure. The American beer market was incredibly large, highly competitive and imported beers were virtually unknown.

On arrival in the United States, the sales promoter was immediately confronted by the enormity of the task ahead. The US economy had reached an all-time low and the beer barons were enmeshed in a life-or-death competitive struggle, fought sometimes using legal means and equally often illegal ones. His enthusiasm was reinforced once he had tasted some of the domestic product, however, since Heineken was clearly superior. Van Munching got down to work... and immediately got a bloody nose. The bank to which he had entrusted his savings, the Stenick Bank of Hoboken in New Jersey, went bankrupt after three months – all that was left of his 5,000 dollar investment was a meager 300 dollars. To stimulate beer sales, he supported a number of agents. Two went bankrupt and another failed to repay his debts. Van Munching had been brought down to earth with a bump. Krol, his colleague from the Amstel brewery, gave up after four months and returned in haste to the Netherlands. He reported to the management of Amstel that it was impossible to make any money at all in the American beer market. The trade was firmly in the hands of bootleggers and gangsters. Van Munching saw things differently and refused to give up. Within two years, he had accumulated a customer base consisting of some 100 businesses. But another factor was required for the real breakthrough... luck!

'THE DUTCH BARON'

Fortune smiled on Van Munching. In 1935 at the New York Athletic Club, he met Tom McCarthy, director of Austin, Nichols & Co. This wholesaler, operating from Brooklyn, held an agency for the Pabst Brewery, making it a good introduction to countless beer businesses in New York. In this city alone, Austin, Nichols & Co. employed some 100 agents, and had regional offices in New Jersey, Illinois and Florida. In February 1935, director Feith visited New York and concluded an agreement with this company. This allowed the unknown Heineken to benefit from the good name of Austin, Nichols & Co. The brewer was responsible for the 10,000 dollar advertising budget and the salary of Leo van Munching, who continued to act as sales promoter. Another favorable development was that the American government lifted the 3.2 percent alcohol content restriction and reduced the import tariff by 50 percent. This opened the floodgates for the real, 5 percent alcohol content Heineken pilsner.

Van Munching's financial problems were over for the time being. Now the organizational ones began. The Austin, Nichols & Co. agents were responsible for selling so many products that they devoted little attention to Heineken. Why spend valuable time on an unknown beer from Holland? Van Munching continued to push, however, and managed to sell the beer to a few businesses... and to convince the agents 'that it could be done'. The fact that the higher-priced Heineken beer offered an attractive margin helped. Using all imaginable means, Van Munching and his team were able to gradually boost sales. The number of hectoliters sold rose steadily from 5,000 in 1935/1936 to almost 11,000 in 1938/1939. The beer was adopted by such illustrious clients as the Waldorf Astoria Hotel, the Astor Hotel, Jack Dempsey's Restaurant and the New York Athletic Club.

6.8

It was during this period that Leo van Munching thoroughly got to know the country and the beer trade. He acquired a good reputation in the beer trade as an honest, active entrepreneur. He was known as 'The Dutch Baron' in the New York cafés. The United States became his second homeland. He was ready to take on a big challenge.

WORLD EXHIBITION

At Leo van Munching's suggestion, Heineken took part in the World Exhibition in New York in December 1939. Time and again, he stressed that the American market made different demands on the sale of beer. Advertising was important. He often referred to Heineken in this respect as 'penny-pinching'. In his opinion, participation in the World Exhibition was an excellent opportunity to make a name for Heineken throughout the United States. The management were slow to come to a decision; after all, the 'American style' promotional plan required an investment of 150,000 dollars – no small beer, even for Heineken. Finally, the brewery gave the go-ahead. Henry Pierre Heineken was appointed to the committee for the World Exhibition.

The Heineken Pavilion at the World Exhibition – 'Heineken's on the Zuiderzee' – was a re-creation of the fishing port of Harderwijk, Van Munching's birthplace. Two rooms in the pavilion were named after Peter Stuyvesant and Kiliaen van Rensselaer, the founders of New York, and decked out with life-like portraits of them. A life-size windmill also proved a great attraction. The American visitors were highly enthusiastic about this little piece of Dutch glory. And more than 10,000 hectoliters of beer were consumed in the pavilion. Heineken had achieved its first objective, namely greater name-recognition and the right quality image – the word at the time was 'The Peer of Beers'. This success story took another turn, however, in May 1940, when the Netherlands was occupied by German troops. This quickly put an end to the export of Heineken beer. For a while Van Munching was able to obtain beer from the Heineken brewery in the Dutch East Indies, but from 1942 this supply dried up as well. War was playing its macabre game.

VAN MUNCHING & CO.

On May 5, 1945, the German army in the Netherlands capitulated – the country was free again. Within a week of liberation, the brewery in Rotterdam received a telegram from Van Munching asking when shipments of beer to the United States could recommence? He had no idea at all of the situation in his homeland. The Amsterdam and Rotterdam breweries had suffered greatly during the war years – if not through direct misuse, then through lack of maintenance. In addition, there were all manner of shortages; of people, raw materials, labels, barrels and, in particular, of bottles.

On October 11, 1945, the management decided to give exports to America top priority. The beer had to be shipped out as soon as possible. Export meant dollar income, and with dollars the essential machines, bottles and raw materials could be purchased abroad. Using the argument 'brewing to rebuild the Netherlands' Heineken hoped to acquire additional support and grain allocations from the government. A very useful coincidence in this respect was that Heineken director Stikker had influential contacts within the government. As the period of uncertainty would undoubtedly pass, Stikker wanted to concentrate on expansion abroad. Particularly as many foreign competitors were concentrating first and foremost on rebuilding their home markets. The world was there to be taken by a brewery with vision and courage.

Left: beer mat featuring a picture of the Heineken south-seas village at the 1939 World Exhibition in New York. Top: beer mat showing a windmill, a much-used image of Holland.

On November 21, 1945, the brewery appointed Leo van Munching as exclusive importer of Heineken in the United States. He knew the market like the back of his hand and also had good contacts in both American and Dutch circles. Early in 1946, Leo van Munching and his business colleague Ralph B. Carter set up Van Munching & Co. (VMCo). This import company took up offices at 53 Park Place, New York 7. The office staff consisted of Van Munching, his secretary Grace Arcoro, a bookkeeper and an assistant, a traffic manager and four ladies to take care of the invoices and the telephone. The import company was in place, all that was missing was the beer.

MORE HASTE, LESS SPEED

'When will I finally get some beer?' This was the burning question put time and again by Leo van Munching. At the beginning of January 1946, Heineken answered that it was willing to send, but was simply unable to, owing to a shortage of barrels and bottles. But everything possible was being done – he was assured – to get things moving again. On the other side of the ocean, Van Munching waited impatiently. He was keen to start work, and the market was ready. After all, the war meant that all imported beers had disappeared from the American market – being first would be a big advantage. On February 6, 1946, the importer once again informed the brewery that good business was there for the taking, provided that pre-war quality and quantities could be supplied.

Finally, in August 1946, Heineken shipped the first consignment of beer to the United States. The consignment consisted only of bottled beer. The shipments sent in November and December of that year were disappointing, however, as the quality appeared to be inferior. The Americans dealt with bottled beer very differently from what was customary in the Netherlands. The beer was often put on ice, a harsh treatment that did nothing for the quality of the beer, making it cloudy and impairing the taste. Technical director Jan Emmens subsequently regretted having succumbed to the pressure of concentrating on exports. The fact that he had used a bargain batch of malt acquired by Van Munching was the worst of it. The technical people at the brewery were likewise confronted by an impossible task. The equipment was faulty, raw materials were scraped together from all corners of the earth... the unfathomable brewing process followed its own laws at the best of times. You can't make a silk purse out of a sow's ear! Exports started at a moment when the brewery was simply not ready.

Van Munching subsequently bombarded the brewery with telegrams complaining about the beer. The importer was caught between a rock and a hard place. He had to achieve high turnover to make a profit, but only had poor quality beer with which to do so. He wondered aloud whether the brewer understood the difficult situation he found himself in. Director Feith provided reassurance in a letter dated December 24, 1946, 'As long as we still possess the skill, as well as the good intention to resolve all of our technical difficulties, I believe you are worrying unnecessarily.' During the period from January 1 - March 15, 1947, Heineken sent no more beer to VMCo. Van Munching prowled around with a face like thunder, recalling the bad batches from the market. At the end of the day, this proved an expensive episode in the brewery's history.

6.11

Heineken reappeared on the American market in 1946. A special campaign drew the attention of beer drinkers to this refreshing news.

6.12 Advertisements for Heineken beer, from the late 1940s. The American Heineken importer, Leo van Munching, set the advertising policy for a long time. He associated Heineken with classic images of Holland: tulips, windmills, clogs and blonde women in traditional dress.

A SECOND CHANCE

During his travels through the United States in the spring of 1947, export director Ben ter Haar came to an important conclusion: 'The poor quality consignments of beer we sent to America (and to other countries) at the end of last year were a hard lesson, teaching us once again that if we want to continue exporting Heineken, the quality of our beer must be maintained, in all markets and at all times. The only course of action left open to us and Van Munching when the beer sent turned out to be cloudy, of inferior taste, dark in color and not frothy, etc., was to remove as many of these batches from the market as possible. Carlsberg, Tuborg, Amstel and a number of other export breweries also delivered inferior consignments during this period. They did not take back the beer, however. They lacked the organization to do so and as a consequence these beers were not able to generate any turnover of significance during the following five years. The Heineken name also suffered greatly because of these poor batches, but the measures taken, namely removing the affected beer from the market, had made it possible to start afresh.'

This fresh start came at the end of March 1947. Heineken was able to win back the confidence of the American beer drinker more quickly than expected. In June 1947, Ter Haar was relieved to note that Heineken beer 'is once more superior to all American beers'. In actual fact, this whole episode had a positive effect on the entire company. Heineken's management – not to mention Alfred Heineken himself, who had followed this American affair with great interest – had learned a valuable lesson: Heineken had to be of impeccable quality. Building up a reputation took many decades, whereas it could be lost in an instant. The critical American mar-

ket tightened up the quality standards at the breweries further still. Good business comes from good products.

During the early post-war years, Heineken had the American import market virtually to itself. Its principal competitors were licking their wounds, the German beers were lagging behind and the other Dutch breweries were hardly in evidence at all. In April and May 1947, Heineken accounted for 99 percent of all Dutch beer exports to the United States. It was also during this period that the brand managed to gain a foothold in sunny California. The local sales promoter, Alfred Heineken, was to no small extent responsible for this.

IMPORTED

1948 was a difficult year for the American importer. Falling turnover forced Van Munching to increase wholesale prices. The price differential between the imported Heineken and the American product became even greater. Initially, this led to a further drop in sales, but in the longer term the price increase had a beneficial effect in that the expensive Heineken acquired a 'snob appeal'.

In 1948, unsettled by disappointing sales figures, the brewery management reactivated an old plan to brew Heineken locally in the United States. This option had already been explored during the 1930s, and Heineken executives had never really given up on the idea. Experiences during the war years led to the re-emergence of this plan. The company wanted to ensure that it could not become isolated from all its export markets ever again, particularly the important American market. As exports to the United States were expensive, setting up a brewery there seemed like a sound idea. The locally brewed Heineken beer could be sold at a much lower price, which – it was expected – would stimulate sales considerably. And greater turnover was exactly what the company directors were looking for at that particular moment in time. The brewery was willing to implement the plan, but a lack of dollars hampered its realization for the time being.

During the 1950s, sales of Heineken in the United States really took off. Some of this success was thanks to the import status of the beer. This changed opinions concerning the local production of Heineken. Following an offer to take over an American brewery, Heineken director Honig wrote to Leo van Munching on August 25, 1954, 'The result is that we all feel that we should not go into a venture like this in the USA, as we fully share your opinion that the goodwill of Heineken's Beer in the USA and its attraction as an imported beer would be lost overnight.' It was becoming increasingly clear that Heineken's import status was an asset of inestimable value.

AN INSATIABLE THIRST

In March 1953, Heineken export director Melchior Weymarshausen visited Miami, Chicago and New York and was surprised by the results achieved by Van Munching. By this time, the importer had built up a national network of 207 agents, employing some 2,200 representatives. The head office was in New York, and there were branch offices in Chicago, Florida and California. VMCo had its own publication, The Windmill, distributed in a print run of several thousand copies to business relations both inside and outside the beer trade. Thanks to the efforts of 'super salesman' Leo van Munching and his team, Heineken was the only foreign brewery with a rock-solid national distribution and sales organization. This well-oiled machine ensured a good flow of the product and constantly monitored its freshness. And because this up-market beer had a good profit margin, Heineken offered its agents and wholesalers security and attractive earnings. In return, they were prepared to go the extra mile!

During the 1950s, sales were growing by 20 to 30 percent per year. The beer was sold predominantly in the better class hotels, restaurants and cafés. The price of a bottle of Heineken

Photo left: Leo van Munching with a radiant 'Holland Girl', 1953. Advertising image left: In the land of the pin-up, Heineken naturally couldn't afford to lag behind. During the 1950s, the brewery produced a colorful pin-up series for the American market, all decently dressed in bathing costumes and always with a Heineken product shot.

6.15

was between 60 and 70 cents, whereas an American beer cost roughly 40 to 50 cents. VMCo devoted a great deal of attention to 'educating' its saloonkeepers. Heineken beer was often being served too cold, meaning that the taste could not be properly appreciated. In addition, the importer was trying to get its beer onto the shelves of as many grocery stores and supermarkets as possible. This strategy succeeded, although the turnover per sales outlet was not yet earth shattering. By the late 1950s, VMCo had launched its advertising campaign under the motto 'Heineken Tastes Tremendous'. Heineken was promoted as a beer of the very best quality from the Old World (Holland), and the product was always displayed in combination with typically Dutch products such as windmills, clogs and tulips.

Van Munching's ultimate aim was to take Heineken to the top and keep it there. He was not afraid of a beer fight. Brimming with self-confidence, he wrote to the brewery on May 26, 1958, 'We are being besieged from all sides by competitive beers, but as you know, we are not afraid and we love a good fight!' His closest competitor in the import segment was the German beer Löwenbräu. It was against this beer that Heineken struggled for dominance as the best selling foreign beer in the United States. Van Munching was convinced of the superiority of his position, and assured the brewery 'that nowhere will this competitor get the jump on us.'

Leo van Munching in 1948 in front of his newly opened office in Manhattan.

In 1958, VMCo celebrated its 25-year existence as an importer with a special silver jubilee campaign. In view of the results achieved, Leo van Munching was in terrific spirits. In August of that year, he visited the Netherlands, where the personnel of the Rotterdam brewery presented him with a sculpture. This important customer was pampered with all imaginable luxuries. Gift after gift was lavished upon him. And the Supervisory Board and other directors joined in the party. Leo van Munching made one speech of thanks after another and enjoyed all the gifts and attention to the full. And he was not yet aware of the biggest gift of all, namely the amendment of his contract in 1960.

The cover of 'Vers van 't Vat' (Fresh from the Keg), the Heineken personnel magazine, from October 1950. For Leo van Munching, serving Heineken beer correctly is child's play.

A CONTRACT FOR LIFE

Leo van Munching was both a jovial beer connoisseur and a skilled businessman. Both of these aspects were reflected in his personality with, on the one hand, a humane, hearty, generous, sentimental side and on the other a calculating, self-confident and hard-nosed attitude. The relationship between Heineken and the American importer was exceptional, as VMCo was responsible for a considerable portion of Heineken's exports. VMCo's status as an importer was set out in a contract between the brewery and VMCo.

Upon its establishment in 1946, VMCo's capital stock was in the hands of Leo van Munching and Ralph B. Carter. The contract with Heineken as 'sole United States importers and distributors for Heineken's Holland Beer' had a term of five years. The brewery had an option on the shares if Van Munching and Carter were to die. At an early stage, Heineken let it be known that it would like to take an interest in the import firm, in Carter's place. A shareholding would give the company more influence than the existing option. But Leo van

Munching, who acquired the majority shareholding in VMCo in 1960, continued to keep his distance. He preferred to keep Heineken on the other side of the Atlantic ocean.

Over the years, admiration for Leo van Munching within the brewery increased. Increasing sales on the American market made a great impression. There was a great deal of respect for the brewery's most important beer customer. The fact that VMCo behaved as a completely independent importer was simply accepted. Respect and independence were important to Van Munching. In 1958, he informed the brewery, 'I am the President of an independently owned American company and not an employee of Heineken and, under these circumstances, I want to be respected and treated accordingly. I have from time to time been in a situation whereby Dutch visitors to these shores look upon me as a direct Heineken representative, and although I am proud of being considered as such, I feel that for the record, this matter should be clarified.'

6.17

During the course of 1959, discussions for renewal of the contract got under way. VMCo had the know-how, the contacts and the contracts in the American market – which gave VMCo a position of power. The negotiating process was to last for more than a year, not least because Van Munching wanted to link the term of the contract to his life, and to that of his son. Before agreeing to this, Heineken wanted to build some safeguards into the contract. The discussions went through high and low points, with a great many legal skirmishes and a great deal of grumbling. The parties finally put their signatures to a new contract on September 1, 1960. The Van Munchings got their contracts for life, Heineken got assurances about the sales trend. This put both Leo senior and Leo junior firmly in the saddle. As long as their house was in order, they were untouchable.

Leo van Munching later said about the conclusion of the contract, 'We renewed the contract in 1960. I was increasingly aware that new people were arriving at Heineken who simply couldn't accept my way of doing business. The directors were in complete agreement, of course, but these were very different people. Then I said, and if I had done that now, I would never have got the chance, that the contract I concluded with Stikker was only temporary, it expired every five years. Now that I have proved what we can do, I want a better contract. It took nine months before it was on paper. Now we have a contract with Heineken for my whole life, and then for my son's whole life.'

Three beer heavyweights in 1958, from left to right:
Leo van Munching, Dr. Henry Pierre Heineken and
Alfred Henry Heineken.

Signing a lifetime contract with the importer was a radical concession on the part of the brewery. Seen in the context of the time, this made some sense. During the negotiations, Heineken was assuming a sales forecast of 60,000 hectoliters per year. The actual situation turned out very differently, however. By 1960, VMCo was already selling 100,000 hectoliters. By the end of the 1970s, sales had increased to 2 million hectoliters. Who could have foreseen this at the time the contract was signed? Leo van Munching and his son and successor Leo van Munching jr continued to resolutely defend the independence of VMCo after 1960. From the American importer's point of view, the relationship between itself and the brewery was very simple. VMCo was the customer, so the customer was always right – Heineken was the supplier. As the importance of American exports increased, so did the brewery's desire to take a firm hold of this activity. It was to take until 1991, however, for this goal to be realized. In that year, Leo van Munching jr agreed to the sale of VMCo to Heineken. The brewery was then free to further pursue its American dream, namely to reinforce Heineken's status as the most renowned imported beer in the United States of America.

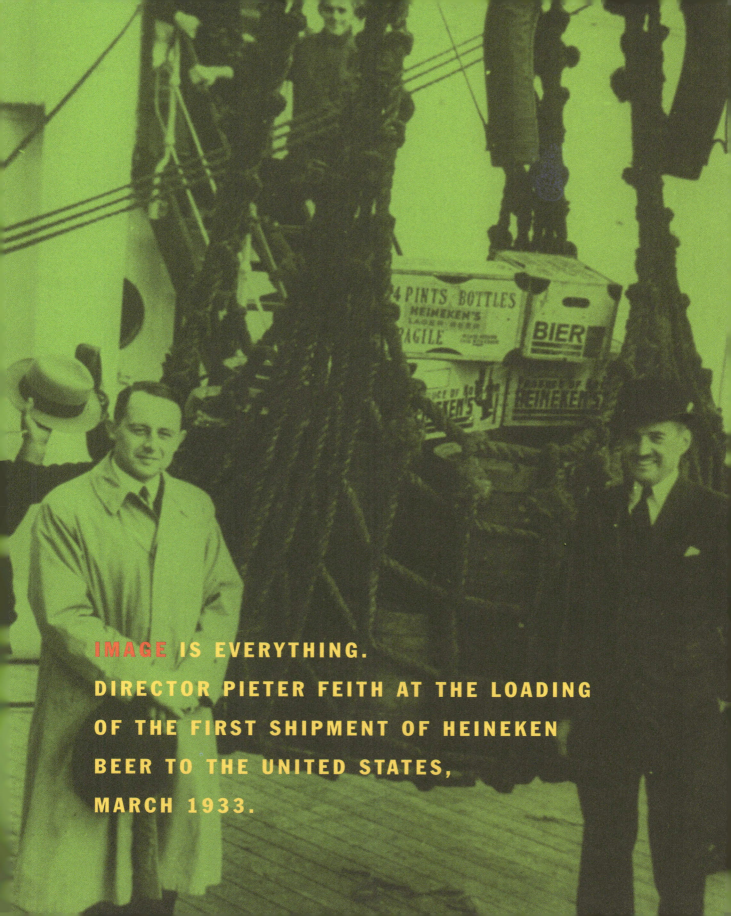

IMAGE IS EVERYTHING. DIRECTOR PIETER FEITH AT THE LOADING OF THE FIRST SHIPMENT OF HEINEKEN BEER TO THE UNITED STATES, MARCH 1933.

IN 1946, HEINEKEN INTRODUCED A NEW GREEN BOTTLE ON THE AMERICAN MARKET. THE BOTTLE WAS OF A CHARMING HONESTY AND HIGHLY EXCLUSIVE.

THE GREEN BOTTLE ACTED AS AN ICON. HEINEKEN BECAME THE MOST EXCLUSIVE IMPORTED BEER IN THE UNITED STATES. IT'S GREAT AT THE TOP.

STATUS

THE BATTLE FOR THE DUTCH BEER MARKET

7

UTRECHT

'... Heineken can go to hell!'. Emotions on the beer market in the Netherlands ran high in the summer of 1948. What was going on? On June 1, 1948, the brewery unleashed a revolution on the beer market. Hundreds of thousands of bottles of 'Heineken's Bier' were on display on grocer's shelves throughout the country. The brewer wanted consumers to enjoy its beer at home, too. Many beer agents and café and bar proprietors were outraged about the sale of beer in shops – in chorus, they accused Heineken of stealing the bread out of their mouths. A rash of protests broke out in Utrecht and in a number of other Dutch towns and cities. The brewery refused to give in, however. The bottles would stay in the stores! With this ground-breaking decision, Heineken had finally made history. The steadfastness shown by the directors, the commitment of the store representatives, the seduction of the housewife, the green label, a shining star, convivial people and the strength of the Dutch advertising campaign 'Heerlijk Helder Heineken'... there's more to a bottle of Heineken than meets the eye.

BOTTLED BEER

7.4

For a long time, the quality of bottled beer had been a thorny issue for brewers. It tended to quickly cloud over and the quality when it emerged from the bottle was never guaranteed – it could be just right, completely 'flat' or too frothy. However, a discovery by French chemist and bacteriologist Louis Pasteur provided a solution. Towards the end of the nineteenth century, Pasteur developed the process of 'pasteurization', a heat treatment that protected products such as milk, beer and soup against bacteria, meaning that they could be kept for longer. This meant it was possible for the brewers to supply better bottled beer with a longer shelf life.

During the first half of the twentieth century, the population of the Netherlands hardly ever drank beer at home. Refrigerators were uncommon and bottled beer was not readily available. For a nice cool beer, beer drinkers went to the café or bar, where beer was available on tap. Only the smaller cafés served bottled beer, as the pump apparatus was too expensive for their limited turnover. This bottled beer was supplied by the brewery agent, who transferred the beer to bottles, or had this work done by a bottling plant. The agents sold the beer under their own brand name or under that of the brewery, stating who had bottled the beer. Bottling often took place in a very improvised manner. Stick a tube in a keg of beer, suck on the end... the beer starts to flow and the bottles can be filled by hand. Often, more beer would flow over the floor than into the bottles, however. Most brewers saw bottled beer as a nice little sideline, but the serious business was done at the pump. Traditional brewers were only really interested in beer on tap in the bars and cafés.

Until 1931, Heineken only bottled beer for export. For the home market, it left this job to the bottling plants, who transferred the beer (often unpasteurized) into 40 cl. swing-top bottles. The Phoenix brewery, from the town of Amersfoort, was the first in the Netherlands to seriously investigate the possibilities of selling bottled beer in the Netherlands, and to stores as well. On December 8, 1925, Phoenix started selling bottled, pasteurized beer from its own brewery in 45 cl. bottles. This raised the profile of bottled beer. By 1928, the Oranjeboom brewery in Rotterdam was delivering 900 hectoliters of beer bottled 'in house'. This sent a signal to Heineken to take a closer look at its bottling operation.

Left: A poster from the end of the nineteenth century advertising a Rotterdam beer bottling plant. Center: The bottling plant of the Rotterdam brewery early in the twentieth century. Right: A swing-top beer bottle for the domestic market, filled by agent Posthuma of Harlingen, the Netherlands.

CLEAR, PURE HEINEKEN

In June 1928, the members of the Heineken Board, Dr. H.P. Heineken, J.Th. Berkemeier and A.W. Hoette, undertook a study trip to breweries in Hamburg, Copenhagen and Berlin which really opened their eyes. In Berlin, 30 percent of beer brought onto the market was supplied in bottles and in Copenhagen the percentage was as high as 98.5 percent. This bottled beer was processed in the breweries' own plants; in Berlin unpasteurized (with a shelf life of 2 to 3 weeks) and in Copenhagen pasteurized. The three directors tasted all manner of beers and decided that the pasteurized beers had a slight aftertaste. This was the challenge facing the Heineken brewers, namely to create a clear, pasteurized bottled beer with a pure taste and good frothy head. At that time, the Rotterdam brewery had an old-fashioned bottling plant used for the export beer. In 1929, an automatic Holstein-Kappert filling machine was installed that could fill 7,200 bottles per hour. In 1930, a second machine was installed. This boosted monthly capacity from 300,000 to 1,600,000 bottles, including exports. The Amsterdam brewery was not yet equipped for bottling owing to a lack of space.

7.6

The bottles for the beer bottled at the brewery were given a new label. This was intended to distinguish the brewery's product in terms of quality from the Heineken sold by the bottling plants. The labels – with their star as the most prominent eye-catcher – had a different background for each type of beer. The neck label bore the text, 'Store in a cool, dark place. Bottled in the brewery.' These new labels were to be introduced worldwide. A number of export customers advised against this, however since the green international label was already well-known on the various markets and furthermore the prominent red star on the new label put a lot of importers off. The directors therefore decided in February 1931 to introduce the new labels only in the Netherlands.

On June 1, 1931, Heineken started selling bottled beer. The introduction was backed up by a consumer brochure and a poster. In Rotterdam and Amsterdam, a separate store advertising campaign was implemented under the alliterative slogan 'Heineken's Heerlijk Hygiënisch Houdbaar' (Heineken's Delicious Hygienic and Long-Lasting) – a predecessor to 'Heerlijk Helder Heineken'. This was the extent of the new campaigns. The brewer did not want to alienate the bottling agents, so the advertising remained subtle. Furthermore, earnings from bottled beer were kept down by the high cost of bottling and transport. For the time being, cask beer continued to be the mainstay of the brewery's success.

During the 1930s, consumption of beer at home increased under the influence of the poor economic climate. Drinking a beer at home was cheaper than going to a café. Would more advertising, the directors wondered, further increase turnover from bottled beer? No immediate action was taken. The fall in beer consumption from 21.6 liters in 1932 to 14.9 liters in 1938 came as a rude awakening to the brewery. Perhaps bottled beer could give turnover a boost? From April 1, 1939, Heineken abandoned the existing 50 cl. bottle in favor of the new 45 cl. tankard. This step was promoted with the slogan 'Flesschenbier overal thuis' (Bottled Beer, at Home Everywhere). But the outbreak of the Second World War was to put an end to further activities.

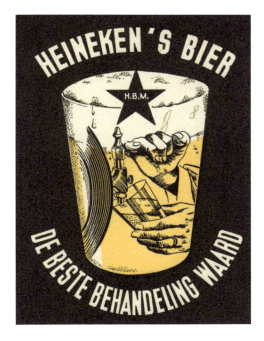

A booklet published by Heineken in 1948 instructing the barman on how to best tap and serve the beer. The text reads: 'Heineken's beer, worthy of the very best treatment.'

POOR BEER TIMES

During the war, brewers were able to continue brewing, partly by reducing the content of the first wort for beer. Owing to the fact that many other drinks were scarcely available, consumption of weak 'war beer' remained relatively high. Shortages of raw materials meant that beer sales sunk to an all-time low of 12.5 liters per capita during the last year of the war. Liberation, on May 5, 1945, gave the brewers new hope. By mid-1947, beer had regained its familiar old quality. Consumption was expected to quickly pick up. But it was not to be. In fact, beer consumption continued to decline until 1950. Many brewers asked themselves despairingly what was going on.

A lot of beer drinkers still associated beer with the weak beer of the war years and had stopped drinking it. Consumers had a strong preference for tea, coffee, lemonade and 'jenever' (Dutch gin), all of which were plentiful again. Coca-Cola in particular became an item of mass consumption. This form of lemonade was new, refreshing and represented a modern, American lifestyle. Beer, on the other hand, was seen by many as an old man's drink. Added to which, many café and bar proprietors preferred to serve Coca-Cola, as the profit margin was higher and the product required less care. Beer, for a time, was not flavor of the month.

YES OR NO?

7.8

Forced by falling beer sales, brewers looked for opportunities to increase turnover. What if consumers were to start drinking more beer at home? The brewers were not completely happy with the idea of bottled beer and home consumption. The question was, who would deliver the beer to the stores, the brewery agent or the groceries wholesaler? The agent had traditionally been the link between the brewer and the café proprietors, the biggest buyers of beer. The agent had always delivered the bottled beer to the storekeepers and was understandably opposed to the wholesaler being brought into the equation. After all, this would affect the agent's turnover. Those familiar with the home consumption market, however, believed that the wholesaler was the best party for the sale of bottled beer to the storekeepers.

Initially, café proprietors were less than enthusiastic about increasing sales of Heineken beer from stores.

At the brewery's offices, brows were furrowed in thought. In addition to a confrontation with agents and café proprietors, the sale of bottled beer also meant serious investments in bottling equipment, sales support and advertising. The thorny issue was whether Dutch beer drinkers would really start consuming more beer at home? Or would the new turnover be achieved at the cost of decreasing consumption in the cafés? Some brewers were singularly unimpressed by the whole discussion. In their opinion, beer belonged in the café and not on store shelves. 'We will not have our beer sold alongside soap and salt,' they cried. These brewers identified with the agents and café proprietors – they favored the grand gesture. Grocers were considered to have a narrow-minded, rubber-stamp mentality, as well as being penny-pinching – totally alien to the grand gesture. This would later prove an expensive miscalculation.

Within Heineken, views were also divided. The average agent did not understand the urge to get Heineken beer into the stores – he was not prepared to risk his vital turnover from the café proprietors for the 80 cents profit on a crate of beer. The predictable result was that Heineken

A grocery store anno 1952. In the early days, these stores made a significant contribution to successful store sales of Heineken in the Netherlands.

beer was not stocked by the 20,000 largest grocery stores. Could the wholesalers do better? At the suggestion of director, Pieter Feith, the Board appointed a special stores commission to resolve the matter. The commission finally recommended involving the wholesalers and commencing sales to and from grocery stores once sufficient bottles were available – one fell swoop would be more effective than an infinite number of small steps. A more surprising recommendation was to market the bottled beer under a name other than Heineken. The pure Heineken brand should not be exposed to this new, high-risk market. Sheer logic.

TRUE COLORS

In the summer of 1946, the brewery carried out a survey among its representatives to determine whether its agents were capable of selling to storekeepers. The response was clear: 26 percent of the agents were assessed as 'moderately capable' and 27 percent as 'not capable'. Various retail associations also stressed 'that the status of Heineken's Bottled Beer should not be impaired by sale in the smaller and smallest stores. Generally speaking, this was precisely the category of retailers to which the agents sold the bottled product. Wholesalers, on the other hand, could sell to the better class of grocery stores, that thanks to their superior fixtures and fittings and better sales techniques were capable of achieving better sales performance.' The message was clear.

7.10 Early in 1947, Heineken's domestic turnover declined sharply. The greatest setbacks were in sales of cask beer; demand for bottled beer still outstripped supply. The Board ascertained 'that the origins of our current decline can be found in our early policy of deliberate abstention from a section of the bottled beer market.' A new course was set, and a plan of campaign drawn up. Heineken decided to contract the best wholesalers, before its competitors joined the chase. Following intensive consultation, it was also decided not to market Heineken bottled beer under a different name and label. The Board took the view that the consumer would see this as second best, a lesser quality 'grocery beer'. Why should this beer not be called Heineken? Was there something wrong with it? In order to win the confidence of the Dutch beer-drinking public, the brewery had to use its most powerful weapon – the Heineken brand.

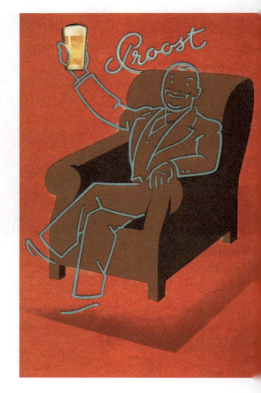

A START

Heineken and Amstel kept the pressure on. The edge over the competitors could not be lost. True, most brewers had stated that they were not interested in store sales, but nothing was certain. The brewery threw all its resources into expanding the capacity of its bottling plant, setting up a distribution division, an office for the new Store Sales division, the purchase of delivery trucks and recruitment of store representatives.

Initially, Heineken and Amstel agreed to commence deliveries to wholesalers in the southern Netherlands from November 1, 1947. Storekeepers would then be able to start retail sales a month later. The Heineken Board was forced to postpone delivery, however. The brewery simply did not have enough bottles. The Board of the Amstel brewery began to sweat – they wanted to get started at all costs, even if on a smaller scale than planned. Heineken tried to change the minds of the Amstel directors, pointing out that it was important to break into the market with one great push. After all, the early bird catches the worm. Amstel was unwilling

Advertising card for the promotion of home consumption, 1947. The text reads: 'Heineken's beer – at home anywhere!'

7.11

to wait, however, thereby forcing Heineken to take another – critical – look at the whole situation. Countless new calculations were made, a number of export orders postponed, second-hand bottles were acquired abroad, a planned upgrade of one of the bottling lines was put back... and, finally, the crucial answer was received from the bottling plant: on May 1, 1948, the beer was shipped to the wholesalers and one month later, store sales officially commenced. A deep sigh of relief reverberated through the brewery.

On April 1, 1948, Heineken officially informed its agents of the plans. The brewery stressed that no other course was open to it. There was no need for the agents to worry, however, as they would continue to form the highly valued link between the brewery and the hotel and catering sector, while the home market offered plenty of opportunities for enterprising agents. In addition, the brewery emphasized that home drinking was no threat to the hotel and catering market, 'If store sales lead to beer becoming a generally valued consumption item, this will in fact only encourage visits to the café.' With these words, Heineken hoped that its agents would accept the inevitable. But the brewery was not entirely sure and it took measures to ensure that it could supply the café proprietors itself in the event of a boycott.

The agents were furious. A number of Amsterdam agents even refused to take part in the celebration of the company's 75th anniversary. The agents' organization, BBM, coordinated the protest. Friendly words were lavished on the sympathetic brewers... and as if this were not enough, veiled threats were made. Most of the breweries bent under the pressure, closed their

7.12　Advertisement for bock beer by the Dutch designer Morièn, circa 1948. The text reads: 'Drink Heineken bock beer. The most pulled pint.'

doors to the wholesalers and ceased store sales – for the time being. The BBM called these brewers the 'true friends' of the agents. Within a few years, it transpired that the price of this title was an irretrievable disadvantage in the home consumption market. Heineken stuck to its guns and now that the decision had been taken, the agents would just have to accept the new situation. What underpinned this resolute attitude? Thanks to the income from exports and foreign shareholdings, Heineken was able to take a harder line with the agents than the other brewers.

As it turned out, the campaigns against the brewery quickly petered out. The collective boycott of Heineken announced in Rotterdam lasted for only two days. A handful of agents persisted in refusing to work with Heineken; the vast majority simply resumed operations. The wheels had to keep turning.

Advertisement for bock beer by the Dutch designer Wubbo de Jonge, circa 1948. The text reads, 'Heineken's bock beer.'

7.13

WHICH BEER DO YOU DRINK?

A good advertising campaign was needed to support in-store sales. Initially, Heineken considered a collective campaign with the other breweries. However, this was not suitable for presenting Heineken beer as a brand, which led the directors to choose their own, striking campaign. Heineken had a clear advertising goal, 'Heineken advertising must move the public to drink beer – in particular, Heineken's beer. They will have to encourage the beer drinker to ask himself, more than he did before, "Which beer do I drink?" and lead him to choose Heineken.' It was also necessary to do this. On June 7, 1948, director Honig spoke words of warning to the personnel, 'At present, the brewery is earning less on its beer than before; in fact, in many cases we are having to support the bottled beer. In particular the sentiment, that I have heard from many people, that "Nothing can happen to Heineken", is just not the case; on the contrary, it is essential that everyone is aware that Heineken is currently having to struggle for its turnover as seldom before. The fact that Heineken's share of total turnover has decreased is a sign we cannot ignore.'

7.14

Heineken and Amstel coordinated their advertising campaigns, which ran from June 1 to September 30, 1948. Amstel's campaign was based around 'Amstel Annie'. A lady who knows where her preference lies, 'Be a man! Drink a bracing glass of Amstel Beer.' Amstel Annie did not pass completely without the criticism that she was too voluptuous and common. And male beer drinkers would not allow a woman to dictate their choice of beer! Philip van Alphen, director of the advertising agency concerned, saw things differently. A touch of sex-appeal couldn't hurt in drawing men away from 'unmanly' lemonade. As its central advertising figure, Heineken used a waiter designed by Eppo Doeve. 'Your Heineken, Sir!' the fat little man would say, popping up in all manner of thirsty situations. Amstel Annie and the Heineken waiter chattered and capered around with gay abandon, but the result was disappointing. The two brewers' turnover hardly rose at all. 'Advertising is a waste of money', was the loud chorus of complaint from the critics of advertising within the brewery.

The waiter and Annie, eye-catchers from the advertising campaigns for Heineken and Amstel in 1948. The texts in the posters read (left to right): 'Heineken's beer. The most pulled pint'; 'Be a man! Drink a bracing glass of Amstel Beer'; 'Your Heineken's, Sir!'

The truth was that both beer campaigns were too strongly focused on the brand, while bottled beer was still a relatively unknown product. Consumers were suddenly confronted by a number of beer brands and wondered which to choose? Sales figures from 1949 illustrate this. In stores, only ten percent of beer clients specifically asked for a particular brand. The attitude of agents and barkeepers also played a role in the failure of the campaigns. Amstel Annie and the Heineken waiter were seen as pillars supporting store sales. The agents and café proprietors therefore did not support the advertising campaigns. Heineken concluded from the failure of the campaign that it was still too early for specific brand advertising. First and foremost, general appreciation of beer would have to be rebuilt. This was problem number one. In 1949, average beer consumption in the Netherlands was still just 10.1 liters per capita. An all-time low!

BEER IS BEST AGAIN

7.16   The Central Brewery Agency (CBK), the umbrella organization of Dutch breweries, attempted to recruit its members for a collective beer campaign. According to the CBK this would 'often appeal to the public more than individual advertising, as the direct interests of the producers would be less obvious. The public would be less skeptical and more willing to accept the informational nature of the campaign. Collective advertising is supremely suited to beer, as the goal is to increase the total consumption of beer, which is only possible by persuading the consumer to drink more beer. Generally speaking, consumers are not drinkers of brand beers. They go to the café because it is pleasant and to seek company and not because a particular brand is served.' The brewers' organization pointed to a successful example from the 1930s, the 'Beer is Best' campaign by the English Brewers Society. A CBK committee contacted the advertising experts at KLM, Unilever and Philips. On the basis of their ideas, the Dutch brewers decided on May 21, 1949 to initiate a collective beer advertising campaign.

On June 18, 1949 – the brewers were in a hurry – the campaign was launched. 40 mm advertisements appeared in all the daily papers, bearing simply the slogan: 'Het bier is weer best' (Beer is best again). In the years ahead, the beer drinker would know that beer was once again of a good quality. All manner of advertising techniques and campaigns were brought into play: special posters, a film, free glasses, instruction leaflets on how to handle beer and the setting up in 1951 of the 'Bierwacht' (Beer Brigade). Information meetings for café proprietors and agents under the motto 'a well-tapped glass sells another' led in 1953 to national beer drawing championships, held to this day. The collective campaign was large-scale, consistent and striking. The efforts had the desired result: beer consumption rocketed after 1950. Beer was best again.

7.17

AND THE WINNER IS...

7.18

'Beer is best again' – this was, and still is, particularly true of Heineken beer. Since the 1950s, the brewer has derived the maximum profit from its head-start in the home drinking market, as well as strong growth in beer consumption and the consumer's increasing preference for bottled beer and pilsner. To this day, Heineken pilsner is the most popular and best-selling beer in the Netherlands – thanks to the beer drinker and the Dutch advertising campaign 'Heerlijk Helder Heineken'.

LEADERSHIP HAS A COLOR.

WORKING ON THE BOTTLING LINE, 1951.

THE TELEVISION AND THE FRIDGE
HAVE MADE HOME CONSUMPTION OF BEER
POPULAR

Red alert !

THE POWER OF BEER COMBINED WITH PLEASURE. DURING THE 1960S, THE 'HEERLIJK HELDER HEINEKEN' ADVERTISEMENTS WERE FIRST AIRED ON THE DUTCH MARKET.

'HEERLIJK HELDER HEINEKEN' IS THE MOST SUCCESSFUL CAMPAIGN IN THE NETHERLANDS. HEINEKEN BRINGS PLEASURE TO PEOPLE'S LIVES.

AUTHORITY

PIONEER IN AFRICA

Heineken made history in Africa. During the 1950s, millions of bottles of Heineken were shipped to West Africa. The brewery was involved in a heroic fight against high waves, rattling crates and crafty competitors. In Lagos, the company built a brewery which, on June 2, 1949, launched the first Star beer onto the market. A star was born thanks to Heineken's technical supervision. Heineken's motto during the 1950s and 1960s was Build and Brew. Aba, Boma, Kumasi, Kisangani, Moundou... a whole series of breweries sprung up in West and Central Africa. Brewing beer under the hot tropical sun was work for real pioneers. The results were there for the tasting: Star, Primus, Gala and Gulder were African beers of an outstanding quality. On the more developed beer markets today, Heineken still brews the Heineken, Amstel, Murphy's and Mützig brands. The company is the second largest brewer on the African continent.

SETTING COURSE FOR AFRICA

8.4

As early as in 1900, Heineken was exporting small quantities of beer to various African countries. British West Africa, which included countries such as Ghana, Nigeria, Liberia and Sierra Leone, was a particularly attractive market. At the end of the 1930s, the brewer was shipping approximately 6,000 hectoliters to Nigeria and Ghana annually. However, at that time, the most important import brands were the German beers Bergedorff and Beck's, alongside English brands such as Tennents, Allsops and Jeffreys. The white colonists were the most important clients. The West Africans drank their own homemade palm wine.

The brewery was also active in an entirely different part of the African continent. In 1935, it acquired shareholdings in two Egyptian breweries via the investment company Cobra. These were the Société de Bières Bomonti & Pyramides in Cairo and the Crown Brewery in Alexandria. Both breweries sold the Stella brand, which completely dominated the local beer market. During the Second World War, these breweries were running at full capacity to meet the needs of the thousands of Allied soldiers. Pre-war production of around 30,000 to 40,000 hectoliters rose towards the end of the war to 200,000 hectoliters per annum. Both breweries paid out high dividends during the war, which were then set aside in a frozen account for Cobra. When Heineken director Stikker visited the Egyptian breweries four months after the war ended, he could scarcely believe 'what enormous changes have taken place in the entire structure, what tremendous expansions have been carried out and what extraordinary profits this has resulted in.' Given the fact that it was only permitted to transfer part of the 'Cobra dividends' to the Netherlands, the brewery had accumulated considerable funds at its disposal locally. What was to be done with all this money?

It so happened that Stikker had recently had a meeting with the management of Unilever in London. This company had, for years, maintained close trading contacts within the African continent. Since the end of the nineteenth century, Unilever's subsidiary, African Trading Co., had been trading by barter in Africa. Salt, flour, exotic fabrics, palm oil and cocoa beans were among the products traded. In 1921, in order to bring an end to their mutual competition, a number of British trading houses joined together to form the African & Eastern Trade Corporation, while a number of French trading houses cooperated under the name Compagnie du Niger Français. On May 1, 1929, these two organizations joined

Label of the Stella brand from the Egyptian breweries Bomonti and Crown, in which Heineken had a shareholding between 1935 and 1963.

forces to create the United Africa Company (UAC), with its head office being Africa House in London. The UAC, a Unilever subsidiary, had for years been the dominant trading power in West Africa.

NIGERIAN BREWERIES

During the meeting between Stikker and Unilever, the possibility of a joint brewery project in Lagos was discussed, whereby Heineken would be responsible for the technical aspects. Unilever emphasized that the conditions in West Africa as far as beer was concerned had never been more favorable. Beer was popular among Africans and the climate made people thirsty. In addition, people's purchasing power was considerable, given the fact the economy was growing due to the increase in raw material prices. Stikker acknowledged the potential. From the psychological point of view it was, however, a considerable step to undertake an unknown foreign venture so soon after the war. Moreover, the brewery was struggling to combat a considerable shortage of brewers and technical personnel. At the Heineken Board meeting on October 24, 1945, the warning was given 'against distorting the organization by imposing increasingly greater burdens on the shoulders of certain departments and people.'

8.6

Nevertheless, Stikker continued to have faith in the brewery project in Nigeria. The draft plan was based on a brewery production of 20,000 hectoliters and an investment of 2 million guilders. The other members of the Board considered this a lot of money during these uncertain times. Stikker on the other hand 'wishes, despite the uncertainty and unrest of these times, which will pass, to continue searching for further expansion opportunities.' A plan began to take shape in Stikker's head. The hundreds of thousands of guilders held by the Egyptian breweries could be used effectively to finance the Nigerian project. Unilever eventually agreed that Heineken should call in a subsidiary in connection with the financial plans. On November 16, 1946, Heineken and UAC signed a contract for the setting up of Nigerian Breweries Limited in the capital, Lagos. Both parties were one-third shareholders. The other shares were held by five trading houses. UAC was made responsible for the commercial aspects while Heineken had technical control and Nathan, a Swiss company, provided the technical brewing installations.

TWO STARS

On June 2, 1949, the first beer – Star – left the Lagos brewery. The inevitable teething problems were solved with great ingenuity by technical manager J. Lens van Rijn. Following a visit to the brewery in 1950, Emmens, Heineken's technical director, sounded the praises of the managers, and in particular Lens van Rijn. It transpired that he 'has brewed a Nathan beer, that, notwithstanding the short preparation time of 17 days, approaches the quality of Heineken beer more than any of our other foreign breweries.' Star beer could easily compete with the imported beers. As far as price was concerned, it turned out to be a favorable alternative for the more expensive imported brands. Within only a couple of years, Star had become a sales success on the Nigerian beer market.

A bottle of Star beer (1950), Nigerian Breweries' successful brand.

8.7

However, Heineken also had a different star in the West African firmament, namely Heineken pilsner. The following figures are a good representation of the conspicuous advance of the beer brand in Nigeria and Ghana. In 1939, beer consumption in Nigeria totaled 70,000 crates of four dozen 65 cl. bottles. Beer sales rose to 900,000 crates by 1954. The market share of the various beer brands was then as follows: 275,000 crates of the local Star beer, well over 200,000 crates of Heineken, and 200,000 crates of Beck's were sold while other imported brands such as Bergedorff, Guinness, Tennents, Allsops together sold approximately 225,000 crates. Sales of Heineken were concentrated in the capital Lagos and Western Nigeria.

In Ghana, the picture for Heineken was even rosier. In 1939, 80,000 crates were sold, while in 1954 this quantity had risen to 550,000 crates. The distribution of sales across the various beer brands in the same year was 125,000 crates of the local Club beer and well over 300,000 crates of Heineken, while Guinness, Bergedorff, Beck's and Allsops together only managed to sell 125,000 crates. Heineken was primarily drunk in Ashanti, the rich northern province and Kumasi, its capital.

8.8 A lorry for the transport of crates of Star beer in a warehouse on the site of the brewery in Lagos, circa 1960.

SUCCESS IS NO COINCIDENCE

In the mid-1950s, half of Heineken's exports were to West Africa, equal to one quarter of Heineken's total production. In Nigeria and Ghana, the two most important beer markets, Heineken was the best-selling imported beer. What was the secret of this success? Immediately after the war, the brewer made export a priority, in particular to the American and West African markets. German breweries were subject to an export ban until the autumn of 1948 and Bergedorff and Beck's only reappeared on the West African market in November and December 1950. Production of local beers only started in the 1950s. In the first instance, therefore, the field was open to Dutch exporting breweries such as Phoenix, Oranjeboom, Amstel and – above all – Heineken. Of all these brewers, Amstel assumed a leading position in the years 1949 and 1950, but thereafter Heineken resolutely moved back to the top, and never relinquished that position.

Heineken pilsner was a big favorite among Nigerians and Ghanaians. The product was promoted as a trustworthy and delicious thirst quencher: 'drinking beer is safer than drinking water' was the core message. Of all drinks, beer benefited most from the increased purchasing power among West Africans. In comparison to spirits, such as Schnapps, cognac and the local palm wine, beer was not expensive. Both men and women liked to drink it. Heineken director Ben ter Haar was encouraged to observe during his visit to West Africa that, 'The quality of our beer, our type of beer, appeals to the African people. If we can maintain our unsurpassed quality, we will continue to be a popular beer in West Africa. Constant quality is a prerequisite. One bad brew could finish us off. It is better for there to be a temporary shortage than to run a risk. Africans work with their senses and are connoisseurs compared to the whites.'

A market in Ghana in 1957. In African countries, the Heineken beer crates are used for a variety of purposes, such as the storage and transport of agricultural products.

Another aspect of the success was based on the good relationship between Heineken and UAC, Heineken's partner in Nigerian Breweries. The West African beer market had some unusual twists. Whereas Heineken managed with one or two importers in most countries, in West Africa they had to work with various large and small trading houses. Most had an English background, such as UAC in London and John Holt in Liverpool and J.B. Ollivant in Manchester. These trading houses all imported the same articles and brands and, in addition to being wholesalers, were also often retail traders as well, selling beer to consumers. Similarly to the other breweries, Heineken sold its beer to all the trading houses in order to have maximum access to the market. This situation sometimes demanded considerable diplomatic skills since, if preference was given to any one trading house, others became jealous.

Another point of note was that the African wholesale and retail trade, unlike elsewhere, had no fixed prices. The price of beer was determined by the popularity of the brand, the competition between the large trading houses and the quantity of stocks held. Large stocks at the trading houses immediately resulted in lower prices. Trading margins that were too low were dangerous because the trade then lost interest in the product. A number of Dutch beer brands therefore failed in Africa because, in their enthusiasm, they accumulated too much stock, resulting in the trading houses dropping these beers like a hot brick. Trading houses operating on this market imposed a hard and fast rule, namely that a beer whose sales were declining must not be saved and should be immediately removed from the range. Without mercy! Heineken's export department was therefore very focused on preventing the accumulation of large stocks in the various regions – traders had to keep generating a decent profit from the beer. Nothing is as stimulating for sales as good margins.

8.10

UAC provided Heineken with a great deal of support, but not directly in the field of active beer sales. Trading houses and the beer trade involved in the markets, which were primarily controlled by women, preferred to wait and see what happened. The wares were set out and it was simply a question of waiting until there was enough demand. UAC offices in Africa had other ideas. If a competing trading house had too much Heineken in stock (thereby entailing a serious risk of lower prices), then UAC was often prepared to take part of the excess stock off their hands. The trading house also provided Heineken with detailed information on Heineken's position and that of competing beers. One good turn deserves another and the UAC in London received 'overriding commission' from the brewer, a secret turnover premium that the other trading houses did not receive. 'More than any other trading house, UAC used its powerful position – approximately 33 percent of trade – to assist the producer to achieve success,' Ben ter Haar stated in 1955. If Heineken was the ship, UAC was the tug pulling it along.

ALARM!

As the trading houses were fairly far removed from actual beer sales, Heineken worked in Nigeria and Ghana on a commission basis with the Liverpool firm Eastwood & Sharples. The sales promoters Norman Eastwood and Bill Sharples perfectly matched the image of the English colonial trader. A 'stiff upper lip', a khaki tropical suit and a bowler hat to ward off the sun. Both men carried out excellent work both before and after the war. They generally went on a thorough inspection trip every year, which lasted one or two months and covered the West African coast and inland areas. Eastwood and Sharples were the lubricant between the brewers on the one hand and the various trading houses and local saloons and beer shops on the other.

Other brewers also brought in European sales staff. This was the case at the Beck's Brauerei with its base in Bremen in Germany, which sold the Beck's brand. In 1952, in an attempt to capture part of the lucrative African market, the German brewer appointed the Dutchmen Morsink and Van Papen to the post of sales promoters. The duo had no success in Ghana and Liberia, but things went a lot better in Nigeria. Particularly in Western Nigeria and the capital Lagos, Beck's took the market by storm and gained considerable ground on its competitors.

The pair visited shops, saloons and traders handing out expensive publicity items such as umbrellas, watches and lighters. For a long time, Heineken was unaware of Beck's success. In 1952, Melchior Weymarshausen, head of Heineken's export department, visited Lagos. He was welcomed with the words 'Heineken is losing ground and Beck's is gaining ground', but the brewery did not pay much attention. Why should it? The export department could scarcely cope with the existing orders. No single Heineken representative visited West Africa for well over two years. The brewer was busy, busy, busy.

How great a threat the situation was for Heineken, was only discovered when an export member of staff Plooij visited Nigeria in November 1954. 'Phew! It is always so difficult to compile proper reports!,' Plooij wrote to the export department in Rotterdam. 'It is a common phenomenon that headquarters and local offices have to be on the same wavelength and I have not been away for that long, have I? Do not for a moment think that there is reason to panic. I am certainly not panicking (albeit that the heat and the total lack of the most elementary comforts sometimes make it difficult to stay calm). Your figures are completely correct, I have checked them meticulously. However, I cannot agree with your interpretation. We have definitely lost ground in Nigeria! I hope that you will be able to understand my report as it is meant to be understood, that is as a reflection of "the boys at the front". We are not afraid. We have gained ground in the East but have conceded a great deal in Lagos. The enemy has better ammunition and more equipment.' Alarm bells started ringing in the Netherlands.

THINGS HAVE TO IMPROVE

Plooij's final report gave the management food for thought. Could improvements be made? Plooij calculated that Heineken was almost 20 percent more expensive than Beck's due to the packaging used. The crates in which the German brewer shipped its export beer to Africa were much better than those used by Heineken – both with regard to construction, materials used and dimensions. There was too much room in the crates for Heineken beer bottles to move around. Because unloading in Africa was certainly carried out heavy-handedly, the extra space was causing a lot of breakages. The crates were also susceptible to warping and breaking open. In addition, these excessively roomy crates meant that Heineken was not

8.12   Poster from the advertising campaign launched in West Africa in the 1950s, 'There is happiness in Heineken's'.

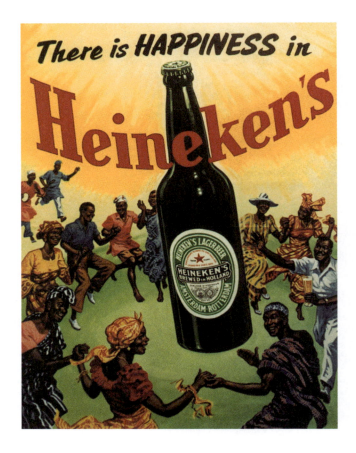

making optimal use of the space in the holds. That meant an even greater financial loss. Beck's was passing the benefits acquired from shipping costs on to the trade. The trading houses were therefore more eager to include this beer in their ranges.

Heineken had also been somewhat asleep as far as advertising was concerned. Heineken's promotional material was not that impressive compared to its competitors'. Beck's in particular outdid Heineken both with regard to quality and quantity. Plooij also wanted a couple of sturdy salesmen to be sent out to visit the shops and saloons to promote Heineken beer. These salesmen would have to be self-confident and also of an easy-going disposition. 'I recommend looking for large, stocky types since physical superiority counts for a great deal here,' Plooij suggested. This comment caused a few doubts to be raised at Heineken regarding Eastwood and Sharples. The two Britons were well over sixty and they were finding it more and more difficult to traipse for weeks through the hot Nigerian landscape.

8.13 Heineken used this enamel sign during the late 1960s to stress the importance of good stock management to its African customers.

Head of advertising Timmer, who visited a year later, reached the same conclusion. 'We are entrusting a quarter of our turnover to a relatively small company, run by a couple of men who could drop dead tomorrow and who are operating in the field themselves with only a couple of sales staff, who have to try to cover an incredibly large area. I can only say that I have qualms about the commercial organization, on which sales of 25 percent of what we brew is based. The people at Beck's once (hypocritically) declared that the place was big enough for the two of us. Nothing is further from the truth. We conquered this market and we have had to adapt our production mechanism in line with the demand that has been created here. We cannot lose any part of this market without it causing us serious damage.'

VICTORY WITH AN AFTERTASTE

'Beck's is concentrating its attack on the capital Lagos, aware of the old maxim that what happens in the capital is accepted within a period of 3 or 4 years throughout the country as a whole. The capital city sets the stage in any country. If they win over the capital, they will win over the country, and if they win over this country their next attack will be aimed at the Gold Coast. We must not hold back at all in foiling these plans,' was the conclusion of a Heineken report compiled in 1956.

The cellars of the brewery in Bukavu in the former Belgian Congo, August 1950. The beer is stored in tanks.

No half measures were taken. The brewer terminated the contract with Eastwood & Sharples and, in 1958, set up its own sales department under the name Nigeria Limited. Sales, which were directed by Gerard van Os van Delden, were based on canvassing, entailing an African sales team in old Volkswagens 'making raids' on coastal locations, where everything and everyone was then placarded and covered with Heineken paraphernalia. Using a comprehensive card system, all 1500 sales locations of 'greater Lagos' were visited street-by-street and neighborhood-by-neighborhood. Wherever these flying squads went, they left a green trail behind them. They did not hold back from organizing entire parties, as long as the brand was publicized and was on display. 'There is happiness in Heineken's' was therefore an appropriate motto for the publicity campaign. Heineken was also one big party, for the brewer. Between 1956 and 1960, Heineken saw its market share in Nigerian beer imports increase from 30.7 to 34.5 percent, while Beck's share receded from 40.2 to 16.4 percent. Beck's tried to stem the tide with price stunts and free beer, but it was fighting a losing battle.

By 1960, Heineken was market leader. In that year, the brewery exported 100,000 hectoliters of beer to Ghana alone, making it Heineken's most important export market. However, there was an unexpected end to the golden export story. Ghana gained independence in 1957, with Nigeria following suit in 1960 and Sierra Leone in 1961. The governments of the independent states strove to achieve rapid industrialization. By doing so, they intended to save hard currency on imports and also improve employment opportunities for their own populations. Industrialization therefore often started with the production of goods which up to then had been imported, such as textiles, cigarettes and beer. In order to protect their own industries and employment opportunities against competition from cheap imports, the governments increased their import duties – often substantially. In 1961, high increases – of more than 125 percent – and economic difficulties brought Heineken exports to Ghana to a complete standstill. The same occurred in Nigeria in 1965. Luckily, the brewery still had a few more trump cards to play on the African market.

8.15

A NETWORK OF BREWERIES

Nigerian Breweries' Star beer was a favorite among Nigerian beer drinkers. This success made them eager for more. UAC and Heineken developed plans for the construction of a new brewery in the country. In 1957, Nigerian Breweries opened a second brewery in Aba and in 1963 a third was operational in Kaduna. These new breweries were funded entirely from the profits of the Lagos brewery. New breweries were established in other countries in West Africa as well. Unilever and Heineken employed the same trustworthy division of tasks and applied the same financing policy as in Lagos. Breweries were successfully opened in Ghana (Kumasi, 1960), Sierra Leone (Freetown, 1962) and Chad (Moundou, 1965). These local breweries made a considerable contribution to the brewery profit and compensated for the absence of Heineken exports.

In Central Africa, Heineken, together with a different partner, also followed the route of building and brewing. Since the 1930s, Heineken had had an interest, via the investment company Interbra, in the Brasserie de Léopoldville, established in 1923. The Primus beer this company brewed measured up well against the best imported beers, Heineken director Emmens concluded during his visit to the Belgian Congo in 1949. 'Given the fact that Léopoldville beer is

8.16

truly of an excellent quality, it is clear that importers of European beer will not find things easy here. The theories of the gentlemen at Léopoldville might have sounded a little revolutionary every now and again, but I can only confirm that their results both from the technical and commercial points of view are excellent. I have never come across a brewery, whose entire staff are so enthusiastic, original and nevertheless critical as at the Léopoldville brewery.'

In 1957, Brasserie de Léopoldville, which had by then already opened a second branch in Bukavu, was renamed Bralima. Thereafter, new breweries were constructed – under Heineken's technical supervision – in Kisangani and Boma (1958) and Mbandaka (1972). Moreover, Bralima also brewed its Primus brand at breweries in the Congo, Rwanda and Burundi. With its brewing interests in Western and Central Africa, Heineken continues to maintain a special link with Africa and African people.

PRIMUS.
ELLE FAIT MOUSSER LA VIE.

RESPECT

THE MAN
AND
THE BRAND

9

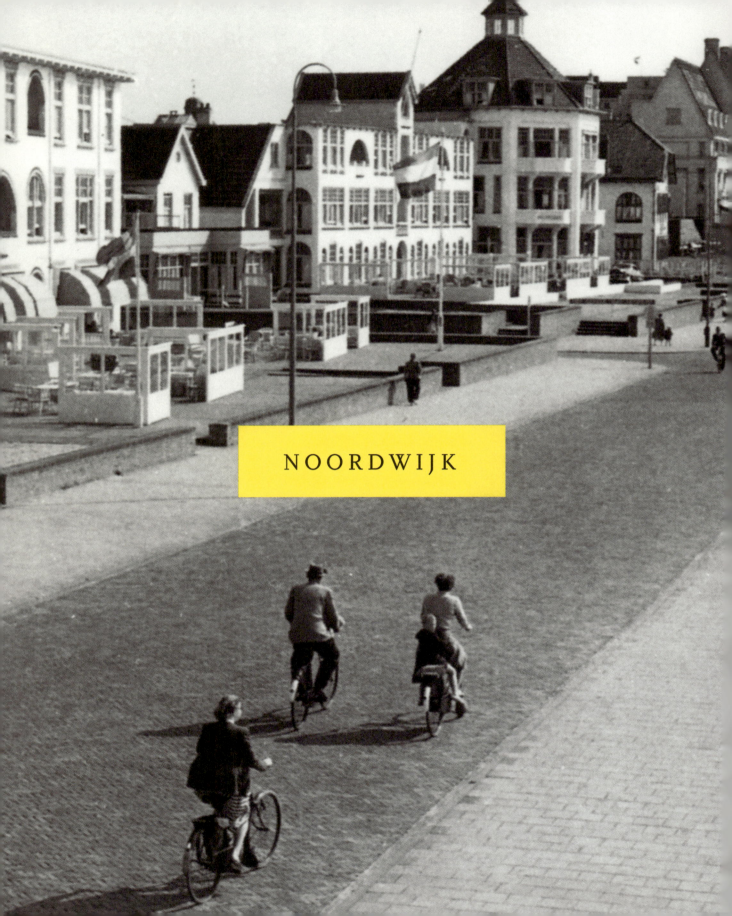

He is a phenomenon and that is how we wish to present him to you. It was a question of one man, one company and one brand. Heineken, Heineken and Heineken. The man was born in 1923 and entered the employment of the brewery at the age of eighteen. In 1954, he ensured that the company returned to family control and expanded it to world-wide proportions. The Heineken brand was his life's work. Is it even necessary to present him to you, we could ask. Without his creativity, the world would look a lot less green. He liked to make people happy and considered that beer should be brewed by contented people. His motto would perhaps have been: behave normally, and you'll end up behaving oddly enough. He described himself as an authoritarian with a human face and as a man of intuition. On April 27, 1989, when he left the company and gave up his post of Chairman of the Board of Management, he was awarded a royal distinction. In the Netherlands everyone knows him, while in the rest of the world there are still many people who are surprised that he actually exists: beer brewer Alfred Henry Heineken.

ALFRED HENRY HEINEKEN

'People often ask me when I am going to write my autobiography? I like to fob off such inquisitiveness with a drole remark. I don't understand why people want to dig around all the time. I mean there is nothing more you need to know than that the man makes beer – makes good beer – and that is what you should be drinking... for the rest, there is nothing to report. I have never really cared what people think of me. I consider myself to be thoroughly unimportant, but no-one believes that. I am more of a clown. Being successful in business is basically nothing more than common sense.'

Alfred Henry Heineken was the product of the marriage of Henry Pierre Heineken and Carla Breitenstein, and was born on November 4, 1923. Together with his sister, Mary Francesca, and brother, Robert Felix, he grew up in the family home on the Jan van Goyenkade in Amsterdam. His younger brother, Robert, died prematurely in 1944 and Mary Francesca had more affinity with the cello than with the art of brewing; the opposite could be said of Alfred Heineken. From the age of four onwards he was regularly to be seen foraging around in the brewery in Amsterdam. Machine rooms, cornlofts, storage cellars... he was fascinated by it all.

Alfred Henry Heineken grew up in a world of contrasts. During the years 1917-1940, his father was Chairman of the brewery's Board of Directors and was responsible for the company's first international venture. He left the actual running of the brewery in the hands of a number of efficient directors, whom he had personally selected. He preferred to spend his time on artistic matters such as the chairmanship of the Resident Orchestra in Amsterdam and on playing the piano. He was often too trusting in business matters. Alfred's mother kept well away from the brewery. It was primarily his grandmother, Lady Mary Tindal, who made her presence felt within the company.

Dr. Henry Pierre Heineken gives Prince Bernhard of the Netherlands a guided tour during his visit to the Amsterdam brewery in 1937.

Alfred Heineken aged 12, 1935.

Mary Tindal made an enormous impression on the young Alfred. She was a descendant of a family of Scottish soldiers and looked after herself in every respect. After her husband, Gerard Adriaan Heineken, died in 1893 she ensured that the brewery remained in the family's hands. When HBM was set up in 1873, Gerard Adriaan Heineken possessed almost 70 percent of the share capital. At his death in 1893, he was privately more or less bankrupt. His shares were largely being used as collateral. Mary Tindal then insisted that the new directors relinquish half of their shares to her. This enabled her to eventually redeem the pledged Heineken shares. Because she was feared and respected, Mary Tindal acquired the nickname 'Her Majesty' within the brewery. She pulled all the strings within the company right up to her death in 1937 – her son Henry Pierre simply accepted the situation without grumbling.

In 1938, the brewery's character changed. For tax reasons, Henry Pierre Heineken floated the company's shares on the stock exchange. The close-knit family character was exchanged for a public company. The share capital was increased from 2.4 to 12 million guilders. At the start of 1939, 2,000 shares with a nominal value of 1,000 guilders were introduced on the stock exchanges in Amsterdam and Rotterdam. Interest in purchasing these shares was so great that only 1 percent of the applications could be accepted. Following the flotation, Henry Pierre Heineken still owned around 52 percent of the shares issued. A threatened tax law – that was eventually not introduced – meant that he did not take the opportunity to issue priority shares. The company's family character was further weakened by the fact that the company's articles of association assigned more power to the Board of Directors and the supervisory directors.

In 1942, the company's share capital had increased even further to 15 million guilders. For tax reasons, Henry Pierre Heineken was advised to subscribe for less than half of this new capital increase and thus the family lost its majority share ownership. In addition, Henry Pierre Heineken's divorce further reduced the family's ownership.

ALFRED, FRED, FREDDY

9.6

'My name is Alfred and at school I was called Fred. To me that was a kind of rodent ['fret' is Dutch for 'ferret']. Then people started to call me Heintje, as my father was often called. However, if they called out Heintje, I simply pretended I hadn't heard them and kept quiet. Then I started calling myself Freddy and insisting on the y at the end. People would often ask me, 'How do you spell that?'. With a 'y' and why not, I would then reply.'

In 1936, Alfred Heineken left the close-knit family surroundings and started attending secondary school, first at the 'Hervormd Lyceum' (High School) in South Amsterdam and then the 'Kennemer Lyceum' in Bloemendaal. He managed to survive using a certain amount of bluff and quick-wittedness. In 1942 – in the middle of the war – he obtained his 'HBS-A' (Dutch High School) diploma. His teachers predicted, primarily on the basis of his personality, that 'Fred' could develop into an intelligent leader. 'He doesn't allow anyone or anything to force him to do something and absolutely does his own thing.' In short, he is a cocksure lad, with all the bravura that an 18-year-old should have.

Sailing on the Kaag, a Dutch lake, 1943.

In order to avoid the German Employment Service, Alfred Heineken and Dick Stikker, the son of Heineken director Stikker, were put to work in the brewery in Rotterdam a week after they had finished school. Their salary was 600 guilders per year. In the beginning there was not that much work for the two boys, who staff referred to in jest as 'part-time girls'. The young brewer's son made the best of it. Every day he traveled from his home on the Amazonelaan 14 in Wassenaar to the brewery and back, first by train and later by motorbike. To him, working at the brewery was one big adventure. He enthusiastically lugged bales of barley, got his hands dirty, learned how to make test brews, gave guided tours, set up a photographic archive, worked on the bottling line and regularly discussed all kinds of beer matters with the director, Pieter Feith. The correctly brought-up lad had the time of his life – he laughed a great deal

In the 1960s, the combination of beer and tobacco was still acceptable.

with the workers. 'As a resident of Amsterdam, I was able to get on with everyone quite easily and clowned around with everyone. I was not someone who made it known that I was the boss's son. Behave normally and you'll end up behaving oddly enough. If you are unsure of yourself, you start to show off, but if you have a little bit of self-confidence then you can cope with a lot more.'

There were also serious matters to be dealt with. Although the occupying German forces allowed the breweries to continue producing, in exchange beer also had to be supplied to the German army. Alfred Heineken's task was to maintain the administrative contacts between the Rotterdam brewery and the German army, and this exempted him from being sent to work in Germany. Every delivery of beer was signed for by a German officer, who thereby agreed the purchase of the essential raw materials. During the last six months of the war, travelling to the brewery was too dangerous and young Heineken stayed in Wassenaar.

Liberation on May 5, 1945 meant a new start. It was some time before life returned to normal. Work was not immediately available at the brewery. Given the fact that he spoke good English, Alfred Heineken became a jack-of-all-trades for the Canadian army. Via a correspondent for a Canadian magazine, he managed to acquire a nice Opel and a few weeks later he was also the owner of a motorbike and a Jeep. He discovered that he was good at wangling things and that he had a talent for sales. Money he had earned himself gave him a feeling of self-respect and independence – he was extremely successful and enjoyed life as a bon vivant, to the increasing concern of his family and the brewery management. They decided that the time had come for 'Mr. Independent' to get involved again in the serious side of beer. The brewery asked Leo van Munching, Heineken's importer in the United States, to teach 'little Freddy' the finer points of the beer trade. The 22-year-old Heineken, who had had to keep a low profile during the five long years of occupation, responded very eagerly to what to him sounded like an offer of adventure – it was time for him to spread his wings.

I HAVE SEEN THE FUTURE

'In 1946, the brewery management sent me to the United States, partly to get rid of me. That is something they should never have done, because I learned an enormous amount while I was there. The beer industry is not that difficult you know, as long as you keep looking to the future.'

On March 6, 1946, the brewery appointed 'Freddy' to the post of sales promoter in the United States, at a salary of US$ 6,800 per annum. Alfred Heineken considered the amount a little on the stingy side, certainly in view of the high additional costs, but a quiet request for a rise was firmly rejected by director Stikker. In his opinion, the amount was 'exorbitant' by Dutch standards and he advised Freddy to approach his father if he needed additional funds.

Alfred Heineken's business card as a representative of the American Heineken importer Van Munching & Co., 1946-1947.

A little to the surprise of the management team, Alfred Heineken emerged in the United States as a diligent and hard-working trainee salesman. In September 1946, he even applied for a place at Columbia University in New York with a view to attending a number of courses, and in the evenings he attended a course at the Advertising Club. He discovered a whole new advertising world. In April 1947, he started work as a sales promoter for the Heineken brand on the West Coast. 'I hope to show them in Holland sometime', he wrote on April 2, 1947, 'that I am not just the boss's son.' He was perfectly suited to the task of selling beer to the trade. In one and a half years, he sold exactly 22,213 boxes. In doing so, he had increased sales on the West Coast (for the full year 1947) by 260 percent compared with 1939. This achievement did wonders for his self-confidence. Sunny California provided him with even more, since it was there he met Lucille Cummins, daughter of a Bourbon whisky producer from LaRue County, Kentucky, whom he married on August 28, 1948.

Alfred Heineken with his bride Lucille Cummins on their wedding day in a restaurant in the New York area, August 28, 1948.

While in America, Alfred Heineken acquired an insight into what he wanted to get out of life. From Seattle, he wrote a candid letter to his father on April 2, 1947 in which he explained, 'As you know, the whole Heineken affair has been very close to my heart during the past year and I hope to achieve great things in the future. Since the day will come that Cesca [Mary Francesca] and I will inherit your block of shares in HBM, it is not so much the capital as the percentage that we will then own together in HBM that is also very important for my ideal, namely the financial interest that the Heineken family will have in the future. I aim to achieve a great deal for HBM and I believe that I will be able to do so in the future. Due to the various things that have occurred in recent years, such as the divorce from Mum and the large amount of money that the tax authorities got their hands on, your interest in HBM, the percentage compared with that which Otie [Lady Mary Tindal] had, has been considerably reduced. There is nothing you can do about this, circumstances were to blame. My intention, however, is to try during my lifetime to ensure that the majority of HBM shares are returned

to the family. I know this to be a very ambitious plan but one can only try and it is always a good idea to have an ambition. Do not misunderstand me, I am not that interested in becoming very rich since one can live just as well from a couple of hundred thousand guilders as from several million. It is more a question of pride that I can leave a percentage in HBM to any children I might have, just as I inherited from my father and you in turn from yours. This might all sound foolish but I just have this idea in my head.' In September 1948, Alfred Heineken returned to the Netherlands together with his wife. The future was his for the taking.

FROM FATHER TO SON

9.10

'When I arrived back from the United States, I found my father sitting at his desk – an accountant had gathered together all sorts of documents because the whole situation was a frightful mess. I still have a few frightening documents from that time, sent by advisors who claimed that all the capital had gone. My father was sitting there quite forlorn... and that was not what he deserved, since he had done a great deal for the company. I said to him, "Let me and my sister inherit and then I will try to look after you as best I can and take care of things from then on." My father then asked, "Is 48 hours sufficient time to arrange the transfer?" I think that would be more than enough time, I said.'

When Alfred Heineken returned to Holland in September 1948, he was a long way from having it made. Although his father still held 45 percent of the shares in the brewery, his father's debts were considerable. In 1946, the Dutch government introduced a special tax on assets and profits acquired during the war. This measure also had consequences for the expansion increase implemented by the brewery in 1942. Henry Pierre Heineken was suddenly swamped with tax assessments. In 1948, in order to be able to pay these, he borrowed 2 million guilders from the brewery. However, the tax authorities regarded this as a dividend payment which meant that even more tax was payable. The tax assessments ran into well over 5 million guilders. Tax advisors calculated that, if the assets were reorganized, the Heineken family would receive an annual dividend of around 46,000 guilders. 'Not too bad, but I considered it not to be enough', said Alfred Heineken.

Alfred Heineken agreed with his father that he would look after the finances from then on. Within a matter of days, Henry Pierre Heineken transferred his stake to his son and daughter. The state of affairs was soon clear to Alfred Heineken. He was personally entitled to around 20 percent of the share capital and a mountain of debts. Following the example of his grandfather Gerard Adriaan Heineken – 'It has to be all or nothing! Anything else is nonsense' – he decided that the best form of defense was attack. The majority of the shares were to be brought back into the family. 'My father knew very well that he could not do it himself; the war had broken people. He probably would not have believed that it was possible. I was not entirely sure either. I then purchased an expensive car with which to visit banks – a Jaguar with a lot of wood finishing. A bit of bluffing does no harm...'

I DO NOT WANT TO BE NON-EXISTENT

'I was 25, but I had already gained quite a lot of experience. I had lived through the war and that had made me grow up quickly. Since I was four years old, I had heard of nothing else than that brewery. I was an 'old' man for my age, married at 24, had a household to look after and leading a more or less stable existence.'

This waiter from 1948 was developed against the wishes of Alfred Heineken, who saw this as a textbook example of a psychologically bad advertisement for beer: an overly fat man.

Heineken's Board of Directors and the supervisory directors did not really know what to do with the young Heineken following his return to the Netherlands. They found him too unpolished and precocious and did not understand his sense of humor and witticisms. Moreover, over the years, they had become used to having more or less sole charge of the company. They would have preferred not to have to deal with an ambitious heir apparent. Some people within the company treated him in a simply condescending manner, as an ignorant son of rich parents who had been kicked upstairs. This only reinforced his determination to eventually have the last laugh. The brewery Board sent Alfred Heineken – slightly against his will – on a work placement lasting six months with the 'Nederlandse Handel-Maatschappij' on the Vijzelstraat in Amsterdam. At the head office of this bank, he was made responsible for checking requests for loans from sub offices. As a subordinate member of the credits department, he came into contact with the hard-working attitude of accountants and business consultants. That knowledge would prove to be invaluable.

9.12

After a period of time, 'Freddy' had well and truly had enough of the boring side of life. He wanted to be involved with beer and the brewery. The management told him, however, that his training was not complete. They had planned additional work placements in the shipping and banking sectors. Alfred Heineken felt he was being belittled and regarded the whole work placement issue as a diversionary tactic designed to keep him away from brewery matters. Being the headstrong person he was, he made it clear to the management, 'I do not want to be non-existent!' The result of this heartfelt cry was that he was appointed to the head office in 1949 as a sales department assistant for the hotel and catering industry in the province of Northern Holland. With a boss who preferred to spend as little as possible on advertising, Alfred Heineken soon found himself with a struggle on his hands. After a couple of months he had had enough. One Saturday afternoon he left a notice stuck to the door of his office bearing the text 'Advertising Department'. From that moment on, his period of 'non-existence' was over.

Alfred Heineken, Heineken director Dirk Uipko Stikker and Cees Laseur (right) in the New York Copacabana club, 1946.

PUTTING THE CAT AMONG THE PIGEONS

'The focus is always on people. I often use the analogy of the cockerel in the hen house – there is only one boss, the rest tag along and try to become the boss.'

From 1949 onwards, tensions between Alfred Henry Heineken and the Board of Directors increased. On January 3, 1949, Henry Pierre Heineken sold a block of Cobra shares, on the basis of mutual consultations with the brewery Board, with a nominal value of 90,000 guilders. The shares were sold at a rate of 170 guilders to the brewery's Board members and supervisory directors, as well as a number of corporate executives. Alfred Heineken heard that ex-director Stikker had referred to this transaction as fraud. In a letter, he asked Stikker whether this was the case and whether this sale had reduced the Heineken family's stake in HBM. Alfred Heineken also added, 'As far as I personally am concerned, if dad has been swindled, and I know just as well as you do that that is simplicity itself, then something should be done, even if it were to mean that serious steps would have to be taken.'

9.13

Alfred Heineken was distraught when his father informed him during a lunch that he had agreed to the low rate believing that these shares were to be sold to the brewery. That was also why he had not informed his son and daughter about the sale. As a result of all the commotion, Stikker wrote a letter to Heineken's Chairman of the Supervisory Board, Baron Collot d'Escury. Heineken's ex-director let it be known that the rate of 170 guilders was 'absolutely too low' and that the former management team 'had often discussed how easy it would be to get Henry Pierre Heineken to agree to transactions that would be beneficial for the management – but detrimental to him. I can only deduce that something of this nature has taken place and I would like to urge most strongly that you consider rectifying this matter in some way, which I am convinced has been distorted.'

However, the Board of Directors and supervisory directors vehemently denied these allegations. Eventually, they agreed to accept the declaration issued by Alfred Heineken on April 7, 1949, 'that no blame can be attached to any of those who purchased the shares.' The tone between the parties had been set, however. What was eventually at stake was possession of the brewery. Who was to become the majority shareholder? Alfred Heineken suspected the incumbent management team of trying to acquire possession of the brewery for itself. In his eyes, it was make or break time.

This show card makes no bones about it: Heineken is delicious at home.

In the early 1950s, Alfred Heineken's influence was still limited: according to the current market philosophy, a pilsner-like beer, Pale Ale, launched under the Heineken label would be a mortal sin.

THE FIRST MOVE

'It is fun to checkmate people.'

In 1950, Alfred Henry Heineken set up the 'Heineken Beleggings- en Beheermaatschappij' (Heineken Investment and Management Company, HBBM), in which he deposited his minority shareholding in HBM. He secretly started to buy up HBM shares and transferred them to HBBM. 'I was very much enjoying working as an assistant in the publicity department. At the same time, I was involved in borrowing money from the large pension funds in order to be able to purchase the shares. I had no money but things were going o.k.... it was just a question of holding my nerve. I bought the shares to acquire control. When your own name is at stake, you don't want other people to start doing strange things with it.'

He bought out his sister Cesca, a move that increased his shareholding as well as his debts in one go. One major problem was that most family shares had been pledged in return for short-term loans subject to high interest rates. Because Alfred Heineken was not able to redeem these debts in the short term, he gambled everything on being able to convert these short-term debts into long-term loans with comparatively low interest rates by pledging his shares as collateral. The amounts he borrowed from the pension funds were considerable, certainly for those days. Many people thought he would eventually fail and were therefore prepared to sell their shares or lend him money in the expectation that these shares would eventually be up for sale again at a reduced price. It was like walking a tightrope. He was either going to become 'filthy rich' or become totally bankrupt. 'What was I to be afraid of, I had already lost control anyway. Once you are no longer scared you dare to gamble more. I had nothing to lose and I knew for certain that I could find another job to keep earning money', Alfred Heineken commented looking back.

In the 1950s, Alfred Heineken acquired a flying license, exploring European airspace with the 'Ambassador'. During the 1960s, he bought a Piper Comanche, an American four-seater, with the call sign PH-RED (pronounced: FRED).

9.15

WHO IS THE BOSS?

'At a certain moment in time, I let it be known that if I did not get my way, they could all leave. Of course, it is not funny when a young lad of 28 starts bossing people around... that is something I fully understand. But I was polite to them and they were slightly condescending towards me – that did not make things easier. If they had continued to resist I would have thrown them all out. Without mercy, is the expression. But I had also worked out beforehand that, when all was said and done, they were most unlikely to leave.'

In 1951, Henry Pierre Heineken resigned as the delegated member of the Supervisory Board and his son Alfred was appointed to the Supervisory Board. Although the young Heineken was the heir, he still had to gain authority. He was met by a great deal of resistance from those at the top of the company. The parties had an uneasy hold on each other. Alfred Heineken had a considerable number of shares, while the management had the know-how, the confidence of the market and the experience. There was certainly no heartfelt cooperation between the two parties during the first few years. Pawns and other pieces were moved around tactically in a mutual 'game of chess' – sometimes openly, sometimes covertly.

At the Board meeting on January 23, 1952, a joint meeting of management and supervisory directors, Alfred Heineken announced that he wished to become the delegated member of the Supervisory Board. Such a position would give him additional powers, including the right to attend directors' meetings. The Board was against the change however. On February 20, 1952,

9.16 the Board of Directors and supervisory directors rejected a proposal by Alfred Heineken to implement a favorable share recapitalization to his benefit, or rather they understood 'completely the difficult position in which the Heineken family finds itself due to the more than crippling tax levies it faced after liberation, but HBM's situation does not permit the implementation of the proposed recapitalization.'

In the 1960s, Heineken created a series of humorous beer cartoons. The text reads: 'Heineken – most served everywhere'.

Well over six months later, Alfred Heineken was able to pronounce a definite 'no' for a change. At a Board meeting on September 24, 1952, the management announced that the large competitor Amstel had agreed to a takeover offer. The cost of this acquisition was approximately 5 million guilders, largely to be financed by the issue of new Heineken shares. However, for Alfred Heineken there was a serious problem. In order to be able to retain his stake, he had to subscribe for almost 50 percent of the new shares to be issued. Given his existing debts, he was unable to do this – something that the existing management had undoubtedly realized. The whole plan seemed to have been devised to cause him financial difficulties. At the Board meeting of October 30, 1952 he therefore refused to agree to the proposal, to the considerable amazement of the Board of Directors and the other supervisory directors.

Alfred Heineken went one step further. The day after the Board meeting, he informed director Honig that he would not be attending any more Board meetings because the other supervisory directors were 'always against him'. Moreover, he wanted to call a meeting of shareholders to implement the dismissal of the incumbent supervisory directors. The Board of

Directors and the supervisory directors discussed the consequences of this 'one-man crusade' at their meeting on November 1, 1952. It really was an absurd situation – the youngest member of the Supervisory Board and assistant in the advertising department was threatening to fire them. Eventually, the Board bowed to the decision of the most important shareholder. The Amstel transaction was cancelled and the supervisory directors were allowed to remain. A cold-war was better than an all-out conflict.

At the beginning of February 1953, Alfred Heineken once again expressed his preference for the position of delegated member of the Supervisory Board. At this meeting, as director Feith wrote to his colleagues a few days later, 'Heineken was forced to do some talking and, as we all know from experience, his words at the green table are not always chosen with the greatest of tact.' Feith considered the appointment of Alfred Heineken to the position of delegated member of the Supervisory Board unacceptable at the time. 'It will only be possible to consider such a request once he has proven in practice that he is prepared and able to adapt to the style and method of working of HBM, instead of the opposite, and to use his position of power reasonably and first and foremost in the interest of HBM. If we were to give way in that respect, it would be a complete capitulation of the Board, which would be in no-one's interest, not even that of Alfred Heineken. We will have to make it clear that the issue is one of personal cooperation with Alfred Heineken and not the creation of a shadow Board of Directors under the auspices of HBBM.' In order not to bring the conflict to a head, the management agreed that the young shareholder should be permitted to attend all Board meetings 'so as to engender a good understanding between the two parties.' Feith had the wisdom of age.

GAME OF POKER

9.18 *'Shares were therefore sold, or loaned using shares, loaned again or used. I am pretty good – at poker, that is. I was in no hurry and timing is the most important thing... I was not thinking of power, nor money. What are you supposed to do with money if you already have enough? I was once asked in an interview what I thought about money. I never think about it, I only thought about it when I didn't have any. It is not a matter of money, but rather of control.'*

By the start of 1954, Alfred Heineken's secret share transactions produced the desired result. His private holding, HBBM, acquired a majority of the shares in the brewery. This thanks to the inclusion of a batch of Heineken shares belonging to H.F. Hoyer. But success came at a price. HBBM's debts were around 22 million guilders. Paying off the debt was something to worry about in the future. What counted for Alfred Heineken was that the brewery was once again in the family's hands. 'With my name', Alfred Heineken emphasized, 'I could not hang around as an assistant in the advertising department. That was something I could not allow with respect to my family. A batch of shares such as this carries with it the obligation to pass it on and not use it up.'

Alfred Heineken played for high stakes and he had won – 'the masterpiece of my working life, that was what it was about', was his conclusion. 'I had complete control of the situation and had carried out everything according to plan.' He allowed himself a small moment of glory. 'I went to director Honig to tell him politely that I was going on a six week holiday to the United States. I asked him if he thought that was alright. "What are you going to do if I don't agree", Honig asked. "I will go anyway", was my answer. He got a bit angry... and when I was about to leave the room, I said, "I almost forgot to tell you something. As of yesterday, I have a majority shareholding in this company." Then I walked out of the room... Later, he called me to ask me to come back and told me, "this is rather a strange situation." I said, "Yes, but that has more to do with you than with me."'

Alfred Heineken might have had control, but that was not enough. 'It was not only a question of acquiring a majority share, but of ensuring thereafter that the majority shareholding also worked. That was the next part of the story.'

EVERYTHING HAS TO CHANGE

'The time I spent in the US changed my life. I had been able to look into the future. I very much enjoyed the way of life there. I was inspired and enthusiastic about beer. The management team at the time was made up of people who had no direct affinity with advertising. Advertising as such did not yet exist. Sometimes adverts were made depicting a young lady and a bottle, but that missed the point which was what was happening emotionally. I came straight back from America and had read everything there was to read on the subject. Then I thought: if it works in America, then it will also work here.'

9.19

HEINEKEN'S

Heineken's

Heineken's

Heineken

Over the years, the Heineken trademark has undergone considerable changes. Alfred Heineken was responsible for the most characteristic steps: tilting the 'e' into a smiling 'e' and doing away with the 'apostrophe s'. Heineken is now simply Heineken.

Alfred Heineken had to fight his way into the brewery during the 1950s. He also found himself up against considerable resistance in the area of advertising. In those years, advertising was just a big word at Heineken. Although the company had an advertising department, its role was very limited – partially as a consequence of a limited budget. The export department organized its own affairs, whereas the most important export market – the United States – arranged its own advertising. Many within the company considered that advertising only cost money and produced very little return. This conservative mentality was at odds with what Alfred Heineken had learned in America, namely that advertising can make or break a brand.

Alfred Heineken started launching all kinds of advertising ideas at regular intervals. His initiatives were not appreciated. 'Turnover is growing so why change a winning formula', was the usual response from people at all levels of the company. He continued to keep pushing the idea however and succeeded in implementing a number of changes, which at first sight may seem to be far from spectacular. The brand name 'Heineken's' was changed to include three beautifully styled, laughing es and the apostrophe and the 's were scrapped. 'I do not want to be known as Heineken's. After all, there are no Droste's or Verkade's', was his succinct explanation. 'I had to fight for around six years to get rid of that s. It was an endless struggle. I wanted everything to change. When I realized that the trucks bore the words Heineken's breweries, I asked, "are we selling breweries or beer?" People thought I was being stupid... I didn't share their view! When it was changed to read Heineken beer I asked, "is that word beer really necessary? Do people think we are selling Chocomel or Coca-Cola... if we just change it to Heineken we can write it in larger letters." It was all very simple stuff, but I encountered a great deal of resistance at every turn.'

His greatest achievement was to introduce a new label for use on the Dutch market. Since 1931, the brewery had used two different labels. Internationally, beer was sold in bottles bearing the familiar green label, while in Holland the star label was used – a large red star on a gray background with black letters. A lot of people within the company were very happy with this formula, but Alfred Heineken was definitely not. 'If I might say so, I have great taste. I simply knew the Dutch label to be incredibly ugly and crass. The green label was chic, powerful and trustworthy!'

He proposed using the green label in the Netherlands as well. 'Well, that turned out to be a revolutionary proposal. They thought I had gone crazy. But I kept thinking that consumers are very conservative when it comes to what ends up in their stomachs and red is the color of danger as far as foodstuffs and drink are concerned. Green is the color of safety. The earth is green, as is grass and trees... green is safe. I foresaw that green would become a symbol for nature and safety, long before the environmental lobby started drumming it into us.' He had to use all his powers of persuasion and perseverance – 'I often had to get angry, they simply did not understand' – but eventually he got his way.

On October 1, 1954, the new green label was introduced in the Netherlands. It was, in a number of respects, a day of celebration for Alfred Heineken since, on the same day, the management appointed him to the position of advisor to 'Heineken's Bierbrouwerij Maatschappij NV' at a salary of 30,000 guilders a year.

A decisive measure by Alfred Heineken: in 1954, the label with the big red star (from 1931) was replaced on the Dutch market by a new, green Heineken label.

MOTHER AND DAUGHTERS

'I once had a director who did everything wrong and had an aquarium full of fish in his office. I said to him, "the mistake you are making is that you are swimming in your own aquarium. If you are running a business you have to stand and look at the aquarium from outside."'

9.22 Alfred Heineken with jazz musician Lionel Hampton in the Palace Bar in St. Moritz, 1958.

Alfred Heineken and his wife arrive in New York, 1956.

From the 1950s onwards, Alfred Heineken was more and more in the public eye. His way of life, assets and eye-catching deeds appealed to everyone's imagination. As a master of the spoken word he knew how to win over outsiders with his humor, striking quotes and one-liners, which made everyone stop and think. 'Freddy' was the talk of the town. His luxury cars, private jets, parties and beautiful houses distorted the image however. To get the right picture, you have to look at the brewery – the aquarium – from the outside. The view is then very clear. During the 1950s and 1960s, Alfred Heineken left a definitive mark on the company.

At the Board meeting on September 15, 1954, Alfred Heineken presented his ideas on the future of the company. In his eyes, the existing organization was not fit for the future. The Board was not immediately enthusiastic, but agreed to his proposal to have an outsider examine the organization. Soon afterwards, this outsider was appointed: Ernest Dale, professor of Business Administration at Cornell University in the United States and also one of the first organization advisors. Dale started his work at Heineken in 1955.

Prior to Dale's arrival in the Netherlands, Alfred Heineken wrote him a very extensive letter. Given that he had given his thoughts free rein, he asked Dale explicitly 'to treat this letter as super-confidential and would even suggest you leave it out of the Heineken dossier that you will lug around in your briefcase when doctoring this beloved company.' Alfred Heineken

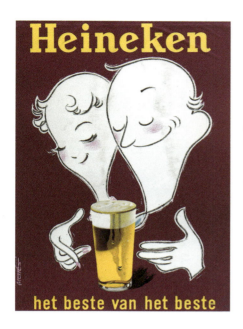

A poster created in the late 1950s by the renowned Dutch designer Frans Mettes. For people in love.

9.23

unfolded nothing more or less than a blueprint for the future structure of the company. He asked Dale to provide, among others, an answer to the question of whether he was 'crazy' – as critics within the company used to say he was – by maintaining that the existing organization was no longer in line with the considerable growth the company had experienced during recent years. The breweries in Amsterdam and Rotterdam were two more or less separate companies operating independently but parallel to each other and also imposing decisions within the existing parent company. Too much attention was being paid to Dutch interests and too little to the interests of the company, with all its foreign participations. To Alfred Heineken everything boiled down to one thing, 'to relieve the mother company of the Dutch twin daughters with which she has been pregnant for over 75 years, since otherwise both mother and daughters' health could be seriously impaired.'

The analysis was as clear as day, but not everyone paid attention to the content. Quite a few people within the company were not enthusiastic about the plans to separate the companies. 'Don't change a winning team' was their creed. Internal discussions meant that the reorganization process proceeded at a snail's pace. One complicating factor was also that a lot of troublesome legal and tax issues had to be solved. A lot of forceful words would once again be exchanged on the subject. However, Alfred Heineken had the loudest voice. The reorganization had to go ahead and he continued to hold on to his position of majority shareholder.

HEINEKEN AND HEINEKEN

'One of my forefathers, Baron Tindal, was a general under Napoleon. I reckon I have some of those general-like qualities as well. Once I know what has to happen, it simply has to be carried out and straight away too. Talking is all well and good, but not in business.'

A number of handy maneuvers helped Alfred Heineken gradually tighten his grip on things. In 1958, he was appointed delegated member of the Supervisory Board, a wish he had had for some considerable time. According to the articles of association, he now had the right to veto any important decisions. He became more and more of a behind-the-scenes director, a task he was perfectly suited to. In 1960, as a result of one of his proposals, the articles of association were amended so that power was returned to the shareholders – 'you cannot run the business if you do not have control', was Alfred Heineken's view.

In 1960, the brewery once again implemented a new organization structure. The Board of Management was at the top of the parent company, HBM, with below four independently operating subsidiaries, namely 'Heineken Brouwerijen Nederland', 'Heineken Internationaal', 'Heineken Exploitatie Maatschappij De Hooiberg' and – a few years later – 'Heineken Technisch Beheer NV'. This was the blueprint that Alfred Heineken had drawn up in his letter to professor Ernest Dale five years earlier. From that moment on, the Board of Management was able to focus attention on general business matters and strategic decisions. The separate subsidiaries acquired their own Boards of Directors with separate tasks and responsibilities. The whole structure increased the economic and legal security of the share capital and made it easier to expand this capital.

In 1962, Alfred Heineken definitively secured his majority stake by means of a flotation of HBBM on the stock exchange. The flotation enabled him to pay off his debts to the institutional lenders. Ingenious fiscal/legal constructions ensured that he continued to control the brewery despite having fewer shares. 50.005 percent of the shares in HBM were acquired by HBBM. 50.005 percent of this holding company's shares were then acquired by an investment company controlled by Alfred Heineken, with its registered offices in Switzerland. Thanks to this staggered construction, Alfred Heineken could exercise control over the entire Heineken group while owning only a quarter of the share capital. The brewery's name, HBM, was changed in 1972 to Heineken NV and HBBM changed its name to Heineken Holding. By reorganizing the brewery as well as his private holding, Alfred Heineken had killed two birds with one stone. The Heineken company was ready for the future and the future of the Heineken family was safeguarded. Heineken and Heineken. Sometimes goals are very closely linked.

THE KISS

'I have always been very happy with the name "Heineken". I certainly cannot imagine a better name for a beer. It sounds German, it is a diminutive, it is a pleasing word and a sweet word.'

At the start of the 1960s, the brewery did not yet have a clear international logo, let alone a worldwide marketing strategy. Although there was a green international label, slightly different labels were being used on two major markets, namely West Africa and the United States. Venezuela and Indonesia even had a totally different variant. Furthermore, there was a wide range of different advertising artifacts and labels. Those at Heineken looked on jealously at other companies such as Shell and Coca-Cola, which had a clear global image.

9.26

An advertisement from 1964, featuring the brewery's new logo: the kiss or 'Heineken lips'.

Heineken had, for years, been using the beer mat motif for all kinds of advertising articles. This was a large red star around which were the words 'Heineken's Bier', arranged in a circle. Consumer research revealed that people primarily recognized the black stripe used on the label. Alfred Heineken therefore wanted to elevate this black stripe, with the word Heineken inside it, to become the universal Heineken logo. This proposal was approved by the Heineken Board of Management on October 29, 1962. The real work could now begin. The stripe on its own did not attract enough attention and was not 'beery' enough. The whole thing had to become more striking and pleasing to the eye. Ed Arendsen, in those days head of the advertising department, was given the job of 'polishing up' the stripe. After a couple of weeks of cutting, pasting and coloring he came up with a design that was to go down in advertising history as the 'Heineken lips', two red semicircles above and below the stripe. After extensive tests, the new logo was launched in the summer of 1964, designed and ready to take on the world.

A MAN OF GENERATIONS

'I am a generation thinker and I think in terms of 25 or 50 years ahead. It is an entirely different way of thinking than, for example, the way in which a director thinks in maximum periods of 5 years. There are no specific targets I have to achieve in 5 years time, nor do I have to ensure that profits rise by a certain percentage every year. The idea is for the business to grow in a stable fashion. I could start throwing money around but that is not in the interest of the brewery. So it is something we don't do. We just keep progressing, not too forcefully, quickly nor madly but in a calm and controlled manner...'

Meeting of the Board of Management of Heineken NV, 1975. From left to right: secretary Pahud de Mortanges, G. van Schaik, Dr. J.P. Ton, Chairman A.H. Heineken, R. van Marwijk Kooy and J. van der Werf.

In 1964, Alfred Heineken was appointed to the Board of Management. Three years later he was Vice-Chairman and, on February 25, 1971, he was appointed Chairman of the Board of Management. It was under his leadership that Heineken and the Heineken brand underwent international expansion. When he reached retirement age he resigned from the Board of Management on April 27, 1989. These days, he does not hold any official positions within Heineken NV. He is still a major shareholder and Chairman of the Board of Management of Heineken Holding. This enables Alfred Heineken to keep alive the dream that he expressed on April 23, 1947 in a letter to his father, namely to gain control over the brewery and safeguard the shares for his heirs.

CONCLUSION

9.28
'Sometimes I am asked whether I would do it all again. My answer is yes! But why do they ask? How should I know. It is sometimes a little mysterious. Often I have watched tongue-tied how certain things developed... it makes you think, gosh! It all went pretty well.'

Alfred Henry Heineken, Amsterdam May 7, 2000.

Alfred Heineken following his appointment as Commander of the Order of Oranje Nassau, April 27, 1989. He is accompanied by his daughter Charlene and his wife.

CHARACTER SAYS A LOT.
THE MAN AND THE NAME JOKE IN PERFECT
HARMONY. A PRIVATE RECORDING BY 'FREDDY'
HEINEKEN IN 1958.

1945

READY FOR THE FUTURE

22-YEAR-OLD ALFRED HENRY HEINEKEN

IN HIS ALFA ROMEO ZAGATO COMPRESSOR 1750 CC

FROM 1934

1947

MY PERIOD IN THE UNITED STATES CHANGED MY LIFE. I DISCOVERED THAT PRICE PLAYS AN IMPORTANT ROLE IN MARKET PERCEPTION. I HADN'T COME ACROSS THIS IN THE NETHERLANDS: CONSUMERS WHO PAID MORE THAN DOUBLE FOR A HEINEKEN. IN AMERICA, THE BEER WAS A 'PRESTIGE ITEM'.

1951

HEINEKEN

"I CONSIDER RETURNING THE SHARES TO THE FAMILY TO BE THE CROWNING GLORY OF MY WORKING LIFE. I BOUGHT THE SHARES IN ORDER TO ACQUIRE CONTROL OF THE BREWERY. I WANTED TO PREVENT STRANGERS FROM DOING STRANGE THINGS UNDER MY NAME. THE RELIABILITY OF THE HEINEKEN NAME IS OF CRUCIAL IMPORTANCE."

1958

ALFRED HENRY HEINEKEN IS COMMITTED HEART AND SOUL TO THE HEINEKEN BRAND. IN 1964, THE COMPANY INTRODUCED A NEW INTERNATIONAL LOGO.

THIS LOGO IS BOTH IMAGE AND PERSONALITY. ALFRED HENRY HEINEKEN HAS MADE SURE THE NAME HEINEKEN IS KNOWN THE WORLD OVER.

1969

"I HAD THE IDEA OF CONQUERING THE EUROPEAN MARKET WITH HEINEKEN AROUND 1970. AND NO SOONER DID I HAVE THE IDEA, THAN IT WAS PUT INTO PRACTICE. PEOPLE OFTEN SAID TO ME: THAT'S NOT VERY SENSIBLE, YOU SHOULDN'T TRY IT. I ALWAYS ANSWERED: IT'S NOT VERY SENSIBLE, BUT DO IT ANYWAY."

1984

   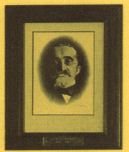

WHEN I HIRE PEOPLE, I DO IT BY INSTINCT. A LOT OF PEOPLE WHO COME IN HERE KNOW IT ALL AND WANT TO CHANGE EVERYTHING. THIS IS WHY I SPEND SO MUCH TIME TALKING ABOUT HOW AND WHY. I HAVE TO IMPREGNATE NEWCOMERS WITH MY VISION. IN THIS RESPECT, I'M SOMETHING OF AN OLD GURU – I JUST DON'T HAVE A CATCHPHRASE!

  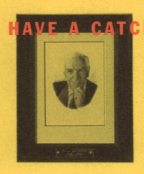 

2000

"PEOPLE OFTEN ASK ME WHETHER I LIKE SEEING MY NAME ALL OVER THE WORLD. IT DOESN'T BOTHER ME. THERE'S A DUTCH SAYING THAT GOES: MADMEN AND ASSES WRITE ON WALLS AND GLASSES. WELL THAT'S EXACTLY WHAT I DO.

AT THE END OF 1999, ALFRED HENRY HEINEKEN WAS LAUDED IN THE NETHERLANDS AS ADVERTISER OF THE CENTURY AND THE HEINEKEN BRAND AS BRAND OF THE CENTURY."

PERSONALITY

10
A BUSINESS OF NATIONAL IMPORTANCE

LOENEN

Chess is a special art form. By the middle of the 1960s, Dutch brewers were looking to reinforce their position through co-operation. Everyone was in discussion with everyone else. Pawns and bishops made strategic maneuvers and even the queen of the chess game was brought into play. There was more at stake than just beer; it was all about market share and power in the beer market. 1967 marked the commencement of battle in earnest. Heineken found itself under attack from an English competitor that was going from strength to strength. Could the beer king be dethroned? At the crucial moment, Alfred Heineken swung into action. Through a sophisticated endgame, he was able to checkmate his opponent within a week. On Monday, August 25, 1968, Heineken and Amstel joined forces. The takeover agreement was signed in Loenen aan de Vecht, in the Netherlands, at the country residence of the former Heineken Chairman. With a domestic market share of more than 50 percent, the brewery had consolidated its leading position. A matter of national importance, in the brewer's opinion.

THE TENSION MOUNTS

10.4

In the 1960s, the beer market in the Netherlands was put under considerable pressure. Beer consumption rose dramatically, in particular that of bottled beer. This forced brewers to make sizeable investments in brewing capacity and bottling equipment. Furthermore, the rise in home drinking was accompanied by increasingly costly advertising campaigns. As virtually all brewers used the same bottles and the taste of the various pilsners was becoming less distinctive, a brand's image was increasingly vital. How else could a beer stand out from the crowd? The ongoing competitive struggle required money, money and more money. If you were unable to keep up, you might go down.

The creation of the EEC in 1958 caused yet more unease within the brewing industry in the Netherlands. The brewers expected the beer market to liberalize over time, putting an end to the existing competitive relationships. Fears arose that a foreign brewer would 'break into' the Dutch market by buying up one or more breweries. Heineken in particular preferred not to see this happen. Given the range of investment programs, the last thing the brewery needed was an upsurge of competition on the domestic market. For this reason, the brewery followed developments in 'beerland' with particular interest.

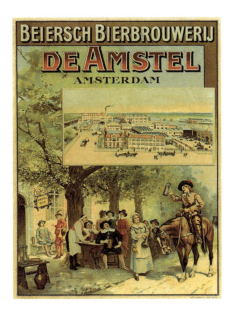

An Amstel poster from the early twentieth century.

Market share was the magic formula during the 1960s. Calculations showed that a brewery had to have a market share of approximately 20 percent to be able to compete as a full player on the beer market. The reason for this was simple: the higher the sales, the lower the cost per hectoliter of beer produced. So brewers were looking for suitable merger partners, to boost their strength. Business mergers are like a game of chess. If you fail to join the hunt for a

The impressive brewing hall of the Amstel Brewery, situated on the Mauritskade in Amsterdam. This photo is from the 1950s.

merger partner, while others are hot on the trail, you run the risk of being left out on a limb. And there is no worse fate since the merged competitors become stronger while, in relative terms, the ones left behind are weakened. During the 1960s, the great merger game began in the Dutch beer market: eat or be eaten – that was the issue.

AMSTEL UNDECIDED

The Amsterdam brewery Amstel, established in 1870, found itself in difficulties during the 1960s, particularly in the home consumption market. The brewery had pursued a half-hearted policy in relation to this market. Between 1948 and 1959, Amstel beer was not sold directly to wholesalers – as was the case with Heineken – but through a separate sales center. Amstel kept store sales as much as possible at arm's length, in order not to offend its agents. This sales organization not only sold beer, but also snacks such as 'Nibb-it' and dried vegetables. Because the representatives received more commission on these products, they made less effort to sell beer. In addition, the brewery was concentrating on selling to independent retailers. However, during the 1960s sales of bottled beer rose fastest among multi-store companies and chains. This meant that Amstel's domestic market share remained around the 18 percent mark, while

10.6

Heineken's grew from 21.7 percent in 1947 to 34.3 percent in 1960. Grolsch also had no grounds for complaint with an increase during this period from 4.6 percent to 10.9 percent.

A striking characteristic of the beer market was the increasing popularity of pilsner. Whereas before the war the respective shares of pilsner and beers such as Münchener, Old Brown and Lager were approximately equal, pilsner accounted for 92 percent of total sales by 1963. Amstel's name as a brewer of dark beers had a negative effect on the sale of its pilsner. Heineken, on the other hand, profited by the shift in tastes since its pilsner had long enjoyed an illustrious reputation. Another factor in Heineken's favor was that it had strong positions in Amsterdam, Rotterdam and the large provincial cities. Here, beer consumption increased more quickly than in the countryside, Amstel's traditional powerbase.

A poster from 1961 by the famous Dutch advertising draughtsman Frans Mettes, who also produced a number of brand-defining posters for Heineken.

Put under pressure by disappointing results, Amstel searched long and hard for the right commercial direction. The brewery did not want to fall further behind its big Amsterdam competitor and attempted to become a jack-of-all-trades. The company, however, did not have sufficient financial muscle nor the international distribution network to really rival Heineken. In the home consumption market in particular, the brewery fell under increasing pressure. Amstel's advertising policy vacillated about the right tone, slogan and target group. A stark contrast with the consistency of Heineken (Sociable people can expect a Heineken welcome), Grolsch (Masters of the craft) and Brand (The beer that is Limburg's pride). On August 22, 1963, Amstel's supervisory directors concluded with disappointment that, 'The Board of Management is unanimous in its opinion that Amstel's position as second among Dutch brewers is not a strong one. Its market share is far behind that of Heineken and the market share achieved by Grolsch in the store market is approaching that of Amstel. As a brand, Amstel does not occupy second, but third place. Profitability is poor.' What could be done?

During the 1950s, all breweries filled their wooden beer barrels by hand.

AN OVERSIGHT

In January 1962, Oscar Wittert van Hoogland, a member of the Heineken Board, was secretly approached by a group of dissatisfied shareholders in Amstel. Would the brewery be interested in merging with Amstel? The answer was 'yes', but Heineken set a precondition that the merger had to lead to 'a discontinuation of Amstel's existence.' Such a demand naturally did not go down well and the negotiations soon stalled.

A change of heart quickly came about at Heineken, however. There were specific worries about commercial policy – low prices – and the position of the Oranjeboom group. Oranjeboom, which saw its market share decrease from 7.6 percent to 6 percent during the period 1947-1960, joined forces in 1960 with ZHB, Phoenix and Keizer Barbarossa. The new conglomerate 'Verenigde Nederlandse Brouwerijen d'Oranjeboom NV' had a turnover of 440,000 hectoliters and a market share of 10.7 percent. In spite of great efforts, the brewery group just could not pull it off, however, and seemed ripe for a takeover by one of the large foreign breweries. The Board of Heineken was in favor of a strong defensive front on the Dutch market. On July 12, 1962, Board member Johan Land contacted Amstel with the following proposal: a combination of Heineken, Amstel and the De Drie Hoefijzers brewery from the town of Breda. His colleagues supported Land's initiative, but Alfred Heineken was against such a merger. Land hoped, however, that once the various Boards had agreed, Alfred Heineken's resistance could be broken.

The management of Amstel was somewhat taken by surprise by this idea. Although they had had similar thoughts themselves in the past, they had never dared to take the initiative, as this would have been seen as putting Amstel up for sale. Furthermore, it was known that Alfred Heineken was against such adventures. Land's suggestion met with a mixed response from the directors of Amstel. Amstel's commercial director Piet Kranenberg was in favor of retaining the brewery's independence. 'What Heineken has achieved during the last 25 years is not one of the wonders of the world. They have worked hard and conscientiously. Is it impossible for us to do the same? Undoubtedly, they will have made mistakes here and there, but they persevered. Is this beyond our reach?' The other directors had their doubts. A counter-proposal was put on the table as a compromise. Amstel was willing, but only on the basis of equality. This meant, among other things, that Alfred Heineken would have to give up his majority shareholding.

Two versions of the advertising campaign, launched in 1960, 'Amstel drinkers do this'. The quality signal with the hand typified the campaign.

At Heineken, the Land committee got down to business. The outstanding capital of the three companies was: Heineken 42 million guilders, Amstel 14 million guilders and De Drie Hoefijzers 5 million guilders. The plan was to set up a new holding company within which the three breweries would take equal stakes. According to this proposal, Alfred Heineken, the majority shareholder in Heineken, would at the end of the day hold just 34 percent of the new holding. The Land committee recognized the problem, but wrote in a report on September 3, 1962, 'We would attempt to draw Alfred Heineken's attention to the fact that ownership of 34 percent of the votes in one company does in fact represent a very significant influence and in fact means that it would be only with the very greatest difficulty that a decision could be forced through against his will.' Alfred Heineken was perhaps willing to discuss a great deal, but not this one decisive point – surrendering his controlling interest. The plan was therefore dropped.

LOOKING FOR A SECOND BRAND

Less than a year later, suspicions surrounding the vulnerable position of Oranjeboom seemed to be confirmed. In October 1963, the Rotterdam brewery hinted to Heineken that a foreign brewing group was interested in taking it over. Owing to national considerations, it was argued, Oranjeboom preferred to cooperate with Heineken. Was this interest reciprocated? After a few days, an answer was received from Amsterdam and it was a negative one. It was cheaper for Heineken to expand its own production capacity than to take over the less efficient Oranjeboom brewery.

10.9

Ideas can change very quickly however. On January 16, 1964, the Heineken Board met at Alfred Heineken's villa in Noordwijk. The Oranjeboom brand appealed to the Board's imagination. At that moment in time, with a total market share of 35 percent – and 45 percent of the home consumption market – Heineken was by far the strongest brewer on the Dutch beer market. This dominant position was almost entirely based on a single product, namely Heineken pilsner. A vulnerable position, it seemed. Thoughts in Noordwijk therefore turned to an expansion of the range in the form of a second brand of pilsner, an extra-strong beer, a light lager beer or an alternative packaging (clasp stopper). It was a cast-iron rule within the brewery however that there is only one Heineken beer, with a few exceptions like highly specialized beers such as Heineken Old Brown. Alfred Heineken himself enforced strict adherence to this policy. However, brewing new beers under another brand name was a different story altogether. Suddenly, the brewery was casting an acquisitive eye upon the Oranjeboom brand, which dated from 1671. Could this perhaps serve as a second brand, alongside Heineken?

Negotiations took place between the Oranjeboom directors and Pieter Feith. The Chairman of the Heineken Board issued a concrete takeover proposal and agreed that Oranjeboom would be continued as an autonomous company and that the brand would be given a prominent position in Heineken's brand policy. Feith, who had a positive impression of the negotiations, agreed that the four Oranjeboom directors and the four

10.10

Happy beer drinkers raise their glasses to a good glass of Amstel, 1964.

members of the Heineken Board would meet for further talks on May 27, 1964. This appointment was not kept, however, since Oranjeboom let it be known in no uncertain terms that it was not interested. Heineken's Board of Management reacted with surprise and thinly veiled anger to this sudden change of course. Shortly afterwards, the brewery heard that Oranjeboom had started initial negotiations with the large American brewer Schlitz. Heineken was not best pleased.

OBSESSION WITH ORANJEBOOM

On July 9, 1964, the Board of Heineken decided to contact Amstel concerning this matter, as 'the manner in which Oranjeboom has treated us assuredly entitles us to now take those measures we think fit.' Four days later, the two Amsterdam brewers met in The Hague. They quickly agreed that Oranjeboom was an attractive target for a large, foreign brewery concern. Heineken and Amstel joined together in deciding to issue a joint take-over offer for Oranjeboom. On September 1, 1964, this was presented to Oranjeboom's Chairman of the

Working on the bottling line of the Amstel brewery, 1951.

Supervisory Board. Heineken's Board of Management then informed its Supervisory Board that, 'Oranjeboom is in negotiation with Schlitz. Heineken has 190 million guilders to invest in production over the next ten years. It would not suit us at all to have to face American-style competition here in this country during that period.'

The three breweries arranged to meet at the airport in Amsterdam on September 21. Heineken and Amstel urged a rapid takeover, but Oranjeboom stated that it needed a week to think things over. A week later, the Rotterdam brewery curtly rejected the proposals made by Heineken and Amstel, believing it would be better off on its own. The Amsterdam brewers 'were amazed that their proposition was rejected without even a trace of a counter-proposal. They were of the opinion that their offer was extremely generous in all areas and wanted to be informed of the grounds for the negative response.' Oranjeboom refused to explain, however. A request by Amstel and Heineken for a 'first right of refusal' if Oranjeboom were once again approached by a foreign brewery was also refused. It was simply impossible to do business with the Rotterdam-based competitor. Heineken and Amstel concluded 'that Oranjeboom is overestimating its own position on the Dutch and European market.'

The truth of these words was demonstrated within three years. Oranjeboom's market share dropped even further, and on October 1, 1967 the company was sold for almost 51 million guilders to the English company Allied Breweries. This puzzled Amstel and Heineken, as their takeover bid in 1964 had been higher than what Allied Breweries was paying now.

FLEEING FROM 'BIG BROTHER'

This move by Allied Breweries turned the brewing world upside-down. The Amstel brewery in particular was dominated by a feeling of pessimism. Internationalization of the brand was not going smoothly and could only be achieved with large sums of money, which were not available. Amstel was still the second brewer in the Netherlands, but was caught between market leader Heineken and the strong runner-up Grolsch. 'Our position is that of an army fighting along a very broad front. Every attack on this front incurs losses on our side,' is how director Piet Kranenberg put it. His colleague Rein van Marwijk Kooy saw no alternative than to merge with another brewery, 'if we want to be strong enough to resist "big brother" and foreign groups.' By 'big brother', Van Marwijk Kooy was referring to Heineken. The Amstel brewery chose to swim with the tide, and at the end of 1967 initiated merger negotiations with the Breda-based brewery De Drie Hoefijzers.

The discussions between the two companies did not go at all smoothly. One of the reasons for this was the future brand policy. The directors of De Drie Hoefijzers had a certain 'Brauersstolz' (pride in the brewing profession). They were not enthusiastic about the plans for their own Breda beer to be the 'B brand', while Amstel would be the 'A brand'. Another reason was that the Breda brewery was also negotiating with other parties, including Heineken, without Amstel being aware of this. On May 3, 1968, final talks took place between Heineken and De Drie Hoefijzers. It was clear that the management of De Drie Hoefijzers wanted to get the best possible price, and was applying the ancient principle of divide and rule.

While Heineken had been more or less been consigned to the waiting room, the Breda brewery intensified its negotiations with Amstel. In June 1968, a detailed merger proposal was put on the table. The name of the new company was to be 'NV Amstel-Breda'. The plan was to exchange the shares in Amstel and De Drie Hoefijzers on a 1-to-1 basis at equal nominal values. At that moment in time the prices of the two breweries' shares were more or less equal. However, following the leak of rumors about the merger, the price of shares in De Drie Hoefijzers rose within the space of a few months from approximately 115 guilders to 150

Advertisement from the magazine campaign from 1965, in which Amstel introduced the flip-top bottle to the consumer. The flip-top meant the bottle could be opened without an opener.

guilders. An exchange of shares on an equal basis was no longer possible for Amstel, so it discontinued the talks at the beginning of August 1968. Somewhat frustrated, Amstel sought a way out of the impasse that had arisen. Perhaps 'big brother' would extend a hand?

ENDGAME

On August 16, 1968, Amstel's Supervisory Board contacted Heineken with a view to a joint takeover of De Drie Hoefijzers. On the morning of Monday August 19, a discussion on this subject took place between Oscar Wittert van Hoogland, Chairman of the Heineken Board, and his opposite number at Amstel, Egberts. During this discussion – chance played a helpful role – news was received that Allied Breweries had made a bid for the shares in De Drie Hoefijzers. The amount of the bid demonstrated that the English brewer was taking its move into the Dutch market very seriously. The directors of Amstel saw the bid price as a scandalous over-valuation – although sour grapes also played a role, of course. Allied Breweries acquired the Breda-based brewery for 84 million guilders. This brought the English brewer's total share of the Dutch market to 18 percent. This was a double blow to Amsterdam. Amstel dropped to third place and now felt really driven into a corner. Heineken was also in the shadow of a titanic competitor, which was clearly out to obtain a dominating position on the Dutch beer market.

10.14 This poster from the mid-1960s shows a festive, colorful Amstel face. The brewer was fighting a bitter battle for market share against several competitors on the beer market, however.

The official announcement of the takeover bid for De Drie Hoefijzers, on August 20, 1968, galvanized Heineken into action. The situation looked ominous. Heineken had a market share of 38 percent. With Oranjeboom and De Drie Hoefijzers, Allied Breweries had a market share of 18 percent. No real threat in itself. But what if Allied Breweries' next target was Amstel, with its market share of 17 percent. Such a third step by the English brewer would have been a masterstroke, as its position would then have been almost as strong as that of Heineken. 'This would force Heineken into a defensive position. Such a state of affairs is considered simply unacceptable by the Board of Management, partly and principally on psychological grounds. The idea has therefore emerged that Heineken must take over Amstel with all possible speed. The time seems ripe for such a move, as Amstel undoubtedly feels itself to be in a difficult situation, sandwiched between Heineken and Allied Breweries. Various negotiations have created a basis that seems acceptable to all the parties involved,' the Heineken Board of Management announced on the morning of Wednesday, August 21, 1968. Amstel was the king that held the key to the position of leader in the beer market in the Netherlands.

During the 1960s, Amstel paid a great deal of attention to Amstel pilsner. More and more beer drinkers were switching from dark beers to the clearer pilsner.

On Wednesday afternoon, Heineken commenced negotiations with Amstel. The partners in the discussion were of course no strangers to one another, and the various contacts over the years ensured that both parties knew precisely what they were getting into. The deal was done at lightning speed. Both Heineken and Amstel realized the importance of the deal. Now that it had dropped to third place, Amstel placed less emphasis on retaining its independence. The position of the major shareholder, Alfred Heineken, was also hardly at issue. Amstel would have been pleased to see its name included in the name of the new company, but this demand was rejected. However, Heineken did undertake to retain the Amstel brand. The discussions centered around the amount to be paid for the takeover and the allocation of seats on the new Board of Management. The deal was concluded on the Monday in Huize Cronenburgh in Loenen aan de Vecht, the Netherlands, Oscar Wittert van Hoogland's country house. The value of the takeover amounted to 150 million guilders.

10.16　On Tuesday, August 26, 1968, it was officially announced that the two largest breweries in the Netherlands were to merge. The joint market share was 56 percent. Heineken requested approval of the merger in a letter of August 29, 1968 to the Minister for Economic Affairs. The brewery pointed out the risk of Allied Breweries acquiring the Amstel brewery, 'In view of the considerable difference in scale and financial resources between Allied Breweries and Heineken, this would in all probability then finally lead to a dominant position for Allied Breweries within the Dutch market. It is not only in the interest of Heineken, but of the nation as a whole, that Heineken take over Amstel.' The government recognized this interest and gave the green light. Heineken green was now combined with Amstel red to create a single new company.

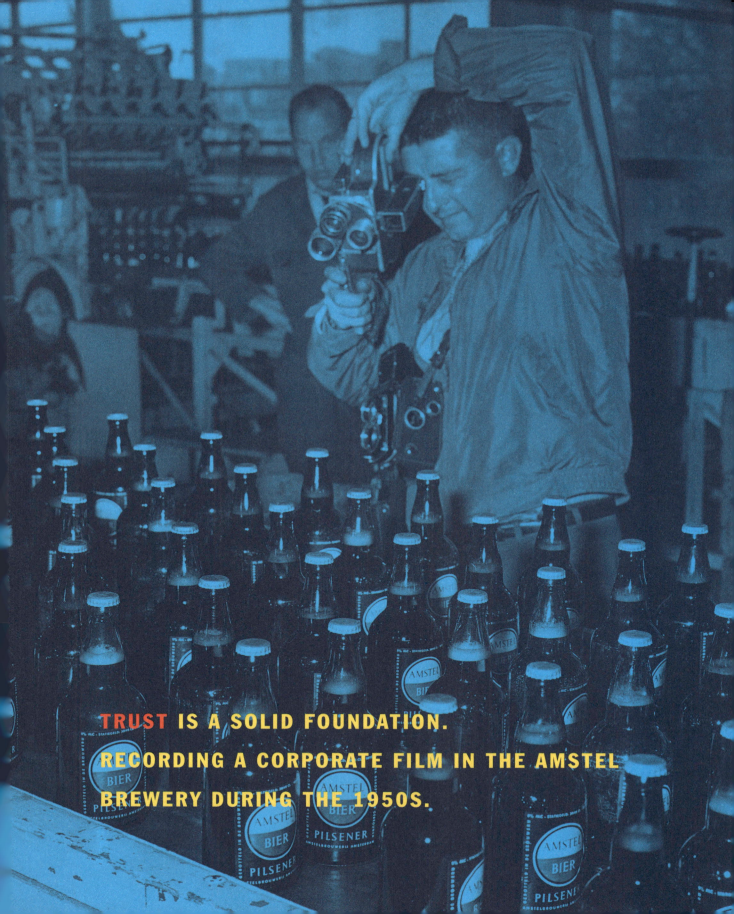

TRUST IS A SOLID FOUNDATION.
RECORDING A CORPORATE FILM IN THE AMSTEL BREWERY DURING THE 1950S.

THE TRADITION OF THE AMSTEL BREWERY BEGAN IN 1870. FOLLOWING THE MERGER OF HEINEKEN AND AMSTEL IN 1968, THE AMSTEL BRAND WAS GIVEN A NEW LEASE OF LIFE AND A CONTEMPORARY FACELIFT.

THE AMSTEL BRAND STANDS FOR QUALITY BEERS WITH A GOOD REPUTATION. BEER DRINKERS THROUGHOUT THE WORLD ENJOY THE AMSTEL FEELING: FREEDOM, PLEASURE AND FRIENDSHIP.

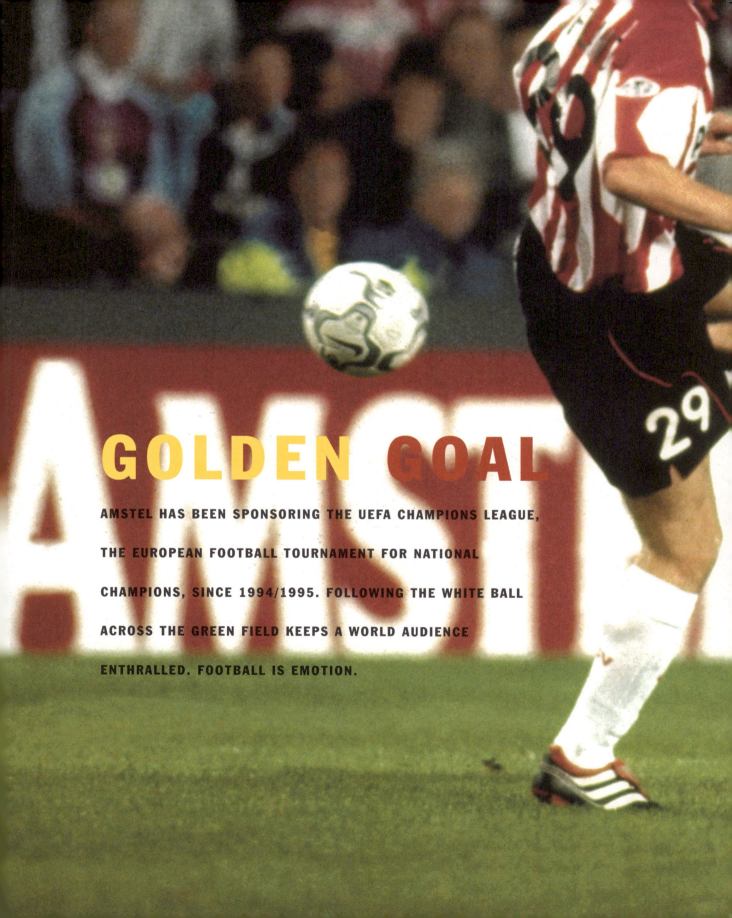

GOLDEN GOAL

AMSTEL HAS BEEN SPONSORING THE UEFA CHAMPIONS LEAGUE, THE EUROPEAN FOOTBALL TOURNAMENT FOR NATIONAL CHAMPIONS, SINCE 1994/1995. FOLLOWING THE WHITE BALL ACROSS THE GREEN FIELD KEEPS A WORLD AUDIENCE ENTHRALLED. FOOTBALL IS EMOTION.

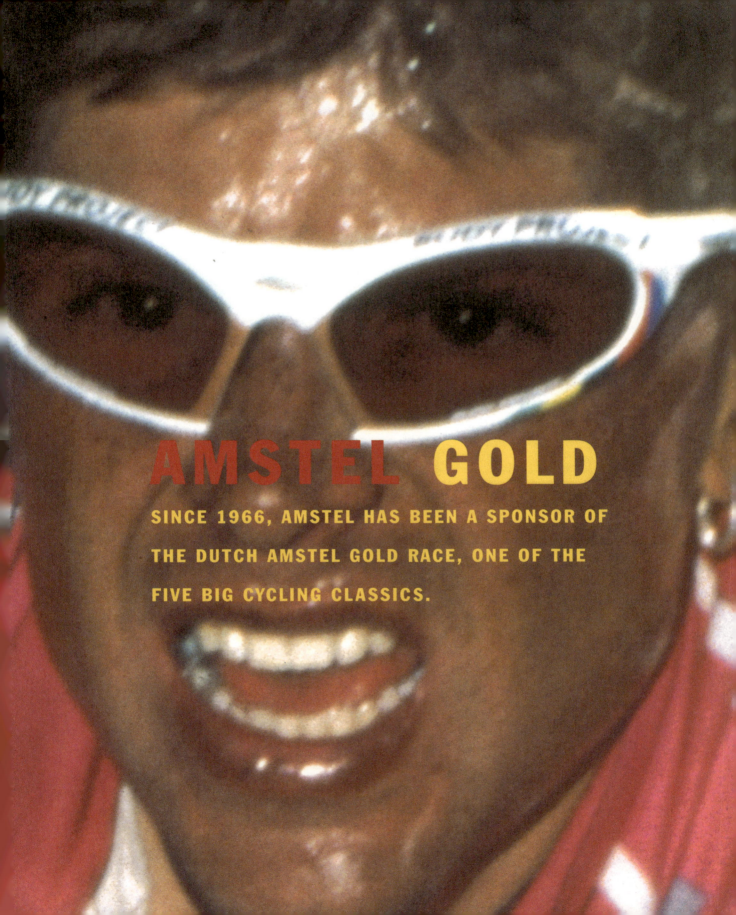

AMSTEL GOLD

SINCE 1966, AMSTEL HAS BEEN A SPONSOR OF THE DUTCH AMSTEL GOLD RACE, ONE OF THE FIVE BIG CYCLING CLASSICS.

IN 1980, AMSTEL LIGHT WAS INTRODUCED ON

THE AMERICAN MARKET WITH THE CAMPAIGN

'95 CALORIES NEVER TASTED SO IMPORTED'.

SINCE THEN, THE BRAND HAS BECOME NO. 1

IN THE IMPORTED LIGHT BEERS SEGMENT.

AMSTEL LIGHT: FOR EFFORT AND RELAXATION.

FRIENDSHIP

STAR STATUS
IN EUROPE

This is a straightforward story to tell. No big deal, you might say. But you still have to come up with it: and that is a big deal! No-one was drinking Heineken during the 1950s in Europe. Americans and Africans knew the brand better than the French, Italians or British. But thanks to the vision and creativity of Alfred Henry Heineken, all this changed. While traveling through Europe during the 1970s, he had a feeling that the continent was ready for Heineken beer. In his inimitable manner, he continued his life's work: to place the company and the brand on the European map. The conquest of the continent started in France in 1972 with negotiations in Strasbourg on the purchase of a brewery in northern France. Over the years, Heineken grew to become the largest brewer and the best-selling brand of beer in Europe. With this amazing story, Alfred Heineken made history. You simply have to come up with it.

PIECES OF THE PUZZLE

11.4

Europe, in contrast to the United States, for example, did not yet have a dominant brewery or a dominant brand of beer at the start of the 1970s. In 1970, Heineken had a European market share of just 2.8 percent. Europe was characterized by national beer markets with their own traditions and beer cultures. One beer for all Europeans was therefore ruled out by those in the know at the time. Alfred Heineken saw things differently. He expected European unity to eventually lead to a single large market, which would become the hunting ground of large breweries with plenty of capital and international brands. The brewery wanted to get a head start on the competition and began to expand Heineken in Europe in its own special way.

In the summer of 1972, and at his own initiative, Alfred Heineken entered into discussions with René Hatt and his son Michel, owners and members of the management team of Brasserie de l'Espérance in Strasbourg. This brewery in the Alsace had a capacity of 1.4 million hectoliters and also had a majority shareholding in the Alsacienne de Brasserie (Albra), an association of regional breweries such as Brasserie de la Perle, Colmar and Mützig. With a market share of almost 9 percent, Albra was the third-largest brewery group in France. Mützig and Ancre were its most important brands. Heineken made an offer for the Albra shares equal to 600 francs per share, around 200 francs above the market rate. On September 25, 1972, the majority of the shareholders accepted the offer and four years later, Heineken took possession of the remaining shares. Shortly after the purchase of Albra, Heineken was offered a new opportunity. Since 1960, the brewery had owned a small number of shares in the Italian holding company Cisalpina, with breweries in Pedavena, Trieste, Genoa and Turin. During the 1960s, the various breweries were grouped under the name Dreher. Heineken's role was limited to that of sleeping partner. At the beginning of the 1970s, however, Cisalpina's financial situation worsened considerably. The Luciano family, the majority shareholder, offered to sell its package of shares in Dreher. Heineken took the bait on August 2, 1974, knowing that such a move would open up the Italian beer market. Just as was the case with Albra, the various Italian breweries had to be thoroughly reorganized before becoming flourishing businesses.

For Alfred Heineken, the purchases of Albra and Dreher were two important pieces in his European jigsaw puzzle. A glance at the map of Europe at the time shows that the largest beer market in the world was still fragmented. With the French and Italian breweries, a couple of Heineken green dots were added to the map of Europe. The puzzle was by no means complete, but the Chairman of the Board already had a complete picture, namely that Europe offered golden opportunities to a brewer with vision, strategic insight, daring and a touch of overconfidence. Alfred Henry Heineken was that brewer. His vision was to make the company and the brand so strong in Europe that it would be a nigh impenetrable stronghold for competitors.

A EUROPEAN BEER STRATEGY

Until the early 1970s, the brewery had focused in Europe exclusively on the export of Heineken beer and the achievement of 'segment leadership'. The brand had acquired a favorable position on various markets, but the high price of the imported product and limited distribution were obstacles in the way of a real breakthrough. Alfred Heineken wanted this to change. His vision was clear, but that did not mean, however, that the company had a complete European beer strategy ready for implementation. One important discussion within the organization was raging with regard to the issue of whether the Heineken company wanted to play a strong role in the entire beer market, or would a leading role for the Heineken brand in the premium segment be sufficient? Put in marketing terms, the issue was, should the brewery attain 'broad leadership' or 'segment leadership'?

It was only in the 1980s that the company's focus gradually shifted from 'segment leadership' to 'broad leadership'. Heineken pursued a course of large purchases in France, Italy, Spain and Switzerland. Although attention was initially focused on southern Europe, eastern European markets also became part of the picture following the fall of the Berlin Wall in September 1989. The various acquisitions contributed greatly to the growth of the Heineken company. The strategy was clear: the brewery preferred to focus on becoming the number 1 brewer in each country. One exception to this rule was Germany, where the decision was taken to give the Heineken brand a position in the premium segment. Heineken wanted to be a dominant brewer in Europe. The local brands provided volume, economy of scale and distribution strength. Economies of scale resulted in good profitability and a better grip on distribution, whereby the brewer's range of brands – including the Heineken brand – acquired a better basis of support. It is considerably more advantageous if a crate of Heineken pilsner can hitch a ride on a lorry carrying local brands than when a separate national distribution network has to be built up exclusively for the Heineken brand.

11.6

An image from the French advertising campaign 'l'esprit bière'.

In order to further broaden the basis of support for the Heineken brand, from the 1980s onwards the brewery switched to the local production of Heineken beer in various European countries. Market research revealed that the European beer drinker considered the import image of Heineken beer to be less important than, for example, the Americans. A large-scale redevelopment and modernization program also brought the various breweries in Europe up to the standards of Heineken. Brewers trained in the Netherlands were a guarantee for the quality of the locally brewed Heineken. Quality and image did not therefore form a hindrance to the brewing of Heineken outside the Netherlands. The advantage of this was that local production made greater sales possible and that the Heineken brand became part of a very efficient brand strategy.

Heineken's European brand strategy could best be compared to a pyramid. At the top of each market, the so-called premium segment, the company operated with the international Heineken brand. This brand was the company's crown jewels. No expense was spared in increasing the beer's quality and image. The local brands accommodated the standard segment, the medium-priced part of the beer market. The Amstel brand was positioned in certain countries at the top end of the standard segment. The brewery was hardly present in the lowest part of the pyramid, the lower-priced beers segment. When described as a pyramid, marketing appears to be a straightforward task. The consistent implementation of a marketing strategy in the various European countries is, however, an art in itself. We will now take you on a journey through Europe as seen through the eyes of Heineken.

l'esprit bière

FRANCE

On the home market of the 1970s, the French acquisition Albra was wedged between the large French brewing groups Kronenbourg (BSN) and Union de Brasseries. Albra's market share, of approximately 9 percent, was too small to enable it to take a stand. Eventually, in October 1984, Heineken France and Brasseries et Glacières Internationales (BGI) – comprising the breweries Union de Brasseries and Pelforth – combined their French brewery shareholdings to form the Société Générale de Brasserie (Sogebra). Heineken had 51 percent of the share capital with BGI owning the remaining 49 percent.

France consisted in effect of two different beer markets. Historically, the focus in northern France had been more on Belgium and Germany, with high beer consumption and a rich beer culture. In southern France, where the focus was traditionally on the consumption of wine, beer consumption was a lot lower. Beer had, for a long time, had a bad image among many French people. They regarded the product as a drink for old, pot-bellied men. When beer consumption in northern France and the Alsace stabilized towards the end of the 1970s, the breweries started paying more attention to the image of beer. They joined forces to upgrade the product. Publicity campaigns underlined the fact that beer was a low-alcohol, healthy, natural product. In addition, increased attention was paid to how beer was treated in the hotel and catering sector, to new forms of packaging and new products. This attention improved the image of beer. The Heineken brand, brewed locally from 1980, underwent a relatively favorable development thanks to the increasing share of the premium segment. The slogan 'la bière qui fait aimer la bière' was enough to enable the brand to reach a new, youthful market.

The combining of forces with BGI in 1984 meant that Heineken's market share increased from 9 percent to 25 percent, thereby making it the second largest brewer in France. Its range of beers was expanded to include the brands '33', Pelican, Pelforth and George Killian's. Following a period of far-reaching reorganization at the end of the 1980s, Heineken had things well under control. The brand portfolio had been reduced and production was concentrated in Schiltigheim, Mons-en-Baroeul and Marseilles. This position was reinforced by the acquisition, in 1988, of full control of Sogebra, the purchase in 1996 of the Fischer group,

11.8 The Café Littéraire Les Deux Magots in Paris, which opened in 1885, has long played an important role in the cultural life of the French capital.

the fourth French brewery with breweries in the Alsace, and the Groupe Saint-Arnould, a French brewery and distributor in northern France. In 2000, Brasseries Heineken, the French subsidiary, had a market share of around 22 percent, making it a very strong number two player in the French beer market.

ITALY

In 1980 Dreher, the Italian brewery group, was a wholly-owned Heineken subsidiary. Production was concentrated in the breweries in Pedavena, Massafra, Macomer and Genoa. In April 1980, the Moretti brewery in Popoli was also acquired by Heineken, as was the Ichnusa brewery on the island of Sardinia, in 1986. By 1985, with Heineken, Dreher and McFarland as its brands, Dreher was the second largest Italian brewer after Peroni. Local production of Heineken beer started in 1976.

Italy – the ultimate wine country – had no real beer tradition. Italians regarded beer primarily as a thirst-quencher, with wine always accompanying any serious meal. Nevertheless, interest in beer was increasing. Tourism also helped tremendously to encourage Italian beer consumption. Although in 1975 consumption amounted to around 14 liters per capita, less than ten years later this figure had risen to 24 liters per capita. And the expectation was that this

The Gran Caffé Chioggia on the San Marco square is one of the trendiest cafés in Venice. The café is named after a place in the surrounding area.

increase would continue. It was for this reason that Heineken's management treated the expansion of Birra Dreher as a major priority. In 1988, a merger took place between Dreher and the two Henninger breweries in Aosta and Messina. After the acquisition of Birra Moretti in 1996 – at that time the third-largest brewery in Italy – it became the market leader. Heineken played the main role in the premium segment, Moretti was the standard beer nationally, while Dreher and Ichnusa were the regional beers.

c'è feeling, c'è Heineken.

SPAIN

At the start of the 1980s, conditions on the Spanish beer market appeared to be very favorable. The country had a large population, people had plenty to spend in relative terms, there was political stability and beer consumption – in particular beers in the premium segment, the 'especiales' – was increasing steadily. This was enough to create a strong sense of opportunity within Heineken's management. In 1984, Heineken acquired a shareholding of 36.7 percent in El Aguila. This company had seven breweries and two malting plants as well as a national distribution network and a market share of 21 percent. In the opinion of Heineken's management, it was 'a perfect fit' in the company's European strategy.

With the purchase of El Aguila – the eagle – the Dutch brewery had a clear path into the Spanish market. However, the real work was only just beginning. The breweries were out-of-date from a technical point of view, the products differed per outlet and the Aguila brand consisted of six different types of bottled beer. Confusion reigned! After years of effort, the Spanish organization was centralized, production was rationalized and the brands policy streamlined. Aguila became the new standard pilsner and Adlerbrau the new brand for the specialty beers segment. Local production of Heineken beer started in 1988. What was noticeable was that, as of 1994, the name Aguila was changed to Aguila-Amstel and the beer was sold in bottles fitted with the same label as Amstel. This step was part of the new European brands policy, which entailed the Amstel brand being sold in a number of countries as an extra trump card in the standard beers segment.

piensa en verde

Café Circulo de Bellas Artes in Madrid is a classic grand-café, located in the heart of a museum. It is a meeting place for artists, fashion designers, writers and journalists.

In Spain, beer developed into a well-liked product. In contrast to Italy, Spain had a much larger population of real beer drinkers. They regarded beer – due to its relatively low alcohol content – as an innocent drink to be drunk all day long. Alcohol-free Buckler beer also played an important role in both France and Spain. Average beer consumption was already well over 40 liters per capita in 1990, which meant that Spain had grown to become the third largest beer market in Europe, behind Germany and Great Britain. In the 1990s, the promising Spanish beer market was at stake in a hard-fought battle between a number of large international brewing groups, including Guinness and Carlsberg. Competition was cutthroat. After beer consumption in Spain suddenly dropped sharply following several years of continued growth, newcomers to the market found themselves facing mounting losses. Heineken used all of its resources to keep up with the fight. The company did have the advantage that its strategy had always been focused on the long term. Short-term profit was not the primary objective. The ultimate goal was a stable and strong market position in the long term. In 1999, this policy was to prove the major factor in the brewery gaining a dominant position on the Spanish beer market. The battle-weary Irish brewer Guinness decided to sell Cruzcampo, with a strong position in southern Spain. Heineken acquired Cruzcampo from Guinness, thereby attaining a market share of 37 percent and becoming the country's undisputed number one beer brewer. The brewery owns 78.4 percent of Heineken España, with the remaining shares being publicly quoted.

GREECE

In Greece, the sun was shining. The takeover of Amstel in 1968 presented Heineken with a nice surprise. Until the 1960s, the Greek beer market had been controlled by the Fix brewery, with outlets in Athens and Thessaloniki. Its brands Fix and Alfa gave it a monopoly, as foreign beers were effectively barred by import duties of 600 percent. All this changed in June 1965 when Amstel, enticed by a favorable outlook for the Greek beer market, opened a brewery in Athens. The newcomer immediately put itself on the map with a market share of 7.6 percent. Thereafter, Amstel profited from a political conflict between Prime Minister Papandreou and King Constantine regarding Mr. Garoufalias, who was both minister of defense and the owner of the Fix brewery. Through their choice of beer – Amstel or Fix – Greek beer drinkers were able to make it very clear which party they sympathized with.

let's Heineken

The takeover of Amstel in 1968 meant that Heineken acquired the shares in the Amstel brewery in Greece, whose name was changed to Athenian Brewery. With breweries in Athens, Thessaloniki and Patras, Athenian Brewery was the clear market leader in Greece. Amstel was by far the favorite among Greek beer drinkers. Local production of Heineken started in 1981 amid a blaze of publicity, all the more because many Greeks could scarcely distinguish the name Heineken from the Henninger brand, which was much better known in Greece at that time. With the publicity campaign 'Now that Heineken is here ...' the Greek beer drinker was left in no doubt that a new brand had arrived. Heineken was presented as a new, internationally successful beer for young, socially active, trendy and modern people. The green bottle distinguished the brand from the local beers sold in brown bottles. Variety is the spice of life.

A good sense of Heineken

The Palace Bar goes back to 1843, making it one of the oldest pubs in Dublin.

IRELAND

Ireland has always been a market for top-fermenting stout. Pilsner only arrived in the 1970s and Heineken spotted opportunities for its brand on the Irish beer market. It made an agreement with the Murphy's Brewery in Cork about brewing Heineken locally. Following a number of substantial changes to the brewery, the first Heineken beer in barrels was supplied in April 1978. When Murphy's encountered financial difficulties, Heineken took over the brewery in April 1983, thereby ensuring access to the Irish lager market. This market – accounting for around 10 percent of the total beer market – was dominated at the time by the Harp brand produced by Irish competitor Guinness. Heineken transformed the antique Murphy's brewery into a modern company and then started intensive promotion of the Heineken brand on the Irish lager market. The work soon bore fruit and these days the Heineken brand, with a market share of 35 percent, is the undisputed number one in the lager segment, which accounts for almost half the Irish beer market. Pilsner continues to attract more and more beer enthusiasts the world over and Heineken is profiting from this as well.

ENGLAND

In England, the Dutch brewery had to compete against a typical beer culture after the Second World War. The English primarily drank top-fermenting ales and only very exceptionally pilsner or – as the English call it – lager beer. English lager is, with an original wort content of 1030, also weaker than the Heineken pilsner, with a content of 1048. In 1951, the brewery decided to market a Heineken lager adapted to English tastes. This solution was, of course, entirely contrary to the brand's philosophy, but the brewery yielded to the wishes of the obstinate English beer drinkers. In order to avoid consumer confusion, the Heineken lager was packaged differently and sold at a lower price.

How Refreshing. How Heineken.

In 1969, in order to stimulate sales of Heineken lager further, the brewery issued a license to Whitbread for the local production of the beer. With backup in the shape of the successful advertising campaign 'Heineken refreshes the parts other beers cannot reach', Heineken lager was a gigantic hit. Within three years, sales reached more than 700,000 hectoliters and by the 1980s, sales rose to well over two million hectoliters. Heineken beer had become the most popular lager brand in the British beer market. Nevertheless, this success did not mean that all in the garden was rosy. The awfully plain British Heineken contrasted considerably with the prestigious character of Heineken sold worldwide. An increase in international travel meant that more and more consumers came into contact with this deviant English brand. That detracted from the image that beer drinkers had of Heineken. Whitbread, however, was more than happy with Heineken lager. Its opinion was 'never change a winning beer'.

During the 1980s, the English lager market developed at lightning speed. As early as 1988, the segment accounted for 46 percent of the total beer market. Demand arose for high-priced premium beers of the pilsner type. In order to be able to meet this demand, Whitbread wanted to bring a super-deluxe Heineken onto the market. However, the Dutch brewer put a stop to such plans – there was no desire for a further undermining of the philosophy of a single worldwide Heineken beer. This is why the Dutch brewery decided, in 1985, to launch the 'real' Heineken beer onto the market. The brewery therefore pursued a dual Heineken policy in England. Heineken Lager was a volume beer in the standard segment; the imported Heineken pilsner was sold under the name of Heineken Export as a premium beer. In 2000, things changed. The Belgian brewery Interbrew acquired English brewer Whitbread. Heineken, faced with the reality of its English licensee being swallowed up by an immediate competitor, decided to reconsider its position on the English market.

THE NETHERLANDS

The Dutch market occupied a special place in Heineken's world. Due to the strong market position that had developed over the years, the brand was positioned very differently in the Netherlands. While Heineken beer was sold abroad as a premium class product, on the home market the beer competed with beers in the standard segment. Packed in brown bottles and sold in plastic crates, the Dutch Heineken looked very different to its international cousin which was packed and supplied in green bottles and six-packs. The taste, however, was the same.

Heerlijk Helder Heineken

Since 1968, 'Heineken Nederland', with the brands Heineken and Amstel, had been the absolute market leader in the pilsner segment. However, the Heineken brand was under pressure during the 1980s due to the appearance of lower-priced beers and the emergence of specialty beers. Within 'Heineken Nederland', plans were therefore drawn up in 1983 for the introduction of a 'super Heineken', intended to compete with the beers in the premium segment. Everything was ready to launch this product except for the approval of Alfred Heineken, the Chairman of the Board. Alfred Heineken, however, totally disapproved of these plans, which were immediately consigned to the rubbish bin. No-one should be allowed to experiment with the Heineken brand and, above all, no-one should suggest that there is a beer of a better quality than the existing Heineken pilsner. To do so would be commercial suicide. The Heineken name should be used exclusively for the pilsner product and only very exceptionally for a number of darker, non-pilsner products such as Heineken Old Brown and Heineken Bock beer. Nevertheless, in order to respond to the changes on the beer market, the brewery

The Café Americain has been part of the hotel of the same name in Amsterdam since 1902. Close to the Leidseplein square, it is surrounded by a lively area rich in museums, theaters, restaurants, cafés, cinemas and shops.

chose an alternative policy. Using the Amstel brand, which offered more possibilities, various beer specialities were brought onto the market. In addition, 'Heineken Nederland' acquired two Limburg breweries – De Ridder and Brand – which were rich in tradition and with which the company could considerably expand its range in the growing market for specialty and premium beers. The 400 or more types of beer sold by the specialty beer trading house De Brouwketel, established in Breda in 1992, allowed the brewery to cater to any beer enthusiast.

'Heineken Nederland' was deliberately reticent about introducing new beers. In contrast, the brewery was quite daring as far as packaging was concerned. Every now and again, consumers wanted something other than simply beer out of a brown bottle or the famous can. In the 1990s, the brewery marketed its beer in all manner of new packagings. The orange can, the ice can, the talking can, the millennium can, the James Bond can, the long-neck bottle, the special 75 cl. bottles for 'Tarwebok' and 'De Belofte', the various packaging variants such as the cube, the Amstel beer-be-que and the now-famous yellow CD crate. Heineken extended the idea of surprising beer drinkers to cover its communications policy. Using special music and sports events, the beer brands became associated with an identifiable type of experience. Heineken NightLive grew to become the largest music festival in the Netherlands with performances by well-known international artists. Amstel presented itself more as the traditional Dutch brand and concentrated on football, bicycle races and music made in the Netherlands. In 2000, Heineken was still the largest brewery in the Netherlands by far.

SWITZERLAND

11.16

Switzerland actually consists of three separate regions with the division being largely based on the language spoken. The cultural differences are therefore also expressed on the beer market. The northern, German-speaking districts are areas of high beer consumption and this is where most breweries are located. The local beer is a little sweeter, has a different hop taste and is drunk slightly cooled or even at room temperature. In the Italian districts less beer is drunk and the taste of the beer is more pronounced. In the French-speaking districts, beer consumption is also moderate with the beer having a similar taste to the white wines produced there, namely light and dry and always served cool.

Sounds good. Heineken.

Heineken beer has been available in Switzerland on an import basis since the 1960s. In 1993, Heineken acquired a majority shareholding in Calanda Haldengut, whose market share of 12 percent made it the second largest brewery group in Switzerland and also the distributor of Heineken beer in the eastern and southern areas of Switzerland. Calanda Haldengut had two breweries in Chur and Winterthur, with a joint capacity of 600,000 hectoliters. In 1999, the remaining shares were acquired. In addition to the regional brands of Calanda and Haldengut, the Swiss brewery group also marketed the locally brewed Heineken, Amstel and Murphy's Irish Stout and imported the specialty beer Desperados. Heineken had a market share of 19 percent in Switzerland. The Heineken brand is the shining star, with a market share of well over 50 percent of the premium segment.

EASTERN EUROPE

Following the fall of the Berlin Wall in 1989, a number of Eastern European countries underwent periods of rapid economic development. They switched to a free market economy, which meant that more and more attention was focused on Western products and services. There were plenty of new opportunities for everyone... including Heineken.

The world-famous Café New York in Budapest was built in 1894. Many writers, artists and other famous figures have visited the café and used it as their postal address. The guest book is filled with names such as Harold Lloyd, Willy Brandt and Pele.

II.17

The first venture into Eastern Europe took place in 1991 when a shareholding was acquired in the Hungarian brewery Komáromi Sörgyár in Komárom. At the end of the 1990s, the name of this subsidiary was changed to Amstel Hungary and the company started bringing locally brewed Heineken and Amstel onto the market. Buckler, Talleros, Fregatt and Zlatý Bažant were the other brands sold by this Hungarian brewery. During the 1990s, Heineken further expanded its position in Eastern Europe. In Slovakia, where Heineken today has a market share of 26 percent, the brewery had shareholdings in Zlatý Bažant, Corgon, Martiner and Gemer. The range of brands comprised: Amstel, Zlatý Bažant, Kelt, Corgon and Martiner. The Zlatý Bažant brand had a very good reputation in Slovakia and the surrounding countries. The Dutch brewer has also acquired shareholdings in different local breweries in Bulgaria and Macedonia.

The beer market that offered the best prospects in Eastern Europe was Poland. With a population of 38 million people, Poland had enormous consumer potential. Beer consumption was still fairly low and concentrated primarily along the German and Czech borders. Polish breweries were proud of their traditional craftsmanship but one problem was that they were forced to work with extremely outdated brewing installations. Because the import of beer was practically impossible due to high import duties, Heineken only had one option open to it on the Polish beer market, namely cooperation with a local brewery. In 1994, the Dutch brewery acquired a small shareholding in the Polish brewery Zywiec in Kraków. Following the construction of a new brewing house and two bottling lines, brewing capacity increased to 2.5 million hectoliters. The merger of Zywiec and Brewpole in 1998 created a large Polish brewery group that became the market leader under the name Zywiec. The Polish brewery owned strong national and regional brands including the successful premium brand Zywiec and the standard beers EB, Warka, Lezajsk, Brackie and Hevelius. In the meantime, Heineken had also acquired a shareholding of 51.5 percent in Zywiec. The future for the Polish beer market looked rosy. The Polish government tried to change people's drinking habits by encouraging beer and wine consumption instead of vodka. In addition, the Polish economy was growing steadily and more and more consumers were prepared to pay the price asked for a quality beer. Heineken was the perfect choice.

A EUROPEAN STAR

Today, Heineken is the largest brewery in Europe. Market share has grown from 2.8 percent in 1970 to 11 percent in 2000. The Heineken and Amstel beer brands are the number one and number two in Europe respectively and the brewery has a very rich and varied range of local beer brands. In Europe, people most often make a toast with a glass of Heineken beer.

Cheers!

———

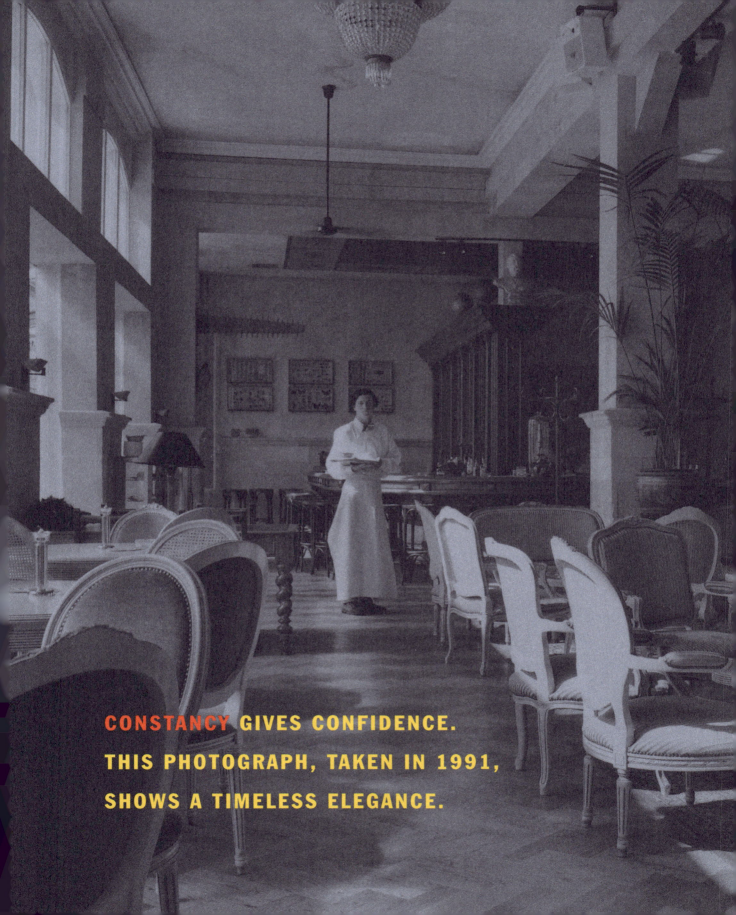
CONSTANCY GIVES CONFIDENCE.
THIS PHOTOGRAPH, TAKEN IN 1991,
SHOWS A TIMELESS ELEGANCE.

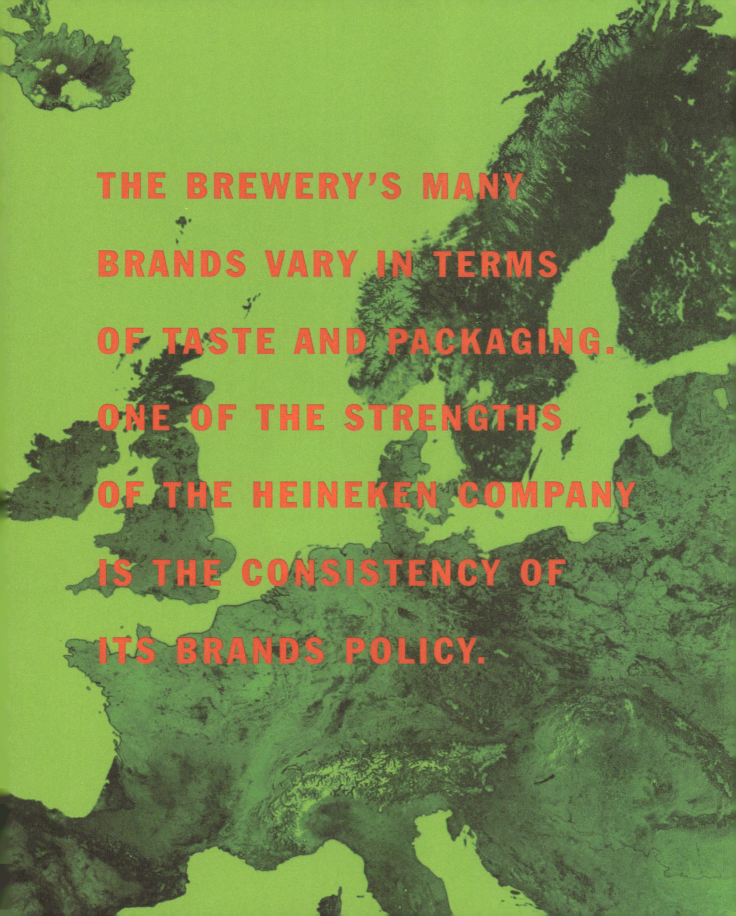

THE BREWERY'S MANY BRANDS VARY IN TERMS OF TASTE AND PACKAGING. ONE OF THE STRENGTHS OF THE HEINEKEN COMPANY IS THE CONSISTENCY OF ITS BRANDS POLICY.

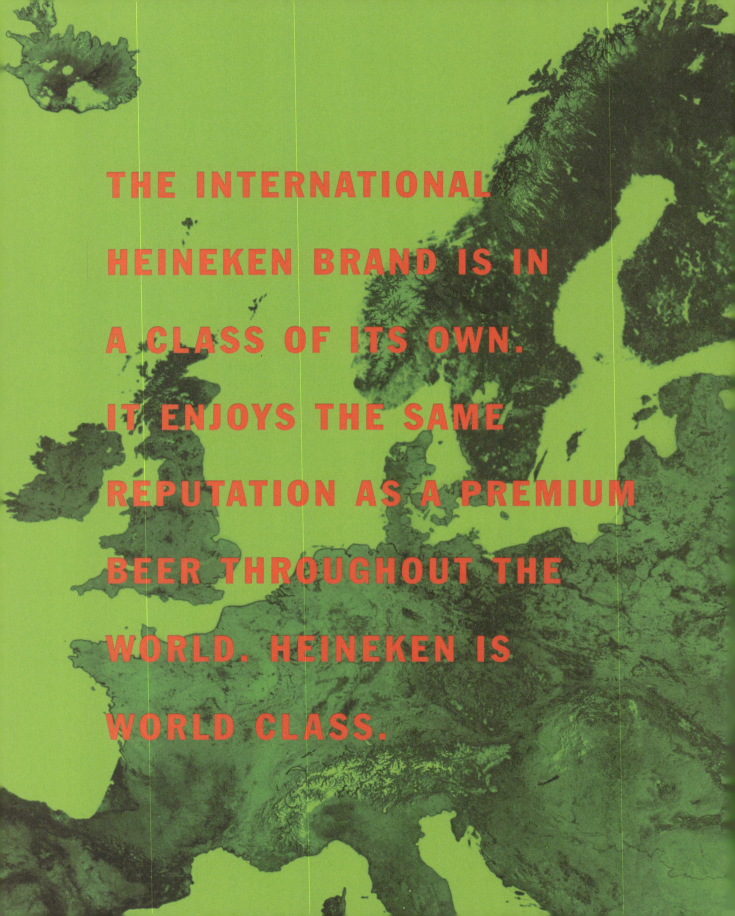

CONSISTENCY

WORLD-CLASS PERFORMANCE

12

What is a business without a goal? Heineken had explicit ambitions at the beginning of the 1990s. The Heineken brand was to develop into the strongest brand worldwide and the company into the best performing international brewery. Two objectives – one name: Heineken. The magic of the Heineken brand became the driving force behind the business. 'Paint the world green' was now the brewer's motto. Europe and the United States have been Heineken green for some time now. But the company wanted more, namely a worldwide presence. New markets were coming into the frame. Hong Kong, Shanghai and Bangkok were starting to color Asia green. And the same applied to Rio de Janeiro, São Paulo and Buenos Aires in South America. Today, Heineken clearly has a global presence. It is a world company. It is a world brand. Two words – one name: Heineken.

WORLD CLASS

12.4

On April 22, 1989, Alfred Henry Heineken resigned as Chairman of the Board of Management. Under his leadership, the Heineken brand had acquired an international resonance and the brewery had achieved spectacular results. The figures spoke for themselves. During the 1970s and 1980s, the world beer market expanded by 181 percent, but Heineken's turnover grew by 465 percent. The company's global market share increased from 2.8 percent in 1970 to 4.6 percent in 1990. Heineken was now the third largest brewery in the world, after American brewing giants Anheuser Busch and Miller. In 1990, the world of Heineken consisted of 90 breweries in more than 50 countries. Under its supervision, a total of 53.5 million hectoliters of beer were brewed. If this amount were to be put into 30 cl. bottles, it would amount to 17.6 billion bottles, enough to encircle the earth 25 times. Heineken pilsner was available in more than 150 countries. It was the biggest brand in the Netherlands, the biggest brand in Europe and had the best reputation among imported beers in the United States. Heineken was the number one beer brand, internationally.

WORLD REVOLUTION

On April 22, 1989, Gerard van Schaik, a member of the Board of Management since 1974, became the new Heineken Chairman. His task was crystal clear, namely to further promote the company's position in the world. Upon his appointment, the beer world had only three international breweries: Heineken, Carlsberg and Guinness. All indications seemed to be that concentration and internationalization within the beer industry would increase considerably. The big brewers in Europe and the United States were facing stabilizing home markets and were looking to expand in areas where there were strongly growing beer markets, such as the Far East. The increasing sales of pilsner on the world beer market, the increasing investments in the brand and the rise of home consumption worked in favor of the big brewers, who could profit from their economies of scale. In 1980, the top 5 brewers had a market share of 18 percent of the world beer market, in 1993 this rose to 23 percent and grew further in subsequent years.

On May 1, 1991, Karel Vuursteen was appointed to the Board of Management of Heineken NV, and on April 22, 1993 took the Chair. Under his leadership, the company experienced strong growth and the Heineken brand improved its position on the global beer market.

Increasing competition forced Heineken into a more aggressive policy. The brewer was able to ride the wave of the fame of Heineken pilsner for a long while: the product simply sold itself. The growing conflict between the international brewers in a sense was to bring about a revolution within Heineken. On February 1, 1991, the Board informed the management, 'The Board is of the opinion that the key challenge for the period ahead of us is to make sure that we are a company that is hungry to go after promising opportunities and that it is determined to regain its spirit of superior performance.' Taking chances, using opportunities and responding in a creative manner to an increasingly dynamic world. 'We are good, but we have to be the best', was the challenging precondition laid down by the brewery. The company wanted to be the best. But in what area? Should Heineken aim to be the biggest brewery in terms of volume, or the best with respect to quality and profitability? Quantity or quality, that – in essence – was the question.

The answer could be found not far away. In 1991, Heineken brewed a total of 52.5 million hectoliters of beer, 14.4 million hectoliters of which was Heineken beer. The premium brand was the company's flagship and the source of inspiration for the organization. Care for the Heineken brand demanded controlled growth of the company. Noblesse oblige, you could say. This also corresponded to the company's character. Heineken had always been geared to consolidation and expansion of its market share and consistent positioning of the Heineken brand. In the case of investments, the long-term effect counted for more than short-term profit. The fact that Heineken was a family business was also demonstrated by other financial preconditions. The preferred method of investment was internal finance. The precondition of a highly solid balance sheet was a major prerequisite of the company's policy for expansion.

12.6 The head office of 'Heineken Nederland' and the Heineken brewery in Zoeterwoude, the Netherlands, officially opened on April 18, 1975. The park-style layout of the site makes the buildings and the 40-meter high malt silos and yeast tanks seem smaller than their actual size.

At the beginning of the 1990s, the brewer drew up a clear strategy. Three processes of change were key. Firstly, the company wished to develop from a general beverage company – with activities in beer, soft drinks, spirits and wine – into a brewery group with highly defined beer brands. In other words, concentration on the core activity. Secondly, Heineken wished to grow in financial terms from 'a good performer' to 'the best performer'. The company decided to monitor costs more closely and derive greater benefits from its economies of scale, particularly in Europe. Finally, Heineken wished to develop into a fully international concern. The company wished to take advantage of opportunities in new markets, such as Asia and South America, while at the same time being a sought-after employer for top international talent.

WORLDWIDE BRAND

In its business strategy, Heineken chose to focus on the brands – the growth of the brands would determine the growth of the company. Quality of sales was given priority above pure volume. The brewery wished to be present with strong brands in the most important market segments, and in particular the premium segment, that is those beers of a high quality and strong image. This is the area in which Heineken felt most at home. The premium segment was also the fastest growing segment on the world beer market, offering the best margins, and the brewery owned the strongest premium brand in the world: Heineken. With a targeted premium strategy, the plan was to further improve the international position of this brand. The Heineken brand was distributed widely throughout the world, but in order to expand into a real global brand, the brand would have to become more visible in a number of markets. The

The Heineken brewery in 's-Hertogenbosch, the Netherlands, which officially opened on September 4, 1958, focuses on brewing specialty beers and beer for export.

world had to be painted green. In 1992, Van Schaik summed it up in two sentences, 'All activities will have to take place with the focus on the Heineken brand. What we need is total focus, total dedication and total consistency.'

However, Heineken could not afford to concentrate exclusively on the premium brand. It was important for the premium strategy that Heineken have a broad range of brands and products. In its conquest of the world, the Heineken brand had to have the support of strong local brands and a powerful distribution network. An interesting point is that the company had to think in two different ways, namely like a brewer of standard beers, who had to monitor costs sharply, while at the same time like a brewer of premium Heineken beer, who had to excel in marketing and selling an image of luxury and exclusivity.

The Heineken brand had to represent 'best product, best package, best image'. This philosophy of 'best brand' fits seamlessly with that of 'best brewer'. Everything the brand does reflects on the company and vice-versa. Extra cachet for the Heineken brand was a boost for the brewery. The concept of 'best brewer' meant that the Heineken breweries in the various countries were geared to the best products in every market segment. This also meant that Heineken would have nothing to do with brewing private labels; this does not befit a 'best brewer'. The luxury of a worldwide brand gave the Heineken organization a common source of inspiration. Who doesn't want to work for the best company and the best brand? 'Being the best is very challenging and very exciting. It should be reason enough to wake up every morning and go to work. And to make a personal commitment to be part of a winning team that has attained a world-class stature', is how an internal Heineken report put it.

WORLD-CLASS PLAYER

12.8

The brand policy sets aside a pioneering role for marketing within Heineken. The appointment on May 1, 1991 of Karel Vuursteen, a marketer, as a member of the Board and his promotion on April 22, 1993 to Chairman of the Board reinforced this. Vuursteen was a forceful personality with firm views: 'The public only supports winners. It doesn't like losers. If you are the best you should still strive to be even better. That attitude has to exist, because your competitors aren't standing still. They are trying to topple you from the throne, so you need to keep an eye on them. Beer is a simple product, but we still have to supply better beer than the next man.' With Vuursteen at the helm, Heineken set off to discover new parts of the world.

The Board of Management of Heineken NV in 2000. Left to right: Vice-chair Thony Ruys, Board member Guus Lubsen and Chair Karel Vuursteen.

During the 1990s, the Board of Management drew up a targeted global policy. The position of the Heineken brand thereby gave direction to the company. Alongside the further expansion of its European interests, the company also concentrated on reinforcing the Heineken brand in the United States and building up and expanding positions in new growth markets in the Far East and South America. The company did not avoid risks along the way, but the basic principle of responsible expansion remained intact. During the presentation of the half-yearly figures on September 15, 2000, Vuursteen announced, 'Other brewers go in for spectacular takeovers, but we are more conservative. We are threading together a string of pearls.'

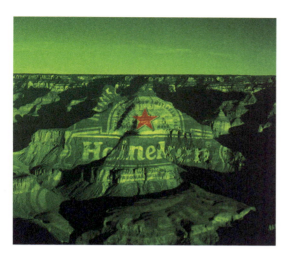

Heineken sets the tone throughout the world. This advertising image from 1998 ingeniously superimposes the Heineken label on the Grand Canyon in Arizona.

12.9

WORLD-CLASS PLAYER: THE UNITED STATES

A particularly precious pearl was the success of the Heineken brand in the United States. In 1973, under the inspirational leadership of the American importer Van Munching & Co. (VMCo), Heineken became the best-selling imported brand. In 1972, Heineken sold 3.5 million cases of 24 bottles, but by the end of the decade this had increased to almost 25 million cases. This gave Heineken a 41 percent share of the import sector. More than half of Heineken exports from the Netherlands went to the American market. The explosive growth during the 1970s was due to a number of reasons. The distribution network was well organized and VMCo switched from spirits agents to beer wholesalers. The extra manpower and the attractive margin on the beer gave the brand a big boost. Heineken also invested a great deal in advertising. At the end of the 1970s, the Dutch brewer became the largest advertiser in magazines of all beer brands, both domestic and imported. But the most important factor of all for the American success was the retention of import status. When, in the mid-1970s, the German Löwenbräu brewery, a big competitor in the import sector, decided to brew its beer in the United States, American beer drinkers turned away from the brand in droves. In their eyes, the beer was no longer special. For this reason, Heineken cherished its import status.

Leo van Munching, the driving force behind the brewery's American success since 1933, was succeeded in 1980 by his son Leo jr. Initially, he too reaped only success. Sales of Heineken beer continued to increase and Amstel Light – 'Never before did 95 calories taste so imported' – introduced on the American market in 1980, became the best-selling imported light beer

12.10 Heineken is highly innovative in the field of packagings. Three exceptional cans in a row, from left to right: the international Heineken can, a 'shaped can' in the shape of a beer barrel for the international market and a special millennium edition.

within just a few years. Where Heineken reflected status, Amstel Light was fashionable. The exclusive character of Heineken beer paid great dividends during the 1980s, the era of the yuppies. An increasing number of American beer drinkers wanted to set themselves apart from the crowd and the instantly recognizable green Heineken bottle proved a highly desirable eye-catcher. Favorable economic circumstances drove up purchasing power and the strong dollar made European import beers even more attractive. Heineken reaped the rewards. However, from 1987 onwards, VMCo started to struggle. The dollar weakened and competition in the import sector increased dramatically. Particularly noticeable was the rise of the Mexican beer Corona, which presented itself as a young, hip outsider challenging the classical Heineken. 'As the leading imported beer for many years, we were simply no longer used to setbacks,' Leo van Munching jr explained in October 1988. This led to a change of course. According to the Heineken Board, the advertising policy could be made 'more playful, younger, snappier and less boring'. The campaign had to demonstrate more aggression and appeal more to the younger beer drinker, without alienating the older Heineken drinkers. The result, in 1988, was, 'When you're done kidding around – Heineken'.

With the takeover of VMCo on January 1, 1991, Heineken took over the running of the business in the United States. Leo van Munching jr left in December 1993. His legacy proved to be a very healthy organization. During the 1990s, the Heineken brand grew far more quickly than the market as a whole and Heineken USA became the sixth largest beer supplier in the United States. At the end of the 1990s, it was time to beef up the brand's image. The local breweries started a price war and a number of breweries were forced to close down. In addition, the number of exclusive local brands increased, as did imports of Mexican and Canadian beers. Because these imported beers had a lower price level and a lesser quality image, Heineken responded gently to these developments. In 1998, the brewery launched a new advertising campaign under the slogan, 'It's all about the beer'. The brand wished to be an exceptional, high-quality beer, but not so exclusive that large swathes of the market were not reached. Alongside the new campaign, the new look of the Heineken can gave the brand an additional luster. Heineken is the brand for everyone who loves beer. 'Heineken – It's all about the beer'.

WORLD-CLASS PLAYER: THE FAR EAST

Heineken had been working with Fraser & Neave in the Far East since 1931 in the joint venture Malayan Breweries Limited (MBL). This cooperation initially concentrated on Singapore and Malaya, now called Malaysia. With breweries in Singapore (1931) and Kuala Lumpur (1962) and the brands Tiger and Anchor, MBL had a firm grip on these beer markets. In 1955, a stake in the South Pacific Brewery in Papua New Guinea was acquired. Outside of these areas, MBL was hardly active at all. However, from the mid-1980s, a new wave of optimism for Heineken swept through Asia. Slowing growth on the Dutch and American markets forced Heineken to change course. Many Asiatic countries – the 'Asian tigers' – underwent rapid economic growth and increasing purchasing power was accompanied by strong growth in beer consumption. In 1986, Heineken and Fraser & Neave entered into a new cooperation agreement in which it was agreed that an active approach should be taken towards developing the beer markets in Asia. Heineken was increasingly involved in the management of the company, and in 1990 MBL's name was changed to Asia Pacific Breweries (APB). Both partners started to develop new activities in Thailand, Vietnam and China: countries with large populations, potential for economic growth and increasing beer consumption.

Hong Kong is one of the special world locations used by Heineken for a global campaign in 1998 and 1999.

Since 1983, Heineken has been active in China, one of the largest and most rapidly growing beer markets in the world. The brand has already made its mark on the Great Wall of China.

China is potentially the most important beer market in Asia. From 1983 onwards, Heineken has been available there as an imported beer, particularly in the international hotels. Annually, this amounts to the sale of only some 10,000 hectoliters. In the 1990s, Heineken decided to take a more thorough approach. From Hong Kong, a national distribution network was set up for the distribution of the Heineken brand in China, whereby the emphasis was initially on the coastal areas. This is where the densely populated cities such as Shanghai are located, and where most economic development takes place. The higher-priced beer was sold predominately in better-class establishments such as western-style pubs, discotheques, karaoke bars and restaurants. Karaoke bars are particularly popular – in Shanghai alone there are some 3,000, over 500 of which have Heineken on the menu. With an export volume in excess of 300,000 hectoliters in 1997, Heineken achieved the status of No. 1 imported beer in China. By this time, the pilsner was available in the 25 largest Chinese cities and their immediate surroundings. Sport sponsoring was employed to further enhance the brand's image. In 1997, for example, the brewery organized the first Heineken Open Shanghai international tennis tournament.

The brewery was also active in other areas in China. In 1988, APB took a shareholding in the Shanghai Mila Brewery in Shanghai, making Heineken one of the first international breweries with a stake in a local Chinese brewery. The Reeb brand, launched by the brewery in May 1989 – in Chinese the name is translated as 'Libo', which means 'strong wave' – acquired a strong position in Shanghai and the surrounding areas within a short space of time. In August 1993, APB took a stake in the TYJ(F) Brewery in the Chinese province Fujian and on May 19, 1997 the new Hainan Asia Pacific Brewery was officially inaugurated on the Chinese island of Hainan. This brewery, built by Heineken, has a capacity of 1 million hectoliters and is an example of a 'greenfield project' in that it was created entirely from scratch.

The brewery also gained a foothold in Vietnam and Thailand. In these countries, APB set up new brewery projects with local partners. In Vietnam, a new brewery was opened in Ho Chi Minh City in November 1993, and started local production of Heineken in July 1994. The brewery's capacity was further expanded in 1997. In Thailand, a new brewery with a capacity of 500,000 hectoliters was opened in the Bangkok area in 1995, concentrating fully on brewing Heineken beer. The Bangkok brewery was a fairly unique project, as Heineken generally first built up brand recognition in new markets through export. The high level of import duties in Thailand made this impossible, however. The gamble in Thailand worked very well for Heineken and the beer developed into a highly desirable premium brand. The new activities highlighted the leading role played by the company in the beer markets of the Far East.

WORLD-CLASS PLAYER: SOUTH AMERICA

Heineken had developed hardly any activities at all in South America until well into the twentieth century. The various beer markets were in the hands of large local brewery groups and exports were often not viable owing to high import levies. A failed brewery project in Venezuela during the 1950s and 1960s also dampened the brewery's appetite in South America. This also meant that the Heineken name was not a familiar one on this continent.

In 1983, the company once again took an important step by taking a minority shareholding in the Brazilian brewing group Kaiser, which started local production of Heineken in 1990. At this time, Brazil was the fastest growing beer market in South America. Beer consumption grew from 23 million hectoliters in 1982 to some 80 million hectoliters in 2000. This made Brazil the fourth

Easter Island, the most easterly of the Polynesian islands, was visited for the first time on Easter Sunday 1722 by a Dutch mariner. A visit by Heineken in 1998 did not go unnoticed.

12.14 The skyline of Rio de Janeiro is familiar throughout the world, like the Heineken label. This advertising image underlines the global image of the Heineken brand.

largest beer market in the world, after the United States, Germany and China. Kaiser profited from this development and grew into a sizeable brewing group with 1,800 employees, 8 breweries, an annual production of 13.5 million hectoliters and a market share in 2000 of 15 percent. The Heineken brand in Brazil was aimed at accessibility, attraction and affordability. Young adults, who made up a quarter of Brazilian beer drinkers, were the most important target group. These consumers wanted to stand out and were open to new experiences. The urban areas of São Paulo and Rio de Janeiro were the most significant sales areas. The initial results were encouraging. Whereas in 1992 Heineken had a market share of just 0.7 percent, by 2000 this had risen to some 2 percent. This may seem a low figure, but with total beer consumption in excess of 80 million hectoliters, this was nevertheless a not insignificant amount.

Argentina was another important South American market. Since 1984, Heineken had had a 15 percent interest in the Quilmes group, with breweries in Argentina, Uruguay, Paraguay, Chile and Bolivia. The most important market for Quilmes was Argentina, with its steadily growing beer market. In 1988, Argentines drank an average of 12 liters of beer a year, but within 10 years this figure had tripled. Here too, beer was a young people's drink. Beer represented a modern lifestyle, having fun with friends, at home and in bars and restaurants. As in other South American countries, most beer is sold in 1 liter bottles – beer is to be shared with others. This is the South American way of life.

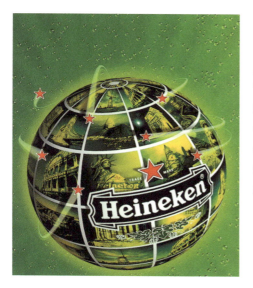

To celebrate 125 years of the Heineken brand, in 1998 the brewery started a promotional campaign in 48 countries, offering as prizes 35,000 air trips to well-known destinations throughout the world. A special campaign that painted the globe and many global locations Heineken green.

Heineken has been brewed locally in Argentina since 1997. Alongside the green 1 liter bottle – a world first for Heineken – the beer is now also sold in smaller size bottles and cans. The main sales focus is in and around Buenos Aires, which is also where half of all the company's turnover is realized. The introduction of Heineken was supported by the 'Pensa en Verde' advertising campaign – think intelligent, think fresh and take a look at things from a different perspective. The campaign illustrates the dynamic and international character of Heineken beer. A great many sponsorship activities were also included under the umbrella of the 'Pensa en Verde' campaign, including rugby, beach volleyball, snowboarding and tennis. Music was also an important means of communication, as represented by the 'Heineken and Vivo' concerts. Since 1997, Heineken's turnover in Argentina has increased by a factor of five. In the neighboring country of Chile, Heineken has been brewed locally since February 1999, also in 1 liter bottles, and promoted as 'La Gran Verde' (The Big Green). The message is: Heineken is the best beer and the strongest brand.

WORLD SUCCESS

12.16

During the 1990s, the brewery achieved impressive results. With a targeted corporate strategy, the brewer has bolstered its position on the global beer market. These cool figures tell their own story. Heineken's strategy is paying big dividends to the company's shareholders. Net turnover increased from 3,667 million euros in 1990 to 8,107 million euros in 2000, and net profit from 166 million euros in 1990 to 621 million euros in 2000. The closing rate of shares in Heineken NV on the Amsterdam Euronext exchange rose from 6.33 euros in 1990 to 64.45 euros in 2000, after restating in connection with a capitalisation issue and splitting the shares.

The Heineken world is built up of solid breweries and strong brands. Heineken has considerably strengthened its position as the leading brewer in Europe. In many European countries, the brewery's market share amounts to more than 30 percent and the brewer is market leader. The Heineken brand is number one in Europe, with Amstel at number two. In the United States, Heineken's status as an imported beer remains unsurpassed. During the 1990s, American beer drinkers provided the brand with annual growth in excess of ten percent, as well as a significant increase for Amstel Light. In Asia too, Heineken stands on firm foundations, with twelve breweries and eight import agencies. In Africa, Heineken is the second-largest brewery with seventeen breweries and one import agent. In South America, Heineken has 3 import agencies and works closely with local brewery groups, making a total of 18 breweries.

In 2000, Heineken is the No. 2 brewery in the world, employing almost 38,000 people and brewing a total beer volume of 97.7 million hectoliters. Its worldwide market share in 1999 was 5.5 percent. Production takes place in more than 110 breweries in over 50 countries. The Heineken brand is sold in more than 170 countries, Amstel in more than 100 countries. Heineken is the leading premium beer brand in the world. Heineken brings life. Heineken gives people pleasure. And this gives color to the future – a great perspective.

DYNAMISM GIVES RESULTS.
INSTALLING A HEINEKEN BILLBOARD ON
THE ISLAND OF CURAÇAO IN 1991.

HEINEKEN IS SEEN AS THE BEST BREWERY IN THE WORLD. THE COMPANY ALSO HAS THE STRONGEST INTERNATIONAL PREMIUM BEER BRAND.

THE MAGIC OF HEINEKEN IS REACHING OUT TO NEW CONSUMERS IN EUROPE, ASIA, AFRICA, NORTH AND SOUTH AMERICA. HEINEKEN IS TRULY A WORLD CITIZEN.

AMBITION

COLORFUL

13 CHARACTERS

WITH

FROTHY HEADS

Beer lovers have an incredible wealth of beers from which to choose. Pilsner remains the big favorite. This cool type with its golden character and light head goes down smooth and easy, and tastes great too. But beer drinkers are also drawn by the countless specialty beers: wheat beer, abbot's beer, amber beer, stout and exotic beers. The same applies to Heineken. In 1982, the brewer acquired the Ridder brewery of Maastricht, the Netherlands; in 1983, the Murphy's Brewery of Cork, Ireland, and in 1996, the French brewery Fischer, as well as acquiring a stake in the Belgian abbey brewery Affligem in 2000. Following extensive renovation work, by 1992 Murphy Brewery Ireland was ready to face the future. Specialty beers bring a little color to life. A refreshing, fruity wheat beer is a joy to drink outside in the summer. A full, harmonious Tripple can pave the way to a good conversation. Enchanted by an amber-colored top-fermenting beer, we can drift away into a tranquil dreamscape. Trendy beer drinkers express their personality with an exotic beer. Strangers become old friends over a glass of Irish stout. Specialty beers add spice to life.

A SPECIAL FAMILY

13.4

Pilsner is the most popular beer type in many countries. The tendency among developed beer markets is towards an even greater variety of beer types. Consumers want choice, and to drink beers that complement their personalities. Beer drinkers use beer to 'communicate' with their environment. As a product with an added emotional value, beer is supremely suitable for this. Tell me which beer you drink, and I will tell you who you are! This applies particularly to specialty beers.

What distinguishes a specialty beer from pilsner? A specialty beer has a different taste and color, sometimes accompanied by a higher alcohol percentage. Pouring such beers usually involves an element of ritual. In the beer drinker's eyes, this is an exceptional beer, to be drunk in select company or even alone. You can enjoy a pilsner any time, whereas specialty beers are for those special moments. Origin and packaging are important elements of the enjoyment of specialty beers. They are associated with countries such as Belgium, Ireland and Germany, and with a traditional brewing process. Discovering a specialty beer for yourself is something of an adventure. Beer drinkers like to see themselves as true connoisseurs.

During the early 1990s, specialty beers started to increase their market share in a number of beer markets. The market share in the Netherlands at that time was in the region of four percent, in France six percent, and in Italy and the United States some four percent each. Although Heineken had a range of specialty beers – the brewer was in fact market leader in this area in France – there was no real clear international strategy in this field. During the mid-1990s, the brewery decided to concentrate its efforts on specialty beers. An attractive range of specialty beers was put together, featuring timeless tastes and beers of clear quality in their class. These specialty beers were marketed in various European countries, the United States, Australia and Hong Kong.

Heineken's range of specialty beers consists primarily of beers of a highly drinkable character: Murphy's Irish Red and the amber beer Vos; the wheat beer Wieckse Witte; Murphy's stout and the Affligem Blond abbot's beer. Affligem Double and Affligem Tripple represent the stronger abbot's beers. These robust drinks should be enjoyed at a relaxed pace. In the trendy specialty beers segment, the brewery also owns the brand Desperados. The world of specialty beers is surprisingly multi-facetted.

A BEER TO SILENCE EVERY CRITIC

The monks at the abbey in Affligem, Belgium, have been brewing their own beer since 1074. They ceased production in 1970 and transferred the brand to brewery De Smedt in the nearby town of Opwijk. The Affligem abbot's beers are still brewed according to Brother Tobias' centuries-old recipe, the Formula Antiqua Renovata. The holy fathers still supervise the process personally and one crate of each new brew is sent to the monastery for approval. In 2000, Heineken acquired the trademark rights to Affligem and took a 50 percent shareholding in the Belgian brewery.

The three Affligem abbot's beers: Tripple, Double and Blonde. Abbot's beers are served in a broader glass – the 'chalice glass' – because the beer's highly carbonated nature makes it foam more than a pilsner.

Affligem beer is available in three types. Affligem Tripple – the flagship brand – is robust and amber-colored, has a rich, powerful taste and 8.5 percent alcohol. Affligem Double has a milder taste, is dark brown and has an alcohol percentage of 7 percent. Affligem Blond is clear, dark blonde in appearance and goes down smoothly. It has the same alcohol percentage as Affligem Double. The beers are sold in 33 cl. bottles. For special occasions, 75 cl. 'champagne bottles' are available, with a real champagne cork. These beers are very popular in Belgium and the United States. In 1996, Affligem received the accolade of best abbot's beer in the world.

A BEER WITH A STOUT CHARACTER

Ireland has always been famous for its stout. Guinness is the leading brand that has elevated stout to the national drink of Ireland. It is only in the south east of the country – in the city of Cork – that two local breweries have managed to continue producing their own stout: these are Beamish and Murphy, established in 1856. In 1978, the Murphy's Brewery acquired a license to brew Heineken beer for the Irish lager market. To guarantee access to this market, Heineken acquired the Murphy's Brewery on April 1, 1983. A successful move, as Heineken became the most popular pilsner in Ireland. But Heineken soon began to wonder what to do about the Murphy's stout.

Drawing a glass of Murphy's Irish Stout has to be done in peace and with a lot of patience. Irish beers are served in the 'pint' glass, which holds 586 ml.

Murphy's stout, famous throughout Cork, was virtually unknown in the rest of the country. Heineken decided to rejuvenate the brand. In November 1985, the beer was launched in a new high neck bottle holding 25 cl., unique in the stout market. 'Tradition in making' was the slogan of the successful advertising campaign. In 1987, the beer was exported to England and rapidly won some 15 percent of the British stout market. The Dutch brewery became convinced that the Murphy's brand was a very potent one. Murphy's was elevated to the brewery's third major brand, together with Heineken and Amstel, and was given the support to expand worldwide.

The Irish pub is a mecca of friendliness, music and beer culture. Drawing a glass of stout is an art in itself. It is done at a leisurely pace, not in one long pull, as is the case with pilsner, but in two or three measured movements. The end result is what counts. The creamy foam head, in which every air bubble is the same size and thickness, takes the edge off the bitter taste of the beer. The Murphy brewery is currently making efforts to establish this beer tradition outside of Ireland. A special team has been charged with setting up original Murphy's pubs throughout the world. These pubs – replicas of old pubs in Cork – are designed in Ireland, where they are also manufactured and then shipped out and put together on site. The philosophy behind these pubs is, 'There are no strangers here, only friends who have not yet met'. The opening of the first of these pubs took place in November 1997 in Antwerp. There are now numerous Murphy's pubs scattered across the globe. It is a wonderful way of promoting the Murphy's brand. Murphy's stout is a way of life.

TIME FOR FRUITY REFRESHMENT

Wieckse Witte, the wheaten beer from Maastricht, the Netherlands, is drunk from a special glass known as 'het Pileerke'.

Some time around the year 1600, Bohemian brewers discovered that a mixture of yeast and wheat produced a delicious top-fermenting beer with a refreshing, sour taste. The recipe spread across Europe, where local brewers introduced it with their own variations. The small Belgian town of Hoegaarden became the center for this Belgian wheat beer – also known as white beer. This name refers to the light color of the beer and the yeast particles suspended in it, giving the impression of a white film in the glass. Belgian white beers have a fruity taste, thanks to the addition of various herbs, including coriander and citrus peel. Towards the beginning of the 19th century, some 30 'white beer brewers' were active in the area. This period was followed by a downward trend, however, and by the 1950s, the town of Hoegaarden was without a single brewery. This situation changed in 1966, when brewery De Kluis revived the white beer tradition. Belgian white beer was given a new lease of life and since the 1990s has made rapid gains in northern France and the Netherlands. The refreshing, highly drinkable white beer is becoming a trendy beer at many a summer pavement café.

13.8

In 1990, Maastricht brewery De Ridder introduced a Belgian-style wheat beer called Wieckse Witte. De Ridder, acquired by Heineken in 1982, boasts a brewing tradition that goes back to 1857. The name and the logo of this brewery are probably derived from Saint Martin, knight and patron saint of the church situated adjacent to the brewery. Wieckse Witte, brewed in Maastricht, the Netherlands, is a very tasty white beer: its 'white' color, citrus tang, mild sour and herby coriander taste make for a deliciously light, refreshing and drinkable beer. Wieckse Witte is the second best-selling white beer in the Netherlands and looks likely to attract fans among beer-lovers in other countries. A fresh passion that never dies.

RED-BROWN PASSION

Amber beers belong to the ale family. In English-speaking countries, ales are top-fermenting beers. Although most ales are amber-colored – owing to the use of red-brown malts – the term ale in fact refers to the fermentation method rather than the color of the beer. In spite of varying characteristics, English ales have a number of elements in common: they are fizzy and have a lower alcohol percentage, have a malty character, a bitter hoppy taste and are often cloudy.

The rich, surprising taste of the amber beer Vos is best enjoyed from this special glass.

Belgian breweries have come up with their own interpretations of the English ale. The Belgian variety is more herby and aromatic, gives a less hoppy sensation, is fizzier and generally somewhat darker in color. Most Belgian ales are brewed in the north-western area of the province of Brabant, where Palm is the number one Belgian ale. The most popular Belgian ale in general, however – although it is not officially called an ale – comes from Antwerp, where the De Koninck brewery has been brewing its red-brown, full malt beer since 1833. As a counterpart to the popular Palm, the De Ridder brewery launched its new beer Vos in the Netherlands in

1994. This is an amber-colored, top-fermenting beer with 5 percent alcohol. Vos has a malty character, a pleasant balance between bitter and sweet tastes and an attractive, dark color. It is highly drinkable, not too heavy and appeals to drinkers of both pilsner and specialty beers. Vos has recently expanded its hunting ground to include Spain.

Murphy's Irish Red Beer combines the best of two worlds: pilsner and stout.

Murphy's Irish Red Beer is a unique amber-colored beer. This beer, based on an old recipe from 1856 for Lady's Well Ale, was introduced in 1995. In terms of taste and ingredients, it is something of a hybrid between English and Belgian ales. In comparison with Murphy's stout, Irish Red is a much more accessible beer with a lighter color, being less bitter and having a real fizz. It could almost be described as a pilsner-like stout. Delicious, and very special. The bottle and special glass give the impression of a premium beer. Although in a class of its own, Murphy's Irish Red Beer can serve for non-Irish beer drinkers as a stepping-stone to the characteristic stout; the ultimate Irish drinking sensation.

BEER FOR FUN

A very different segment of the specialty beer market is that for exotic or 'fun beers', sometimes mixed with a tropical juice extract or other drink. The French Fischer group – acquired by Heineken in 1996 – introduced a highly original new beer to the market during the 1990s: Desperados. A product that reflects the rise of Mexican brands such as Corona and Sol. Trendy beer drinkers in particular have expressed a preference for these exotic beers in the striking long-neck bottle.

13.10 Desperados is not a traditional beer, but rather a mix. Tequila flavoring is added to the beer, giving it a unique taste. Desperados is a classic example of a fun beer. Some beer drinkers need a dynamic beer, a drink that sets them apart. The transparent long-neck bottle and label give this beer the sought-after alternative image. A small sachet of salt is included, as the tequila tradition involves licking salt from the back of your hand before quenching your thirst with the exotic tropical drink. This exceptional beer gives the drinker a feeling of carefree enjoyment. The high price of the beer adds to its exceptional character. Desperados is an extremely popular beverage in pubs, clubs and cafés in France, Germany and the Netherlands. Viva Desperados.

SPECIALTY BEERS ARE
LINKED TO THE CHANGING
OF THE SEASONS.
IN THE SUMMER,
THE SUN BRINGS COLOR
TO LIFE AND WHEATEN
BEER REFRESHES.

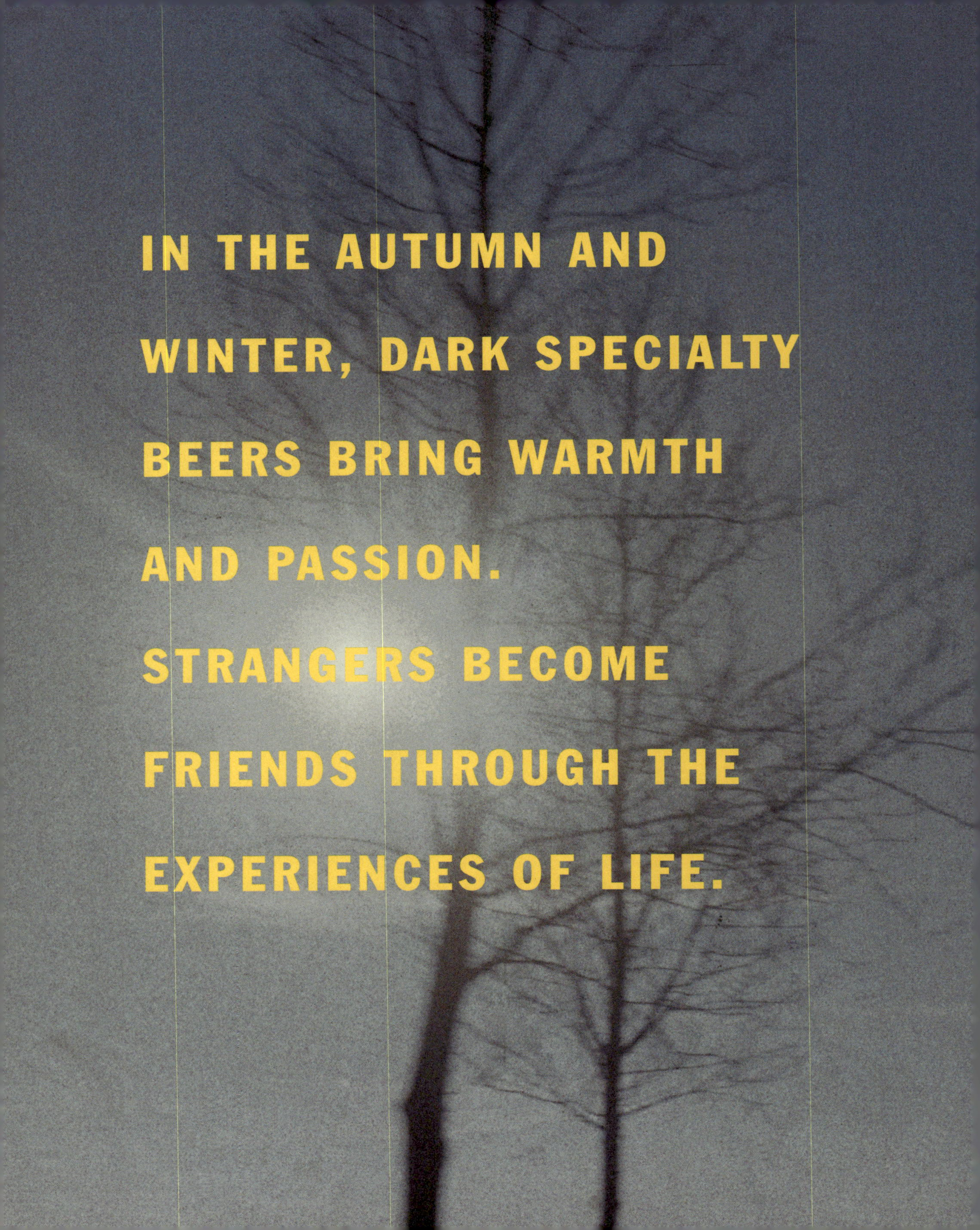

IN THE AUTUMN AND
WINTER, DARK SPECIALTY
BEERS BRING WARMTH
AND PASSION.
STRANGERS BECOME
FRIENDS THROUGH THE
EXPERIENCES OF LIFE.

EXPERIENCE

CROWNING ACHIEVEMENT 14

The magic of the Heineken brand is timeless. It was brewed for the first time in Amsterdam in 1870, 'born' as a brand in 1873 and since then has grown to become a pilsner of global proportions. Heineken is the leading beer brand in Europe, the most prestigious imported beer in the United States and the number one international premium beer brand. This universal appreciation says it all. The company has always remained faithful to the brand's origins: traditional quality, perfect taste and a warm, pleasing image. Perhaps the actual secret of the Heineken brand is the link between tradition and the dynamism of human life, with product quality being an unchanging beacon of reliability and the brand image being a clear reflection of the time. The Heineken brand is linked to the experiences and emotions of millions of people all over the world. People are constantly attracted by the magic of Heineken. But what exactly is this magic? Heineken drinkers know the answer.

PASSION FOR QUALITY

14.4

Heineken beer is brewed from water, malted barley and hops. The natural ingredients and the special Heineken 'A'-yeast are responsible for the specific character of the Heineken pilsner, namely its pleasant bitterness, the clear color and the refreshing drinkability. There has never been any dispute about the taste: the fact remains that, in comparison to other pilsners, Heineken comes out on top in consumer tasting tests all over the world. The Heineken brewing process is a combination of traditional craftsmanship and modern brewing technology. Every year, millions are invested in safeguarding product quality, for which Heineken has a considerable reputation. The beer is therefore more expensive.

Heineken is determined that its beer should taste the same all over the world. Heineken is brewed in the Netherlands and at a number of locations around the world. As far as a lot of beer drinkers are concerned, beer has to come from a traditional beer country, or their own country. Beer drinkers universally regard 'Holland' as a traditional beer country. No matter where it is brewed, the Heineken brewers guarantee the consistency of brewing process and taste. The brewery does not market any other pilsners using the Heineken label as, after all, it is impossible to improve a beer that is already perfect.

WHAT'S IN A NAME?

If a panel of consumers had to choose an ideal name for a beer then the choice would undoubtedly be 'Heineken'. But why? The name Heineken is authentic. The Heineken family is a genuine brewing dynasty, whose ancestors were brewing beer as long ago as the 17th century. However, there is more to it than that. The name has three syllables and sounds like a diminutive, which gives a sympathetic feel. The name, with its Dutch-German sound, exudes tradi-

'Toast with caution' was the title of the Heineken 2001 New Year commercial. Heineken drinkers toast the New Year. But touching glasses involves a certain amount of spillage. So the brewer issued some well-meaning advice: toast with caution. The various photos show images from the commercial.

tion and quality and can be pronounced with ease in a number of languages. The way in which the brand name is written also attracts attention. Originally, Heineken was written in capitals. This produced 11 vertical lines and a brand name that went too far around the bottle, reducing legibility. Alfred Heineken noticed that writing his name in small letters made it easier to read, as well as making it look friendlier. He was not yet completely satisfied however. Beer is a convivial product and people like to look at things. The 'e' in the brand name was therefore tipped to one side in 1951. This operation was extensively tested, the sloping position of the 'e' was the decisive point. If it slants too much to the right, the 'e' looks sad and if it slants too far to the left it looks silly. The Heineken 'e' is perfect, since it appears to smile mischievously.

Proost

BORN UNDER A LUCKY STAR

The five-pointed red star was, to Heineken, a hallmark for quality and beer experience. Legend has it that the origins of the star go back to the Middle Ages, when the brewing of beer was regarded as something magical. A lot of brewers hung a star above the hop boilers to ensure that the brew stayed good. The five-pointed star represents the four elements of earth, water, air and fire – and the fifth, the missing and magic element was intended to safeguard the brew's quality. In any event, the star appealed very much to Gerard Adriaan Heineken. He wanted to get to the bottom of the brewing process and guarantee a consistent quality product. Heineken adopted the star as its personal logo.

The star appeared in the brewery's brand logo for the first time in 1881. A five-pointed star, which included the brewery's abbreviated name (HBM), was printed on the bottle caps. From 1884, the star was included on the labels and from 1891 onwards on the company's stationary. The star's design was influenced by political developments. Since 1917, most export labels included an open contour star. Only the labels on the Dutch and English markets retained the solid red star. However, in 1992, Heineken decided to reintroduce the red star across the board in all its former glory. The star grew to become an important symbol of the Heineken identity and became a striking logo element in numerous forms of company communication. The Heineken brand logo consists of a combination of a star, a stripe and a hop plant, recognizable to all.

SAY IT WITH GREEN

One of the most important characteristics of the Heineken brand is, of course, the color green. Green stands for freshness, nature, life, and safety... an ideal color for food or drink. The Heineken label is green and the beer is sold worldwide in a refreshing green bottle. The standard Heineken bottle is the 33 cl. one. The smallest Heineken bottle, with a capacity of 25 cl., is sold in Puerto Rico, for example. In this hot country, beer drinkers do not want their Heineken beer to become warm. A small bottle can be drunk quickly and also looks charming. Argentina and Chile are countries in the world in which Heineken beer is sold in 1-liter bottles. Heineken cans of beer are also produced in the green house style color.

It is only in the Netherlands that Heineken is sold in a brown bottle, as a result of an agreement among Dutch brewers to work with a uniform brown returnable bottle. Given that Heineken in the Netherlands is positioned differently – the beer is sold in the standard segment – the brewery has been able to accept the fact that 'Dutch' Heineken has a different appearance. Tourists who visit the Netherlands are the lucky ones since they can enjoy a modestly priced premium beer. In order to nevertheless give Heineken in the Netherlands that green family feeling, a green long-neck bottle has been on the market since 1996. This special bottle is very popular among young beer drinkers who visit trendy bars and discos.

Santé

Heineken started emphasizing the color green more and more. In 1999, the Netherlands and Greece were the last two countries to replace the yellow crates with green ones. From then on, the 4.6 million new green crates in the Netherlands bore the entire Heineken logo: star, stripe and hop plant. 'The Netherlands is getting greener' was the new crate's introduction campaign. In Spain, the color green was highlighted most in the campaign: Think Green. In one of Heineken's Spanish commercials, the wolf leaves Little Red Riding Hood alone when he sees the hunter pass by with a green bottle of Heineken.... The concept of 'Think Green' is also used in Argentina. The world is getting greener.

WORLDLY-WISE

14.8

Today, the global beer market is dominated by pilsner. The various brands are all based on the same traditional brewing process, meaning there are only limited differences in quality. In the beer world, brand images and different drinking habits are all important. Beer is a culture-related product. In southern Europe, beer is primarily drunk for its thirst-quenching character and principally at mealtimes. In northern and central Europe, beer is regarded mainly as a sociable drink with a social and relaxation function. In New-Zealand and Australia, beer is regarded more as a product for tough guys who play rugby and football. Chinese people drink beer during meals from a half-liter bottle shared by others. Spanish people drink a couple of glasses of beer after work in the bar on the corner. Germans drink beer at various times of the day. Dutch people drink beer in the evenings while watching television. Brazilians drink beer primarily at parties, while the Irish drink beer until closing time.

The Heineken brand is consistently positioned in the premium segment of various markets. In addition to regulations governing the logo and recipe, close coordination also takes place with regard to price levels, advertising concepts and sponsoring. This does not mean that every country has the same media campaigns or commercials. That would be far from the truth. The

Cheers

way in which the brewery positions Heineken as a luxury beer differs per culture. 'Think global, act local' is the philosophy. In its commercials, Heineken emphasizes values such as authenticity, quality, integrity, enjoyment and humor. The target group on which the company focuses consists of young, well-educated beer drinkers aged between 20 and 35 who are brand-conscious, worldly-wise and dynamic and from an urban environment. Market research in a variety of countries has shown that Heineken drinkers interpret the brand's premium image identically. Heineken is regarded as the brand with the most international image and as a pilsner with the best taste to be drunk by beer lovers. Heineken has prestige without being so exclusive that it is out of everyone's reach. Simply delicious!

RESPECT

In 1960, the brewery changed the words 'Heineken's beer' to 'Heineken beer' and from that moment, the company and brand could be referred to by a single name. The worldwide success meant that all attention was focused on the Heineken brand and the brewery became secondary to the brand. The company's image was reduced to the 9 centimeter high and 7 centimeter wide Heineken label.

During the last 20 years, however, consumers increasingly wanted to find out more about the face behind the brand. Who is brewing this beer? What sort of company is it? What do they stand for? How does the company deal with social issues and the environment? The Heineken brewery started presenting itself more actively and started thinking about its social responsibility. Alcohol abuse, for example, is not beneficial to anyone and the brewery therefore introduced a strict alcohol policy. Consumers were urged to take responsibility and drink alcohol in moderation. However, the brewery's social responsibility went a great deal further. All over the world, Heineken strives to minimize environmental damage by the brewing process, takes account of the wishes of governments and consumers, offers prospects and opportunities to its staff, takes an honest and careful approach to the quality of its products and the emotional power of the various different brands.

The core message the brewery wanted to purvey was respect for quality, people and customers. What is interesting is that these values correspond to those of the brand. This is no coincidence, of course. The worldwide presence of the brand and company can only be appreciated if there is respect for different societies and cultures. The Heineken world is a world of people.

ENJOYMENT

Heineken believes in strong brands. More than any other international brewer, Heineken invests in advertising, promotions and sponsoring. The Heineken brand is an eye-catching feature at a lot of prominent sports events.

While golf was originally the focus of the sponsorship policy, tennis and rugby tournaments have for some years now found a place in the sponsorship policy. Among other events, Heineken sponsors the US Open, the Australian Open, the Davis Cup, the Heineken Shanghai Open, China's first international tennis tournament, and the Heineken Challenger, the ATP tennis tournament in Ho Chi Minh City. As of 1999, Heineken has also been the main sponsor of the European Rugby Tournament. A phenomenon on a smaller scale is the sponsoring of the annual regatta on the Caribbean island of Saint Martin.

Bringing pleasure to people's lives is one of Heineken's core values. The expectation is that consumers will start spending their scarce free time more on special events and experiences. The brewery is therefore becoming more and more active in the field of event marketing. Heineken wants to be present wherever people come together, wherever emotions play a role and wherever unique experiences are acquired and shared. Heineken has gained an international association with large-scale music festivals: The Red Star Concert in the United States, Heineken Music Horizon in Hong Kong and Heineken NightLive in the Netherlands, Spain and Switzerland and the Heineken Jammin' Festival on the Imola race circuit in Italy. There has been a successful relationship between Heineken and jazz for many years in Puerto Rico, the Dominican Republic, France, Switzerland as well as the Netherlands.

Beer is an emotional product. You have to appeal to consumers' hearts. Brands that only offer status or safety will run into difficulties. Today's consumers have greater self-confidence and therefore less of a need for a brand's symbols. Brands are judged more and more on their total image, which encompasses taste, raw materials, recipe, packaging, company, respect and, last but not least, perception. Consumers no longer allow themselves to be dictated to and brands have to be prepared to enter into a dialogue. Heineken's greatest strength is its name. Heineken heads the European list of best-known brands and is the premium beer valued most highly at an international level. A name like this is worth its weight in gold.

Salud

A STAR FOREVER

14.12

What is it that transforms a brand into a global star? Naturally, the brand's character is a major factor, but at the end of the day it is the consumer's taste that decides. The power of the Heineken brand is the power of an honest, delicious, top-quality pilsner. The brand's magic and beer drinkers' preferences mean that Heineken has all it takes to develop into the first global beer brand. Heineken. A star forever.

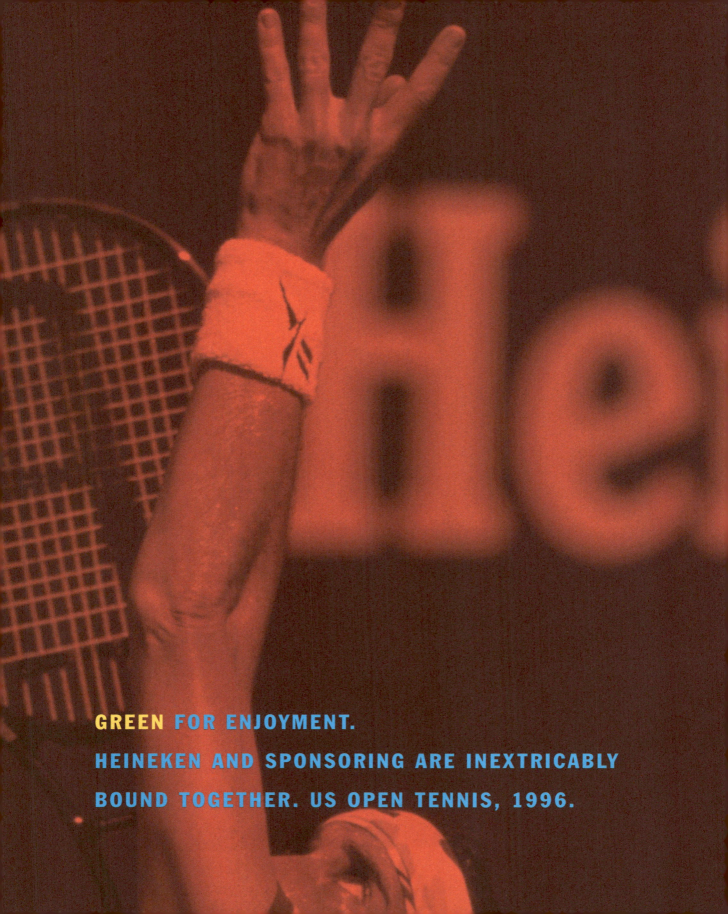

A TRADITION SINCE THE 19TH CENTURY AND STILL AS POTENT TODAY: THE HEINEKEN BRAND. CONSUMERS FROM ALL ERAS KEEP THE BRAND CONTEMPORARY.

THE HEINEKEN WORLD IS A WORLD OF PEOPLE. HEINEKEN BRINGS PLEASURE. HEINEKEN ADDS COLOR TO LIFE. ISN'T THAT MAGIC?

HEINEKEN

MEMBERS OF THE BOARD OF
HEINEKEN NV

G.A. Heineken / 1864-1893

W. Feltmann jr / 1873-1897

J.G. van Gendt / 1873-1876

H.F. Hoyer / 1873-1887

H.P.C. de Balbian / 1890-1898

D.J.A. Petersen / 1894-1904

A. Berkemeier / 1898-1914

G. Dalmeyer / 1898-1917

H.P. Heineken / 1914-1940

J.Th. Berkemeier / 1914-1941

Ch.P.H. Ras / 1916-1934

A.W. Hoette / 1922-1939

D.U. Stikker / 1935-1948

J.M. Honig / 1940-1960

Jhr. P.R. Feith / 1941-1966

J.A. Emmens / 1944-1955

M.H. Damme / 1944-1945

B. ter Haar / 1952-1957

Jhr. O.A.E.E.L Wittert van Hoogland / 1957-1971

J.H. Land / 1959-1963

J.P. Ton / 1963-1976

A.H. Heineken / 1964-1989

E.J. Egberts / 1968-1970

R. van Marwijk Kooy / 1968-1977

J. van der Werf / 1969-1988

G. van Schaik / 1974-1993

R. van de Vijver / 1976-1991

H.F.M. Coebergh / 1983-1994

A. Oostra / 1988-1990

J.H. Drost / 1989-1998

K. Vuursteen / 1991-

L. Schouten / 1991-1993

A. Ruys / 1993-

S.W.W. Lubsen / 1995-

M.J. Bolland / 2001-

J.F.M.L. van Boxmeer / 2001-

A HISTORY AT A GLANCE

1592 / Brewer's widow Weyntgen Elberts founds a brewery in the heart of Amsterdam under the name De Hooiberg.

1864 / On February 15, Gerard Adriaan Heineken buys brewery De Hooiberg and Heineken & Co. starts selling various types of beer, both in the Netherlands and abroad.

1868 / A new brewery is taken into use on the Stadhouderskade in Amsterdam. This brewery operated until 1988, when production is transferred to the brewery in Zoeterwoude, the Netherlands.

1873 / On January 11, 'Heineken's Bierbrouwerij Maatschappij NV' (HBM) is established.

1874 / The new Heineken brewery on the Crooswijkse Singel in Rotterdam is taken into use. This brewery closed 100 years later, in 1974. Production is transferred to the breweries in Zoeterwoude and 's-Hertogenbosch, the Netherlands.

1884 / The green Heineken label is registered as a trademark in many countries. The five-pointed Heineken star makes its first appearance on the label.

1886 / Dr. H. Elion creates the famous Heineken 'A'-yeast.

1889 / At the World Exhibition in Paris, Heineken beer is awarded the gold medal of honor.

1909 / The first collective labor agreement for the workers at the brewery in Rotterdam is concluded: the working hours are set at 54 hours a week, with four days holiday a year.

1923 / To mark its 50th anniversary, Heineken sets up a pension scheme for its employees.

1927 / Heineken acquires an interest in the brewery Brasserie Leopold in Brussels, its first foreign shareholding. In 1964 the interest is sold.

1927 / Queen Wilhelmina of the Netherlands grants Heineken a license to bear the Royal Crest and use the designation 'By Royal Appointment'.

1931 / Together with the company Fraser & Neave of Singapore, on April 15 Heineken sets up Malayan Breweries Limited to operate a brewery in Singapore. This joint venture still exists, under the name Asia Pacific Breweries, and runs brewing operations in China, Vietnam, Cambodia, Thailand, Papua New Guinea and New Zealand.

1932 / Heineken takes a research brewery into use; it is still one of the few breweries in the world with such an extensive research plant.

1933 / Following the end of Prohibition, Heineken is the first foreign brewer to set foot in America, on April 11.

1935 / Heineken acquires interests in breweries in Angola, Egypt, Morocco and the former Dutch East Indies, French Indochina, the Belgian Congo and Palestine. This marks the beginning of the company's worldwide expansion.

1937 / The remaining shares in the 'Nederlandsch-Indische Bierbrouwerijen' in Surabaya are acquired. In December, this brewery launches a locally brewed Heineken beer on the market. A first, as it is the first time Heineken beer is brewed outside of the Netherlands.

1938 / An interest is acquired in the distillery 'Distilleerderij en Likeurstokerij P. Hoppe' in Amsterdam. The remaining shares are acquired during the 1960s. In 1970, Heineken reinforces its position in the spirits sector by taking a 50-percent stake in 'Coebergh's Verenigde Distilleerderijen'. In 1971, the remaining shares are acquired and Heineken takes over the Bokma company.

1938 / The first annual report is published for the financial year 1936-1937. The financial year runs from October 1 through September 30. From 1980, the financial year is brought into line with the calendar year.

1939 / On January 16, Heineken is floated on the Amsterdam Stock Exchange.

1940 / The outbreak of the World War II in the Netherlands puts a temporary end to exports of Heineken beer from the Netherlands.

1941 / Together with Fraser & Neave, Heineken takes over the local ABC brewery and its Anchor brand in Singapore.

1945 / Leo van Munching is made exclusive importer of Heineken in the United States.

1946 / A minority stake is acquired in Nigerian Breweries Limited, and in 1949 a brewery is opened in Lagos. During the 1950s and 1960s, Heineken is involved in the construction of a variety of breweries throughout West Africa.

1947 / The logo undergoes a significant facelift: 'HEINEKEN'S Bier' becomes 'Heineken's Bier'. In 1951, the laughing e's appear in the name 'Heineken's'. In 1960, 'Heineken's' is changed to 'Heineken'.

1948 / On June 1, Heineken starts selling bottled beer in stores in the Netherlands.

1951 / A 50-percent stake is acquired in soft-drinks manufacturer Vrumona in the Dutch town of Bunnik. In 1968, the remaining shares are acquired.

1955 / Malayan Breweries Limited takes a shareholding in the South Pacific Brewery in Papua New Guinea.

1955 / A 50-percent stake is acquired in 'Mouterij' (malting plant) Albert in Wijnegem, Belgium. In 1971, this becomes 100-percent ownership.

1957 / The Indonesian government takes control of the Heineken brewery in Surabaya. Heineken resumes operations in 1967. The name of the brewery is changed to Perusahaan Bir Bintang. From 1981, expansion of activities prompts a further change, to Multi Bintang Indonesia.

1958 / In the Netherlands, a third brewery is opened, on September 4 in the town of 's-Hertogenbosch.

1960 / A 6-percent stake is acquired in the Italian Cisalpina concern, with Dreher as its dominant brand. This shareholding is gradually increased, to 100 percent in 1980. Following the takeover in 1995 of Interbrew Italia and of Birra Moretti in 1996, Heineken becomes market leader in Italy.

1960 / Heineken reaches a milestone in the United States: in one year, the company sells more than 1 million cases of 24 bottles, a total of 85,000 hectoliters.

1961 / On October 1, Heineken enters into a partnership with Whitbread & Co. This English brewery group is put in charge of the distribution and sale of Heineken beer in the United Kingdom. In 1969, a license agreement for the local brewing of Heineken beer is concluded.

1962 / A stake is acquired in Brasserie Lorraine in Fort-de-France, Martinique.

1962 / In Kuala Lumpur, Malaysia, a new brewery is taken into use.

1963 / The Heineken Foundation, aimed at promoting science and culture, is set up on February 6 and introduces the Dr. H.P. Heineken Prize for Biochemistry and Biophysics, which is awarded for the first time in 1964. In 1988, the Alfred Heineken Funds Foundation presents the Dr. A.H. Heineken Prize for Art for the first time. These are followed in 1989 by the Prize for Medicine, and in 1990 for Historical Science and Environmental Sciences. The Heineken Prizes are awarded every two years at a special session of the Royal Netherlands Academy of Arts and Sciences.

1968 / On August 26, Heineken takes over Amstel. This takeover gives Heineken stakes in a number of foreign breweries associated with Amstel in Suriname, Curaçao, Jordan, the Lebanon, Greece and Madagascar. A number of such stakes were subsequently sold, either partially or in full.

1971 / From January 1, Heineken acquires a direct participating interest in the Belgian Interbra group, which has various breweries in Central Africa.

1972 / A majority stake is acquired in the French brewery group Alsacienne de Brasserie. This marks the beginning of Heineken's expansion in France and Europe. In 1979, the brewery's interest is expanded to 100 percent. In 1980, the name is changed to Heineken France.

1972 / The name 'Heineken's Bierbrouwerij Maatschappij NV' is changed to 'Heineken NV'.

1973 / In the United States, Heineken achieves the status of number 1 imported beer brand.

1974 / The position in New Caledonia is reinforced by the takeover of a local brewery. This leads to the creation of Grande Brasserie de Nouvelle Calédonie.

1974 / A stake is acquired in the National Brewing Company on the island of Trinidad, and taken over in turn in 1991 by the brewing corporation of the Caribbean Development Company (CDC). In exchange, Heineken acquires a 20-percent stake in CDC.

1974 / For the first time, a 'social annual report' is produced, for the financial year 1973-1974.

1975 / On April 18, the new brewery in Zoeterwoude, the Netherlands, is officially opened. It is the largest, most modern brewery in Europe at that time.

1978 / In Lagos, Nigeria, Heineken sets up a training school giving technical training to local personnel. In 1987, a training school is opened in Kinshasa, former Zaire.

1979 / 'Heineken Nederland' incorporates its spirits and wine activities into a new distillery annex grain plant in Zoetermeer, under the name 'Gedistilleerd en Wijngroep Nederland' (Spirits and Wine Group Netherlands). In 1989, this company merges with 'Bols Nederland'. Heineken and Bols each take a 50-percent stake in the ensuing joint venture, Bols Benelux. In 1994, Heineken sells its 50-percent stake to Royal Bols Wessanen.

1980 / Takeover of 'Mouterij Ruisbroek', Belgium.

1980 / Leo van Munching jr takes charge of Van Munching & Co.

1980 / Amstel Light is introduced on the American market and within a few years is the number 1 in the light import segment.

1982 / Heineken takes a majority stake in the Bralima breweries in Central Africa. The major beer brand is Primus.

1982 / Takeover of Brewery De Ridder in Maastricht, the Netherlands.

1982 / The Amstel Brewery on the Mauritskade in Amsterdam closes.

1982 / Together with the other Dutch producers and importers of beers, wines and spirits, Heineken sets up STIVA (Foundation for Responsible Alcohol Consumption), aimed at reducing alcohol abuse and promoting responsible alcohol consumption.

In 1990, Heineken is one of the initiators of 'The Amsterdam Group', an alliance of European producers of beers, wines and spirits, with the aim of combating the problems of irresponsible alcohol use and the promotion of responsible alcohol use, together with government bodies and other organizations.

1983 / Takeover of the Murphy's Brewery in Cork, Ireland.

1983 / A minority stake is acquired in the Brazilian brewery group Kaiser.

1984 / Heineken France and Brasseries et Glacières Internationales (BGI) – made up of the breweries UDB and Pelforth – combine their brewing interests in the new company Sogebra. This enables Heineken to increase its market share in France to 25 percent. Heineken acquires 51 percent of the shares. In 1988, Heineken buys out BGI and Sogebra becomes a full Heineken subsidiary.

1984 / A stake of 36.7 percent is acquired in Spanish brewery group El Aguila. This interest is gradually increased to 71.3 percent. The takeover of Cruzcampo in 1999 makes Heineken España market leader in Spain.

1984 / A 15-percent stake is acquired in Quilmes International, a concern with brewing, malting and soft drinks interests in Argentina, Uruguay and Paraguay.

1984 / A stake of 60 percent is acquired in a holding company that has an 80-percent stake in Commonwealth Breweries, newly constructed on the Bahamas.

1984 / A stake of 8.5 percent is acquired in Cerveceria Bohemia in the Dominican Republic. Along with the co-shareholder in this company, a year later Heineken acquires a stake in Cerveceria Nacional Dominicana, the largest brewery in the Dominican Republic.

1984 / A 10.5-percent stake is acquired in Brasserie Nationale d'Haïti.

1984 / A 34-percent stake is acquired in Internationale Brasserie in Cameroun.

1984 / A majority shareholding is acquired in Brasseries et Limonaderies du Burundi.

1984 / Heineken starts the first ever Alcohol and Work program. During the 1990s, this is further expanded and internationalized under the name Cool@Work.

1985 / Takeover of the brewery and malting plant of Breweries of Greece in Patras, Greece.

1985 / A 51-percent stake is acquired in Brasseries de Bourbon on Ile de la Réunion.

1985 / The brewery in Zoeterwoude, the Netherlands, takes its own total energy plant into use, fulfilling a considerable share of its electricity requirement.

1986 / A new joint venture is concluded with Fraser & Neave in Singapore, aimed at active development of beer markets in Asia.

1988 / In the form of Asia Pacific Breweries, a stake is acquired in the Shanghai Mila brewery in Shanghai, China. This marks Heineken's first step into the important Chinese market.

1988 / Introduction of the non-alcoholic beer Buckler in a number of European countries.

1989 / Takeover of the Royal Brand Brewery in Wijlre, the Netherlands.

1989 / Heineken is closely involved in the establishment of the European Recovery and Recycling Association in Brussels, aimed at promoting the collection and responsible re-use of packaging materials.

1989 / In Kinshasa, former Zaire, a medical center attached to the brewery is opened. Ten years later, Heineken opens an extensive medical clinic in the city. The medical care provided by Heineken in Africa covers all employees and their families, a total of some 62,000 people.

1990 / In Singapore, a new, highly advanced brewery is taken into use. The old Tiger and Anchor breweries are closed.

1991 / The American import organization VMCo is taken over on February 19. On January 1, 1995, the name is changed to Heineken USA.

1991 / An interest is acquired in the Magnum Group with Asia Pacific Breweries, the owners of Dominion Breweries, giving Heineken a springboard in New Zealand. In 1993, the majority of the shares is obtained.

1991 / A 50.3-percent stake is acquired in the brewery Komáromi Sörgyár in Komárom, Hungary. Following the fall of the Berlin Wall in 1989, this marks Heineken's first interest in Eastern Europe. The remaining shares are acquired in 1994.

1993 / A stake of 52.3 percent is acquired in the Swiss holding company 'Brauerei Haldengut', which holds the majority of shares in Calanda Haldengut. In 1999, this becomes 100-percent ownership.

1993 / Brasseries du Cameroun takes over International Brasserie. Heineken had a stake in International Brasserie and therefore acquires an 8.8-percent shareholding in Brasseries du Cameroun.

1993 / Official opening on November 19 of the Vietnam Brewery in Ho Chi Minh City, Vietnam.

1994 / Heineken subsidiary Brasserie de Brazzaville in Congo merges with local brewery and soft drinks company SCBK. Heineken has a 50-percent stake in this new company, Brasseries du Congo.

1994 / A stake of 24.9 percent is acquired in the Zywiec brewery in Poland. In 1998, Zywiec merges with the biggest Polish brewing group, Brewpole. Heineken has a majority shareholding in the new joint venture, Zywiec.

1994 / A stake of 39.5 percent is taken in the Zagorka brewery in Stara Zagorka, Bulgaria. In 1997, the brewery's position in Bulgaria is further strengthened by the acquisition of a 30.1-percent stake in the Ariana brewery in Sofia.

1995 / A 66-percent stake is taken in the brewery and malting plant Zlatý Bažant in Hurbanovo, Slovakia. Heineken's position in Slovakia steadily improves during subsequent years: in 1997, a shareholding of 49 percent is acquired in brewery and malting plant Karšay in Nitra, and in 1999 a 51-percent stake is obtained in the Martiner and Gemer breweries.

1995 / The new brewery Thai Asia Pacific Brewery in Bangkok, Thailand, is finished and starts brewing Heineken beer.

1995 / The first Heineken International Business Course is organized. Heineken presents itself as an international employer offering exciting international career perspectives to talented managers.

1995 / 'Heineken Nederland' issues an environment report for 1994. In November 2000, the first environment report is issued for 1998-1999 in Europe.

1996 / In France, the Elzasser Fischer group and its subsidiary Société Adelshoffen are acquired, as well as a 66-percent stake in Groupe Saint-Arnould, a beer brewery, wine producer and distributor in northern France. This strengthens Heineken's position as number 2 on the French beer market.

1996 / The new Cambodia Brewery in Phnom Penh, Cambodia, officially opens in November.

1997 / The company's position in Ghana is reinforced by the acquisition of a 90-percent stake in ABC Brewery in Accra. Heineken already had a majority shareholding in the Kumasi Brewery in Ghana. In 1998, the two breweries merge under the name Ghana Breweries Ltd.

1997 / The Hainan Asia Pacific Brewery – a newly constructed brewery in the province of Hainan, China – becomes operational.

1997 / A new Multi Bintang brewery is taken into use in Sampang Agung, Indonesia, to replace Heineken's first Asian brewery, in Surabaya.

1998 / A 25.2-percent stake is acquired in the Pivara breweries in Skopje, Macedonia.

1998 / On October 1, 'Heye-Glas Nederland', a cooperation between Hermann Heye Glasswerke and Heineken, opens a glass factory in Moerdijk, the Netherlands, to produce the green export bottles.

1998 / The Heineken University opens, a training institute for the company's employees.

1999 / An 18-percent stake is acquired in Tempo Beer Industry in Israel.

1999 / A stake of 28 percent is taken in brewery Dinal LLP, Kazakhstan.

1999 / The Heineken brand is elected 'Brand of the Century' in the Netherlands.

1999 / Alfred Henry Heineken is lauded as 'Advertiser of the Century' in the Netherlands.

2000 / On June 9, Heineken receives the King William I Award for Dutch Entrepreneurs. This prestigious prize is awarded once every two years to a large Dutch company that has distinguished itself through good business sense and making a major contribution to the economy, employment, welfare and the reputation of Dutch commerce.

May 22, 2001 / Festive opening of the Heineken Experience in the former brewery on the Stadhouderskade in Amsterdam. To honor this event, Heineken NV presents you with the book 'The Magic of Heineken'.

PHOTO CREDITS

Unless stated otherwise, all photographs and illustrations are from the Heineken NV collection.

TEXT ILLUSTRATIONS

Algemeen Hollands Fotopersbureau / Stichting FotoAnoniem: 10.5

Lood van Bennekom / Nederlands Fotoarchief: 6.18

Bierreclamemuseum Breda: 4.9, 4.10, 4.11, 4.14, 7.16 (center), 9.14

Egidius van Dun / Stichting FotoAnoniem: 10.7, 10.12

Private collection Alfred Heineken: 1.4, 1.5, 9.4, 9.5, 9.6, 9.8, 9.9 (top), 9.12, 9.15, 9.22, 9.27, 9.28

Maritime Museum Rotterdam Collection: 6.4

Amsterdam Municipal Archive: 1.8, 8.12, 10.6

Rotterdam Municipal Archive: 7.4, 9.23

Eppo Notenboom: 12.7

Cas Oorthuys / Nederlands Fotoarchief: 10.11

Dieter Schütte: 12.8

Sky Pictures: 12.6

Hans Spies / Stichting FotoAnoniem: 3.15

Private collection Jan Stabij: 2.8, 7.6, 7.16 (right)

Eddy van der Veen / Stichting FotoAnoniem: 5.10

Peter van der Velde: 11.8, 11.9, 11.10, 11.12, 11.15, 11.17

Peter Venema: 10.16, 13.6 (top)

Vereenigde Fotobureaux / Stichting FotoAnoniem: 3.13, 3.14

Bram Wisman / Maria Austria Institute: 7.9

COVER / Heineken, 2001.

ENDPAPER / Photograph Dieter Schütte, 1999.

PRELIMINARY PAGES / Poster, 'HEINEKEN'S Bier. Biedt u het beste', circa 1930. Show card for storekeepers, 'Heineken's ook bij U thuis!', circa 1951. Poster, 'Heineken's bier! Smaak en kwaliteit als voor de oorlog', 1947. Poster, 'Bij zomer hoort Heineken', circa 1960. Poster, circa 1955. Poster, 'Heineken het meest getapt!', circa 1960. Advertising sign from the international campaign 'There is happiness in Heineken', circa 1960. Poster, also known as 'Charlie', by the Dutch designer Frans Mettes, 1951. Gerard Adriaan Heineken. Alfred Henry Heineken. HBM logo. Heineken logo. Heineken bottle, 1900. Heineken bottle, 2000.

CHAPTER 1 / Nieuwezijds Kolk in Amsterdam, circa 1900. Bernard Eilers / Collection Amsterdam Municipal Archive. Heineken Exhibition at the World Fair in Paris, 1889. Self-portrait by Rembrandt van Rijn with his wife Saskia, 1636. Collection Staatliche Kunstsammlungen Dresden. Portrait of the young Gerard Adriaan Heineken. Detail of an undecorated beer glass. Indo-Australian Pieridae and Papilionidae in the Entomological Museum in Amsterdam. Photograph Paul Huf, 1984. Waiters in Rotterdam, circa 1900. Collection Rotterdam Municipal Archive. The attic of the millhouse at the old brewery on the Stadhouderskade in Amsterdam, converted into a reception area. Photograph Peter Venema, 1999. Passion. Photograph Fee Arnold, 2000.

CHAPTER 2 / The Coolsingel in Rotterdam, circa 1898. Collection Rotterdam Municipal Archive. A Heineken consumer in 1900. The Rotterdam brewery bowling club, 1887. Gentlemen in Amsterdam, circa 1893. Jacob Olie / Collection Amsterdam Municipal Archive. Workers at the Van Diemenstraat in Amsterdam, 1897. George Hendrik Breitner / Collection of the Rijksbureau voor Kunsthistorische Documentatie, The Hague. The export label, registered in 1884. Starry night. Stone. Two women in New York. Photograph Thomas Manneke, 1997. Daring. Photograph Fee Arnold, 2000.

CHAPTER 3 / Pont Alexandre III on the Seine in Paris, circa 1890. Collection Rijksmuseum Amsterdam. Painters' workshop in the Rotterdam brewery, 1917. Brewery laboratory in Rotterdam, 1900. Yeast cells. Brewing hall of the brewery in 's-Hertogenbosch, the Netherlands. State portrait of Queen Wilhelmina and Prince Hendrik of the Netherlands, 1901. Spaarnestad Fotoarchief. Attention. Photograph Fee Arnold, 2000.

CHAPTER 4 / Brussels 1935. Spaarnestad Fotoarchief. HBM management and personnel on the football field, circa 1935. The choir of the Royal Brand Brewery in Wijlre, the Netherlands. Photograph Peter Venema, 2000. Portrait of Dr. H.P. Heineken. Sky with cloud in Provence, France. Photograph Peter Venema, 2000. Slide in the swimming pool. Benelux Press. Female portrait. Benelux Press. Social. Photograph Fee Arnold, 2000.

CHAPTER 5 / View of Singapore from the Elgin Bridge, circa 1890. G.R. Lambert & Co / Collection of the Wereldmuseum Rotterdam. Building work at the brewery in Surabaya, the Dutch East Indies, now Indonesia, 1938. The 'retourschip Pieter en Paul' belonging to the Amsterdam Chamber of the Dutch East Indies Company on the river IJ close to Amsterdam, painting by Abraham Storck, 1698. Collection of the Nederlands Scheepvaartmuseum Amsterdam. Dutch colonists on the Indonesian island of Java, 1899. W. Koenecke / Collection of the Wereldmuseum Rotterdam. •'Heineken's Bier', brewed in the Dutch East Indies. •Detail of a brew kettle in the brewing hall of the old brewery on the Stadhouderskade in Amsterdam. Photograph Peter Venema, 2000. •Master brewer in the brewing hall of the brewery in 's-Hertogenbosch, the Netherlands, 1994. •Smoking volcano in Alaska, photographed at dusk. Fotostock. •Barong and Kriss dance on the Indonesian island of Bali. Benelux Press. •Tiger. Benelux Press. •World class. Photograph Fee Arnold, 2000.

CHAPTER 6 / •Wall Street in New York, with the Trinity Church in the background and on the right the statue of George Washington, 1929. Spaarnestad Fotoarchief. •Loading barrels and crates of Heineken beer in the Port of Rotterdam onto the ship the S.S. Statendam bound for New York, March 1933. •View of New York with the Statue of Liberty in the foreground. Benelux Press. •The bottling line at the brewery in 's-Hertogenbosch, the Netherlands, 1998. •Red and yellow tulips in the bulb fields near De Zilk, the Netherlands. Photograph Frans Lemmens, 1997. •Statue of Liberty in New York. Image from Heineken Travel Promotion, a campaign from 1998 celebrating 125 years of the Heineken brand. •Cheerleaders. Photograph Peter Venema, 2000. •Fair in Arnhem, the Netherlands. Photograph Peter Venema, 2000. •Status. Photograph Fee Arnold, 2000.

CHAPTER 7 / •The Oude Gracht close to the St. Jans Bridge in Utrecht, the Netherlands, 1947. Collection of Het Utrechts Archief. •The bottling line at the brewery in Amsterdam. Photograph Paul Huf, 1951. •Image from the first ever advertising film for Heineken shown on the Dutch television, 1968. •Refrigerator, 1956. Spaarnestad Fotoarchief. •Product shots of an empty beer glass. Photograph Arnoud Kor, 2000. •The H in Heineken. •Product shot of full beer glasses. Photograph Arnoud Kor, 2000. •The Beatles during their concert in Blokker, the Netherlands, on June 6, 1964. Bob van Dam / Nederlands Fotoarchief. •Elvis Costello during the Heineken NightLive in Ahoy, Rotterdam. Photograph Alexis Deenen, 1999. •Authority. Photograph Fee Arnold, 2000.

CHAPTER 8 / •Marina in Lagos, circa 1955. Camera Press / ABC Press. •Dock workers in Accra, Ghana, 1953. •Belgian Congo, 1959. Cas Oorthuys / Nederlands Fotoarchief. •Market in Togo, Africa. Benelux Press. •Bottle washing machine in the brewery in Kumasi, Ghana, 1960. •Wall made from Worldbottles (Wobo) in the old brewery on the Stadhouderskade in Amsterdam. Photograph Peter Venema, 2000. •Participants on a course at the Heineken University for Managers of Heineken breweries from all over the world. Photograph Peter Venema, 2000. •Detail of an advertisement for Primus, Zaire, 1988. •High-five in Cape Town, South Africa. Photograph Ingmar Swalue, 1997. •Respect. Photograph Fee Arnold, 2000.

CHAPTER 9 / Koningin Wilhelminaboulevard in Noordwijk, the Netherlands, 1951. Published by Lokaal Boek / Stichting FotoAnoniem. Friesland, 1958. Private collection Alfred Heineken. Amsterdam, 1945. Private collection Alfred Heineken. Washington D.C., 1947. Private collection Alfred Heineken. Alfred Heineken in his office on the Weteringplantsoen in Amsterdam. Photograph Paul Huf, 1951. Lettering on the facade of the old brewery on the Stadhouderskade in Amsterdam. Photograph Peter Venema, 2000. Portrait of Alfred Heineken, 1958. Private collection Alfred Heineken. Detail of a Heineken label with drops of condensation. Outdoor advertising in Hong Kong, 1999. Portrait of Alfred Heineken in Antibes, France, 1969. Private collection Alfred Heineken. Kite. Photograph Peter Venema, 2000. Portrait of Alfred Heineken in St. Moritz, Switzerland, with Corviglia Ski Club tie, 1984. Private collection Alfred Heineken. Portrait gallery of the Chairs of the Board of Heineken NV. Photograph Peter Venema, 2000. Portrait of Alfred Heineken. Photograph Mathieu Jacobs, 2000. Graffiti in Arnhem, the Netherlands, by Sebastiaan Terhorst. Photograph Peter Venema, 2001. Personality. Photograph Fee Arnold, 2000.

CHAPTER 10 / Loenen aan de Vecht, the Netherlands, on the right the country estate Oud-Over, 1965. Collection of Het Utrechts Archief. Recording a corporate film in the Amstel brewery in Amsterdam, 1957. Collection of the Nationaal Foto Persbureau. Advertisement for Amstel beer from the 1950s. Detail of a television picture. A still from the Amstel commercial Football with Three Friends, 2000. Amstel football game, available during the special sales campaign accompanying the European Football Championships in 2000. Photograph Peter Venema, 2000. Football match from the UEFA Champions League. Photograph Matthew Ashton, 2000. Amstel beer mats. Jan Ullrich ascending the Joux Plane in the Tour de France 2000. John Pierce / Photosport International. In-line skating in Santa Monica, the United States. Benelux Press. Friendship. Photograph Fee Arnold, 2000.

CHAPTER 11 / Strasbourg, with the towers of Ponts-Couverts in the foreground. Zefa Visual Media. Café-restaurant De Kroon in Amsterdam, 1991. Collection Amsterdam Municipal Archive. Café Los Gabrieles in Madrid, 1994. A. Soldeville / Ana / ABC Press. Playing darts in the pub, 1992. Marcel Malherbe / Hollandse Hoogte. Thessaloniki, 1998. F. Zanettini / Laif / Hollandse Hoogte. Switzerland, 1991. M. Nascimento / Ana / ABC Press. Beer brands brewed under Heineken supervision in various European countries. Satellite photo of Europe. Fotostock. Heineken beer. Venice, 1992. Marleen Daniëls / Hollandse Hoogte. Restaurant La Coupole in Paris, 1999. Peter Hilz / Hollandse Hoogte. Consistency. Photograph Fee Arnold, 2000.

CHAPTER 12 / •Nanjing Lu, Nanking Road, in Shanghai. Fotostock. •Erecting a Heineken billboard on the island of Curaçao. Photograph Paul Pet, 1991. •Young people having fun. James McEntee / Stone. •Crown cap of the green Heineken bottle. •Young couple in Las Vegas, the United States. Sean Murphy / Stone. •Ambition. Photograph Fee Arnold, 2000.

CHAPTER 13 / •Cork, with St. Finbarr's Cathedral in the background. Zefa Visual Media. •Benedictine monk Maurice Beaugrand in the St. Andries abbey in Zevenkerken, Belgium. Photograph Robin Lutz, 1990. •Sunflower. FontShop. •Spring. Photograph Frederik de Wal, 1999. •Open fire. Photograph Peter Venema, 2000. •Experience. Photograph Fee Arnold, 2000.

CHAPTER 14 / •Amsterdam, with the 'Zuiderkerk' in the background, viewed from the Groenburgwal. Benelux Press. •Tennis at the US Open. Photograph Shaun Botterill, 1996. •Advertisement for the music event Heineken Crossover Award, 1994. •Image from the Swiss advertising campaign Feel the Night, 1988-1998. •Sarah Bettens of the Belgian band K's Choice during the Heineken NightLive in Ahoy, Rotterdam. Photograph Alexis Deenen, 1999. •Appreciative audience. Photograph Rico D'Rozario, 1998. •Kiss. Photograph Arnoud Kor, 2001. •The birth of Venus, painting by Sandro Botticelli, in Galleria degli Uffizi in Florence. Benelux Press. •Heineken consumer. Photograph Peter Venema, 2001. •Advertisement. Heineken Summer 1997. •Surfer in the sea. Fotostock. •Product shot. Photograph Rien Bazen, 1991. •Drinking moment. Photograph Arnoud Kor, 2001. •Heineken. Photograph Fee Arnold, 2000.

APPENDIX / •Image from a magazine campaign for various local markets, 2000. •Product shot. Photograph Pieter Boer, 1996. •Product shot. •Product shot. Photograph Jaap Vliegenthart, 1996. •Product shot. •Product shot. Photograph Jaap Vliegenthart, 1993. •Product shot. Photograph Jaap Vliegenthart, 1993. •Product shot. Photograph Pieter Boer, 1993.

THE MAGIC OF HEINEKEN

2001 marks the beginning of the magic of Heineken in the 21st century. We have presented the story of the Heineken family, the brand and the company to you with deserving pride. We too find it an exceptional story.

Heineken NV hopes that this book has taken you on an equally marvelous journey. As all books, so this one too must end. But the future is unwritten and the journey continues. Open a new world and experience the magic of Heineken.

Production / Historion, 's-Hertogenbosch, the Netherlands
Text / Historion, Mathieu Jacobs and Wim Maas
Translation / Mark Baker and Howard Turner
Concept / Historion, Mathieu Jacobs / Frederik de Wal VOF
Graphic design and typography / Frederik de Wal, Schelluinen
Photo editor / Frederik de Wal, Schelluinen
Photo research / Historion, Wim Maas
Litho and printing / Lecturis, Eindhoven
Binding / Proost NV, Turnhout

© Heineken NV

No part of this publication may be reproduced and/or published in print, by photocopying, on microfilm or by any other means whatsoever without prior written permission from the publisher.

Heineken NV has made every effort to determine the origin of all images and acquire permission for their publication and correctly credit the holders of the respective rights. Parties believing they are entitled to such rights are kindly requested to contact the publisher.

ISBN 90-806280-1-8

PREMIUM

QUALITY